IMAGES
of America

SOUTH PORTLAND AND CAPE ELIZABETH

IMAGES
of America

SOUTH PORTLAND AND CAPE ELIZABETH

Connie Porter Scott

ARCADIA PUBLISHING

ISBN 978-0-7385-9002-8

Published by Arcadia Publishing
Charleston, South Carolina

Printed in the United States of America

For all general information contact Arcadia Publishing at:
Telephone 843-853-2070
Fax 843-853-0044
E-mail sales@arcadiapublishing.com
For customer service and orders:
Toll-Free 1-888-313-2665

Visit us on the Internet at www.arcadiapublishing.com

COVER PHOTOGRAPH: SAILING. At Delano Park, Cape Elizabeth, Jane and Emma Morse are sailing on a small scale near the turn of the century. The punt shown is still at the Morse cottage. (Robert Shuman family)

Contents

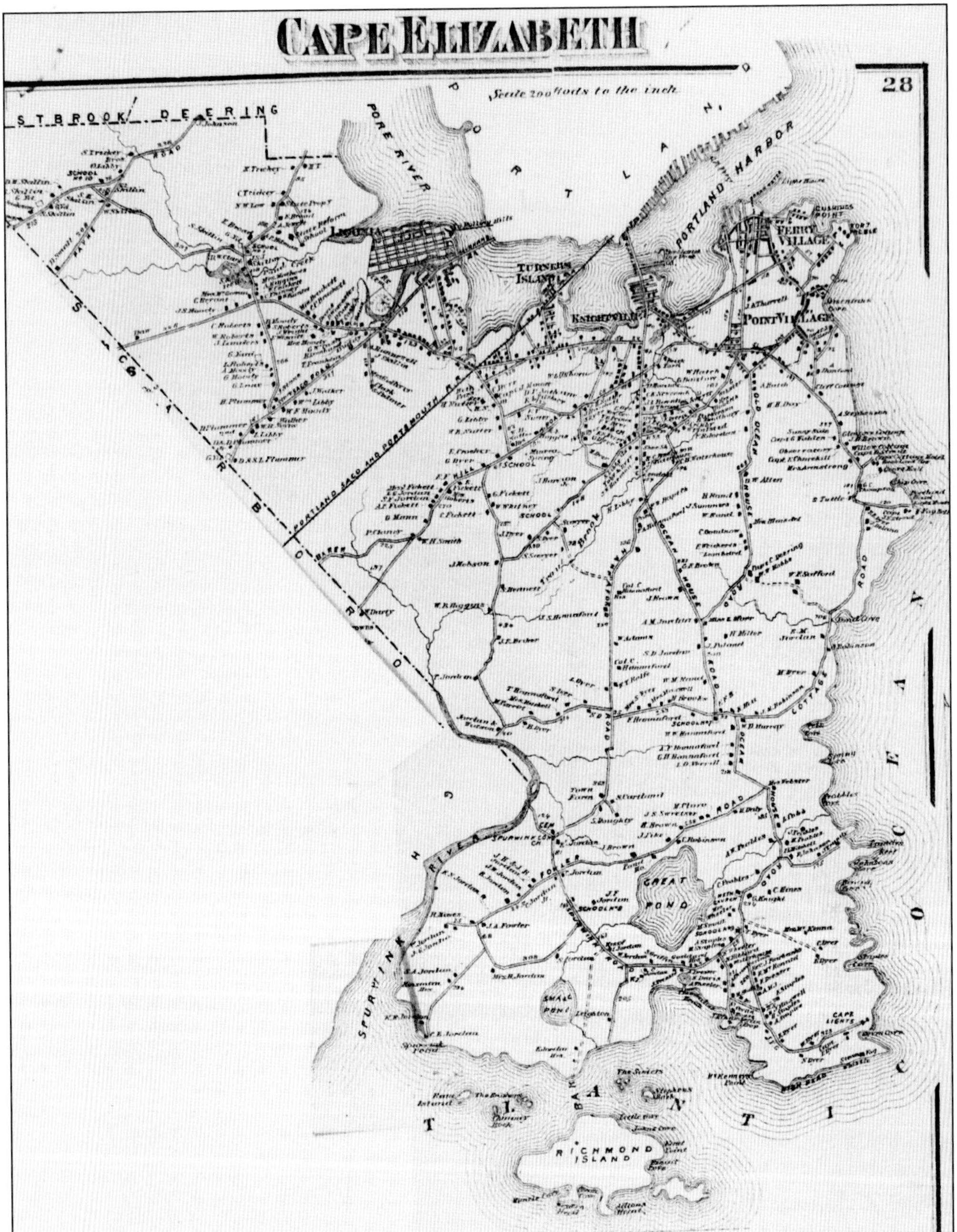

A detailed map of Cape Elizabeth showing Portland Harbor and the various railroad lines in the area. (Thomas Memorial Library)

Introduction

Author's note: Driven out by the Indians, early settlers returned to Cape Elizabeth, then part of Falmouth, following a peace treaty signed with the Indians in 1678 on the banks of Long Creek. These farmers and fishermen, with settlements on Richmond Island and the shores of the Spurwink River, continued to endure hostilities and suffered severe losses during the Revolutionary War. Our story begins with the shipbuilding era of the mid-1800s and takes us up to the 1950s.

Although some shipbuilding had been carried on at an earlier period, it was during the 1840s that shipbuilding became a major part of the Cape's economy. As the shipbuilding era reached its height, the shores of the Ferry Village section of the town may be visualized as one long yard in which some sort of construction was always underway.

Two merchants who were very influential in developing Cape Elizabeth prior to the Civil War were James Cahoon and George Turner. They started a yard in the northeast corner of Ferry Village to the east of the Ferry Slip. This yard, which later became Benjamin W. Pickett's, was the largest on the Cape and ships were built there until 1868.

Other principal yards were owned by Joseph and Nathan Dyer, Nathaniel Blanchard and Thomas Knight, and Cornelius and Alfred Butler. At the latter yard, which was located at Turner's Island, three clippers were constructed during the two-year period from 1850 to 1851.

Maritime activities began to decline following the financial panic of 1857 and the losses of the Civil War period. Furthermore, the advent of steam meant the virtual end of the sailing vessel. By the end of the century, the town had become a quiet suburb of Portland. The shipyards experienced a mild boom during World War I and a decided boom during World War II, at which time the city played a prominent role in the maritime development of the country.

It was during the late nineteenth century that sentiment seemed to crystallize in favor of partitioning the territory of Cape Elizabeth, and the partition finally came in 1895. It was largely occasioned by a dispute over Sebago water, which had been introduced into the town in 1892. This event caused much excitement among the people and the issue was sharply debated between the opposing factions. The accompanying problem of increased taxation proved the final spark. The Cape was divided in 1895, after the state legislature voted in favor of the separation. The South Portland section consisted of about 8,000 acres, while the southern section, which retained the name Cape Elizabeth, consisted of about 7,000 acres.

South Portland remained a town until 1898 when the first city charter was adopted. One of the interesting features about South Portland is its division into distinct areas, each of which formerly exhibited various traits of individuality: Willard, Ferry Village, Knightville, Town House Corner, Pleasantdale, Ligonia, and Thornton Heights.

A ferry across the harbor began in 1718 and in 1734 the Stroudwater Bridge across Fore River was erected. At the turn of the century, Vaughan's Bridge was built, and in 1823, the long wooden Portland Bridge was constructed. This bridge continued in use until replaced in 1916 by the so-called "Million Dollar" Bridge.

The first railroad leading from Portland began to operate in 1842. A landmark was reached in South Portland in 1895 when electric street car service was installed. By 1940 all electric car lines within the city had been replaced by busses. It was during the days of the old trolley cars that casinos were built at Willard Beach (formerly Simonton's Cove) and Cottage Park in Cape Elizabeth.

World War II brought vast changes. During this period, the city played a prominent role in the maritime development of the country. The waterfront of South Portland acquired an entirely new "face" as many buildings were razed or moved to make space for the large development of the New England Shipbuilding Corp., which operated as an affiliate of the Todd Shipyard Corp. of New York.

The progressiveness of any community is reflected in its cultural and recreational advancement. Major strides have been made in South Portland in these areas, and a fine educational system has evolved. In the spring of 1874 the town voted to establish a free high school. The first class to be graduated was the Class of 1877; it consisted of four members, three girls and one boy. The boy was Edward C. Reynolds, who eventually became the first mayor of South Portland.

The oldest church in the area is the First Congregational, United Church of Christ, located on Cottage Road at Meeting House Hill. The origin of this church dates back to 1734 when it was constructed in what is now Mt. Pleasant Cemetery and known as the Second Parish of Falmouth. A new building erected on that site in 1835 was moved across the street to its present location in 1891.

Rosella A. Loveitt
Local Historian

One

People and Places

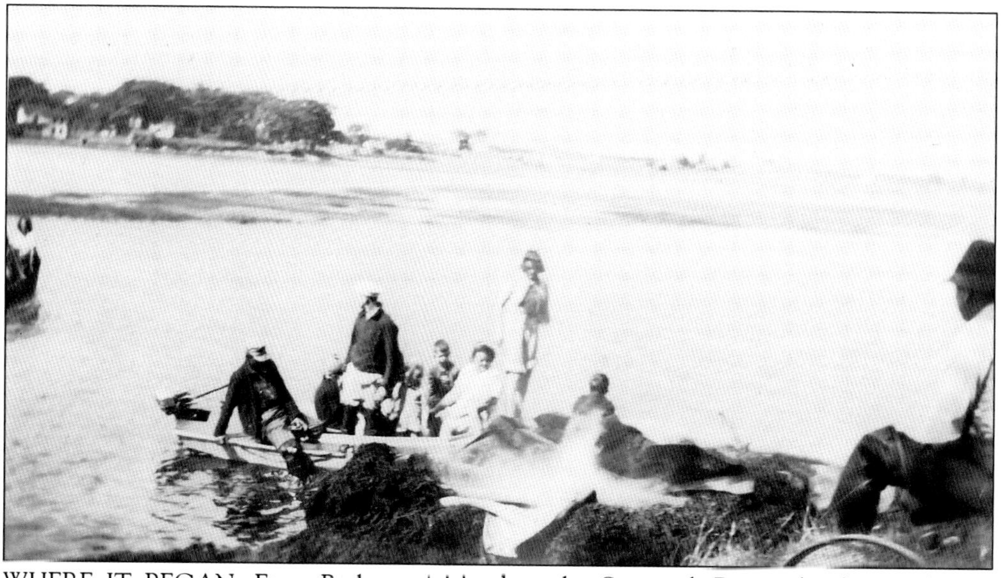

WHERE IT BEGAN. From Richmond Island to the Spurwink River, the first settlers of Cape Elizabeth were fishermen and farmers. Here at the mouth of the Spurwink in the 1940s, ancestors of those early settlers gather for a family clambake under the watchful eye of Roy Jordan (far right). From left to right at the boat are Art Kennedy, unknown, Randall Jordan, Linda Wainwright Mullin, Dwight Jordan Jr., Emma Jordan Kennedy, Dorothy Jordan Dixon, and unknown. Scarborough can be seen on the far shore. (Ted & Norma Wainwright)

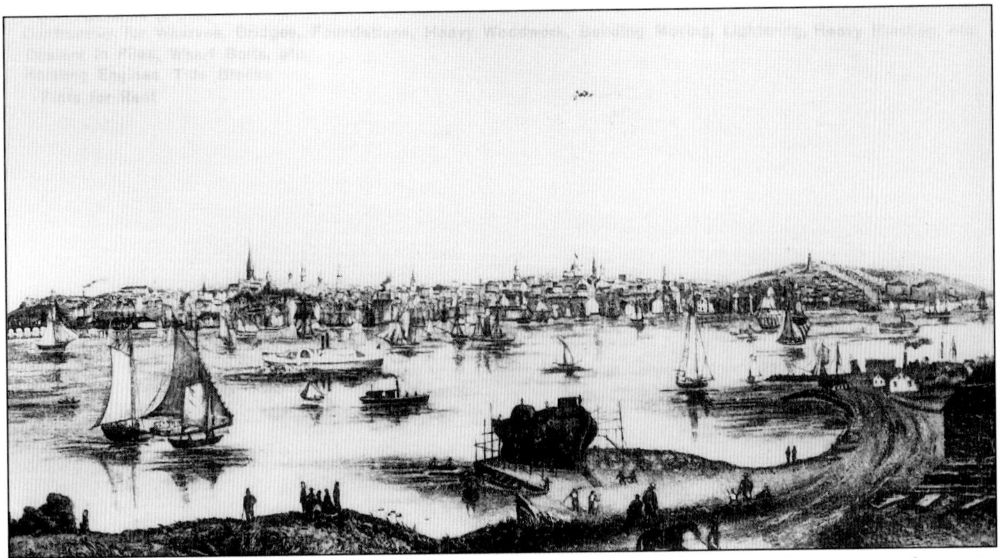

BUSY BUILDERS. From the early 1800s to the 1860s, shipbuilding was a booming industry in Cape Elizabeth, as seen in this *c.* 1815 view looking from the Ferry Village shore across the Fore River toward Portland. Prominent names in the industry were Dyer, Cahoon, Turner, Pickett, Knight, and Butler.

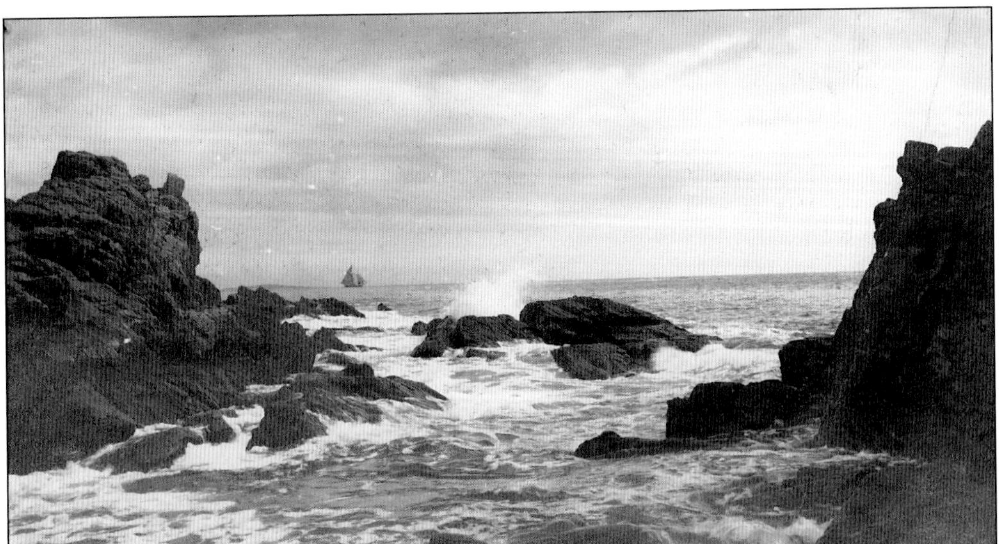

OFF SHORE. Ships sailing Maine's rocky coast and coming and going from Portland Harbor were a familiar sight to those on the Cape shore in the 1800s. One of the most notable of the clipper ships built in the area in the mid-1800s was the *Snow Squall*. After being run aground in the Falkland Islands in 1864, its bow was recovered in 1987 and is the only clipper bow in existence. (Robert Shuman family)

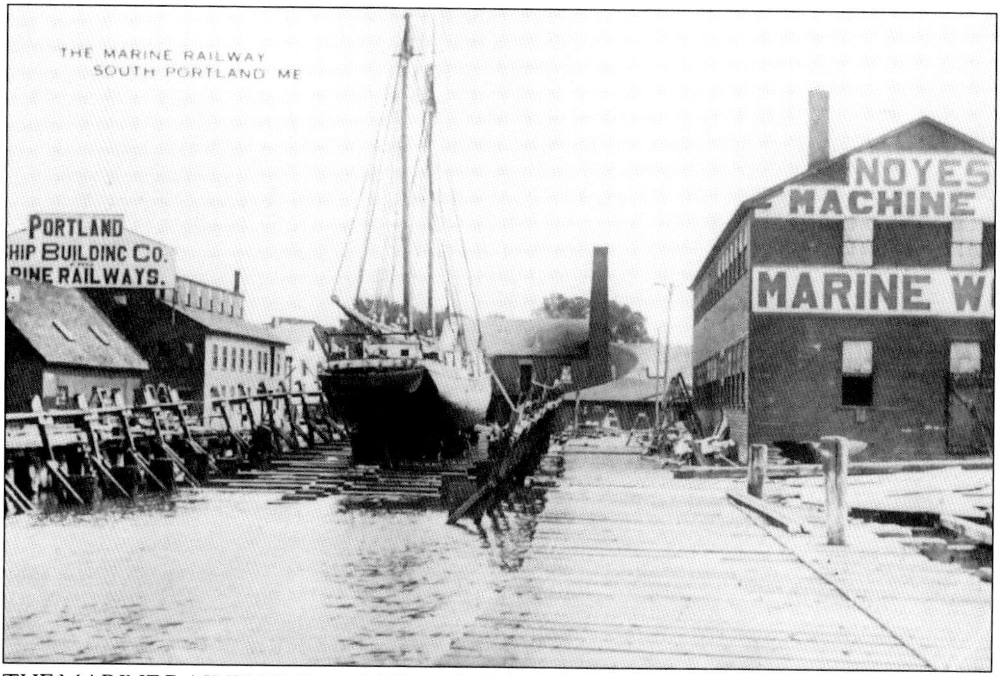

THE MARINE RAILWAY. From 1850 to 1883 the Marine Railway was located at Ferry Village, which was at that time the hub of Cape Elizabeth's shipyards and marine-related industries. The Marine Railway later became the Portland Merchants Marine Railway and, in 1887, the Portland Shipbuilding Co. (Sullivan Photo Collection)

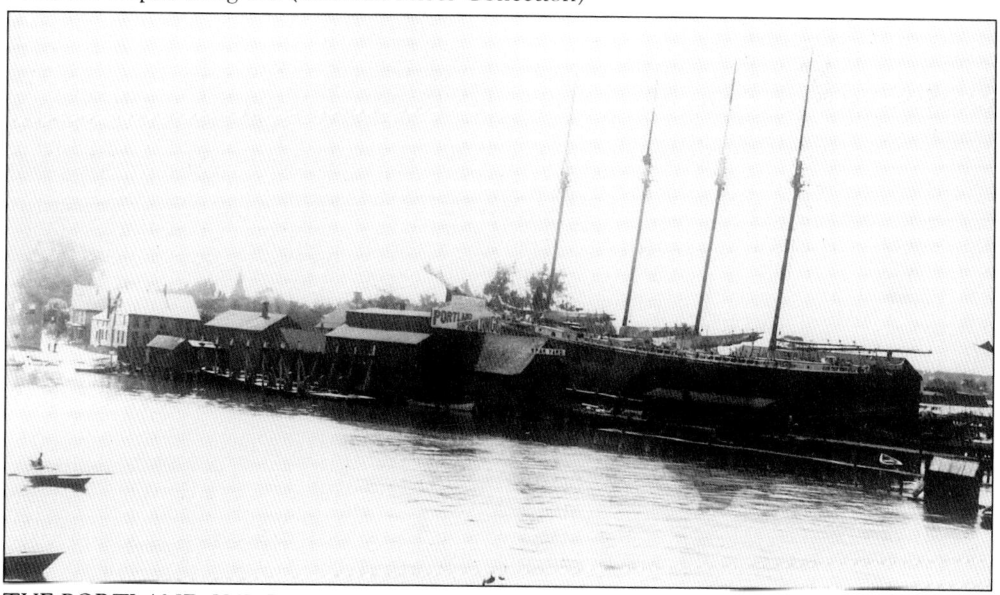

THE PORTLAND SHIPBUILDING CO. A four-masted sailing ship is docked at the Portland Shipbuilding Co. at Ferry Village near the turn of the century. With the advent of the larger steam-powered vessels, shipbuilding soon came to a halt in the Cape Elizabeth area, as it did in other Maine villages. In 1895 Cape Elizabeth was divided into two towns, and its northern end renamed South Portland. Resettlement and urban development were about to begin. (Sullivan Photo Collection)

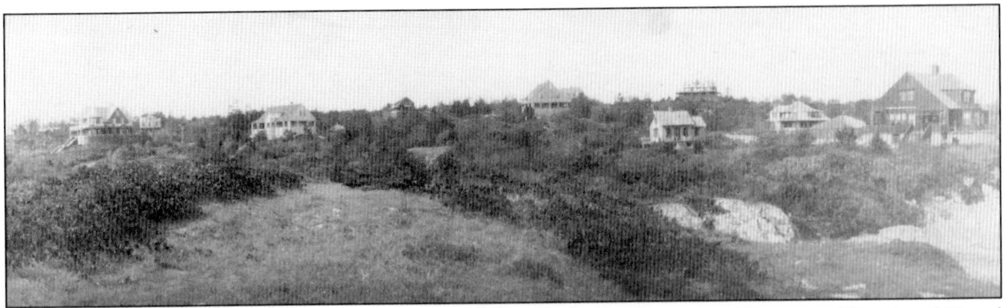

DELANO PARK. Once farmland owned by James Delano, the second keeper of Portland Head Light, this area was developed on the Cape Shore in the late 1880s by a group of Portland businessmen. Originally consisting of 15 acres, the area has grown to approximately 32 acres and 27 house lots. Several of the homes were designed by Portland architect John Calvin Stevens, who was renowned for his gable-roofed, shingle-style design. Early cottages were owned by Brill, Swazey, Millett, Goodridge, Gignoux, Morse, and Denison. (Robert Shuman family)

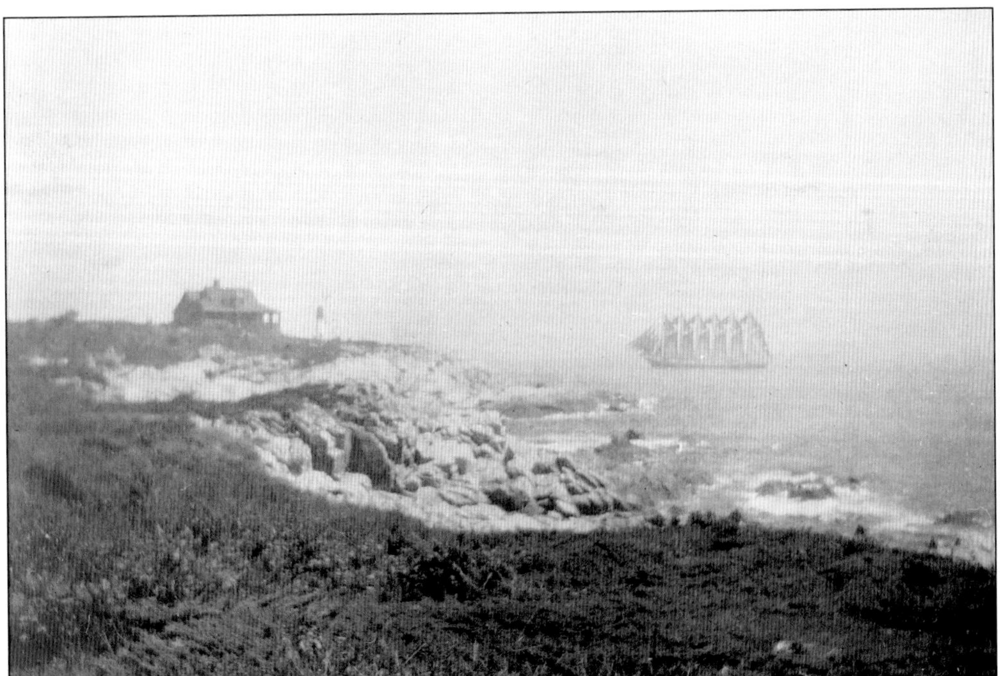

MAJESTIC. A six-masted schooner is captured on film off the rocky Cape Shore. The Coyle house, later destroyed by fire, is on the point, *c.* 1890. (Robert Shuman family)

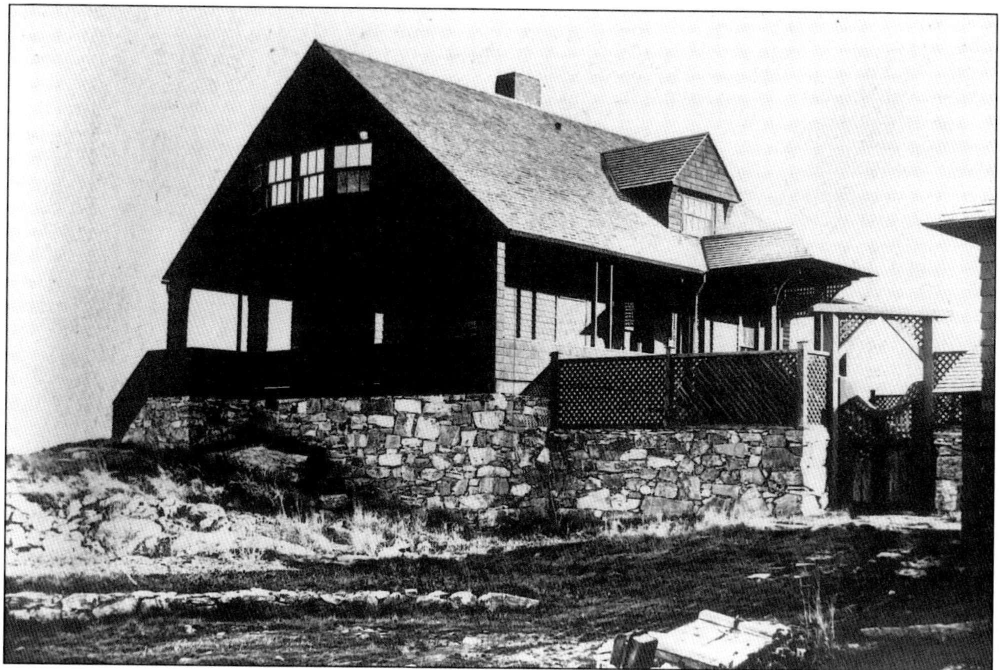

THE GEORGE F. MORSE HOUSE. The first summer cottage in Delano Park, Cape Elizabeth, was built in 1886 by George F. and Rhobie Morse. The treasurer and chief operating officer of The Portland Company on Portland's waterfront, George F. Morse (known by his family as Fred) was a friend of Portland architect John Calvin Stevens, and was an admirer of his nationally-acclaimed shingle-style design seen here. Since 1987 the house has been owned and occupied year-round by Morse's great-grandson, Robert Shuman, and his wife Elizabeth. (Robert Shuman family)

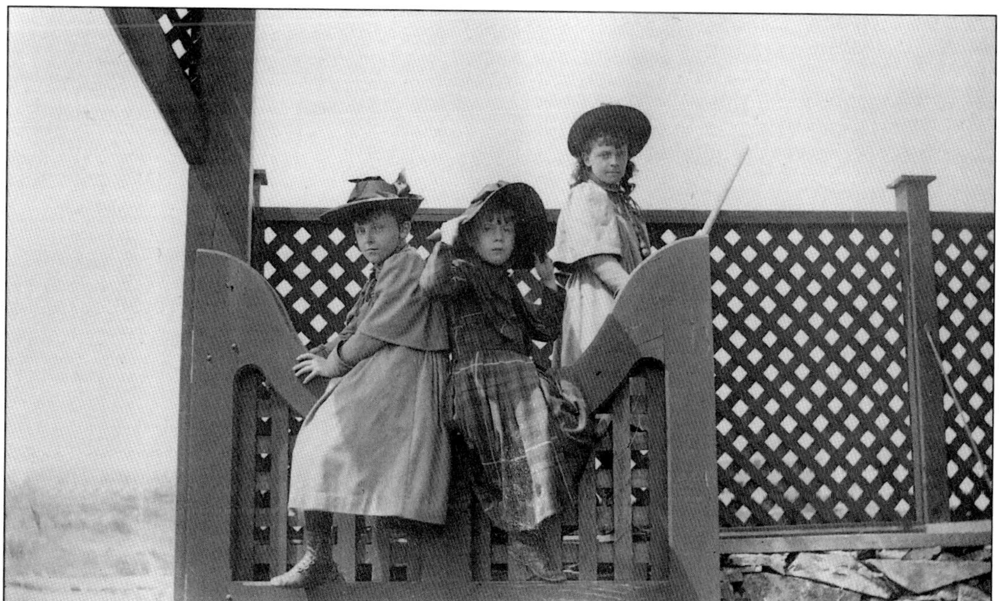

GATEWAY. Reflecting a Japanese influence, the fencing and gate to the Morse home at Delano Park provide an unusual "settee" for these three girls. (Robert Shuman family)

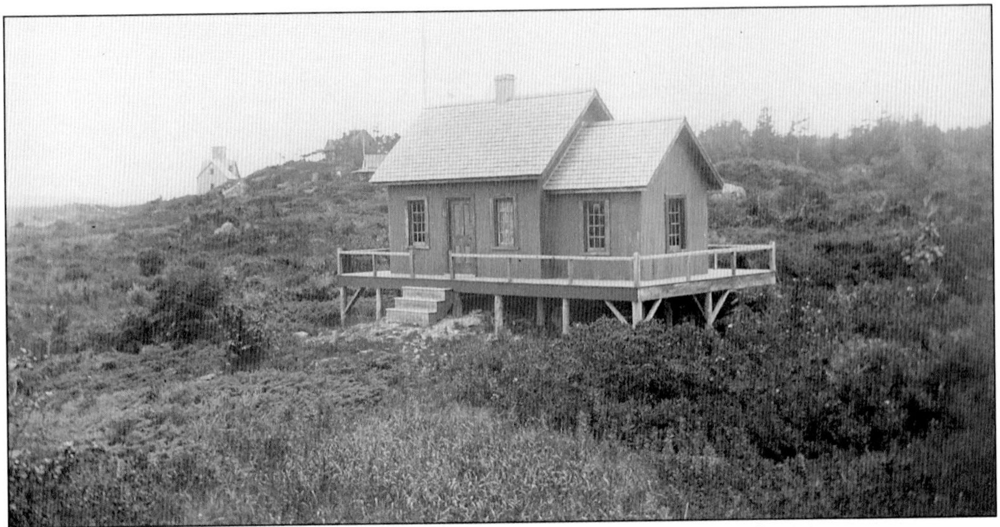

PLAYHOUSE. Known as the "children's cottage," this playhouse on the Morse property was built "child-scale," c. 1888, for George F. Morse's daughters Jane and Emma. The playhouse features a living room, a kitchen with a sink, and an upstairs room. It was restored by the Shumans and is now a favorite hideaway for their visiting grandchildren. (Robert Shuman family)

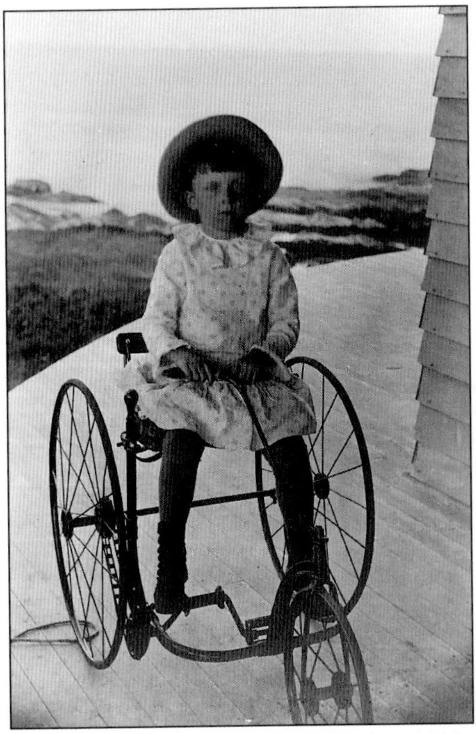

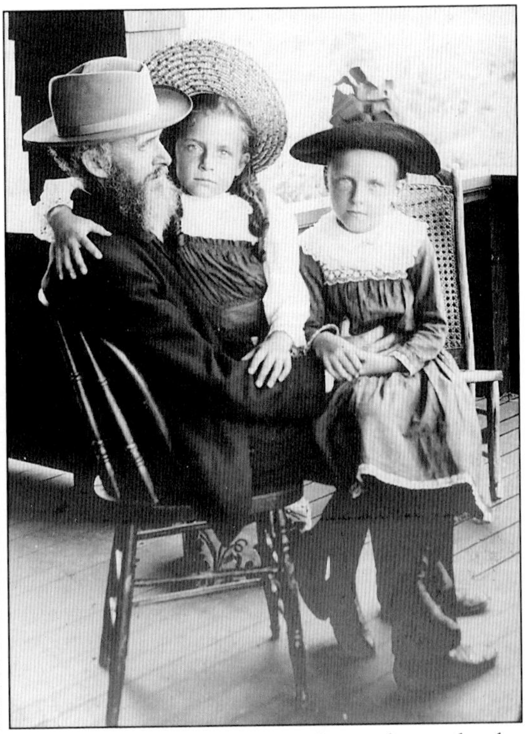

LEFT: 'ROUND AND 'ROUND. A *c.* 1890s photograph of Emma Morse riding a three-wheeler around the circular piazza surrounding the family cottage at Delano Park. Her younger brother George F. recalled that twenty laps equaled a mile. (Robert Shuman family)
RIGHT: LAP TIME. George F. Morse sits with daughters Emma and Jane on the piazza circling the family cottage in Delano Park, *c.* 1890s. (Robert Shuman family)

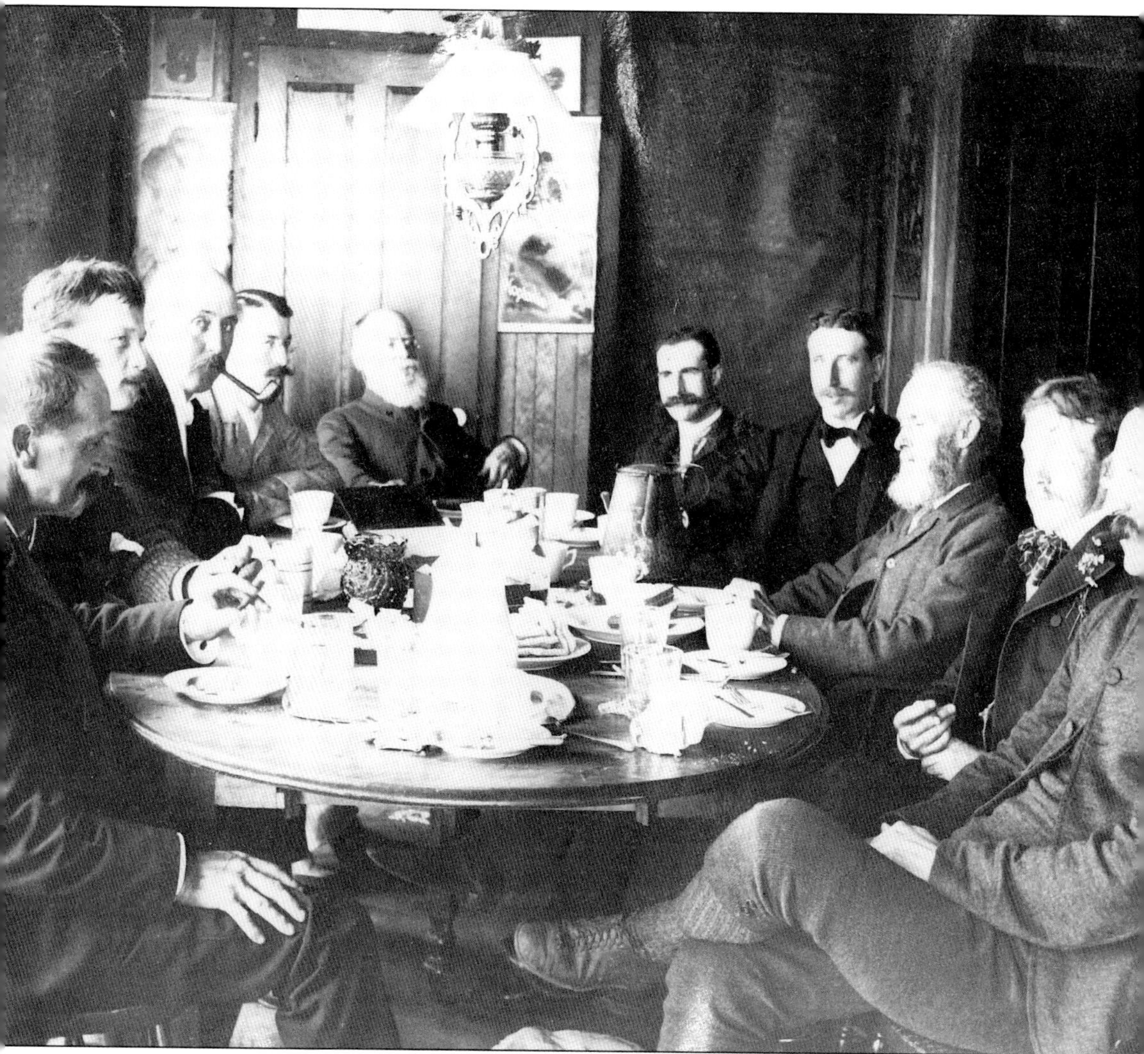

BRUSH'UNS. Local artists, who referred to themselves as "Brush'uns," gather at the home of George F. Morse at Delano Park, Cape Elizabeth, around the turn of the century. In addition to Morse were architect John Calvin Stevens and Charles F. Kimball, founder of the Portland Society of Art. (Robert Shuman family)

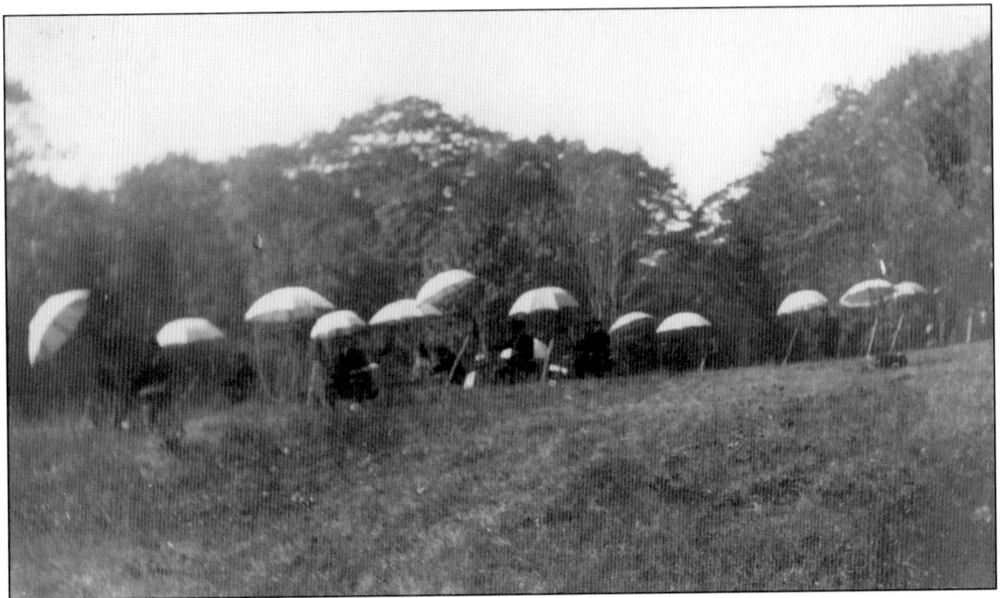

UNDER THE WEATHER. Sprouting like giant mushrooms atop a knoll in Delano Park, white umbrellas provide shelter for the Brush'uns at work, *c.* 1890. (Robert Shuman family)

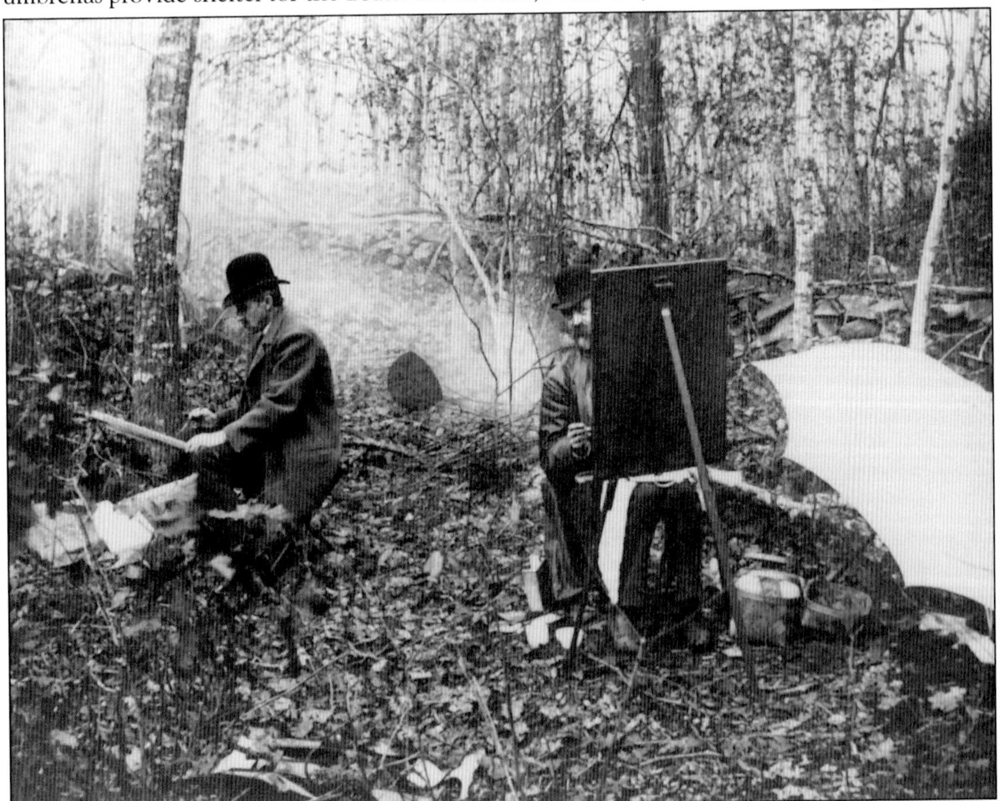

INSECTICIDE. Smoke from burning smudge pots protects the Brush'uns from insects in the wooded area known as Delano Woods, located across from Shore Road, *c.* 1890. (Robert Shuman family)

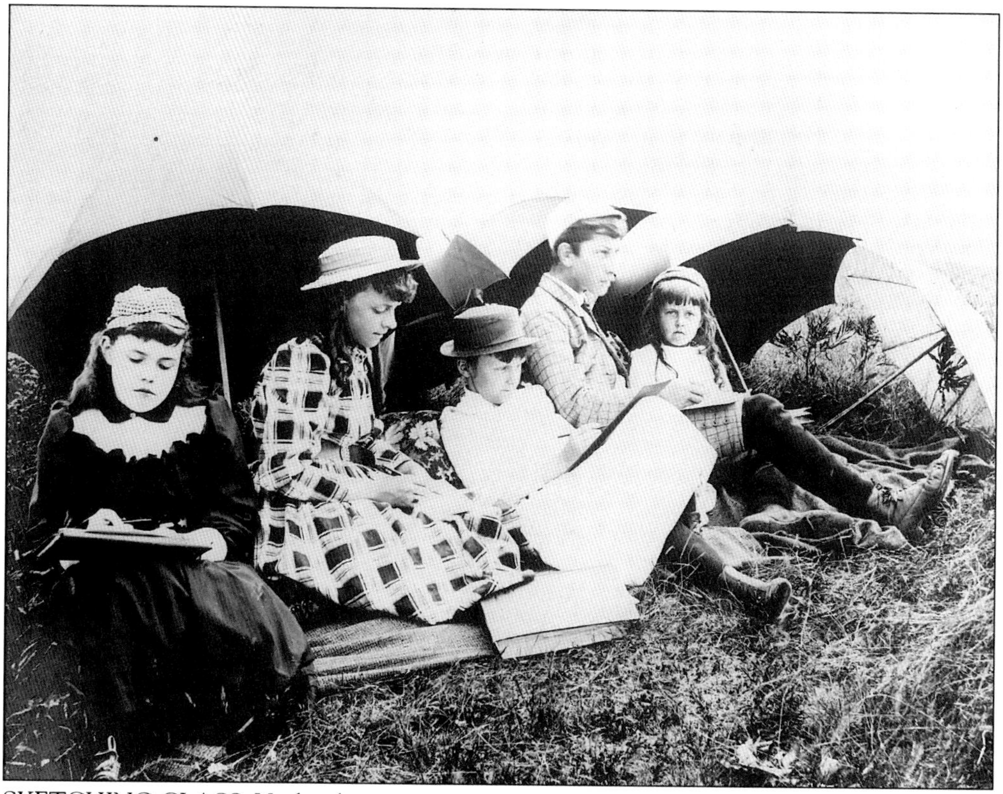

SKETCHING CLASS. Under the direction of George F. Morse, children and friends of the Morse family learn sketching techniques at Delano Park, Cape Elizabeth, c. 1890. (Robert Shuman family)

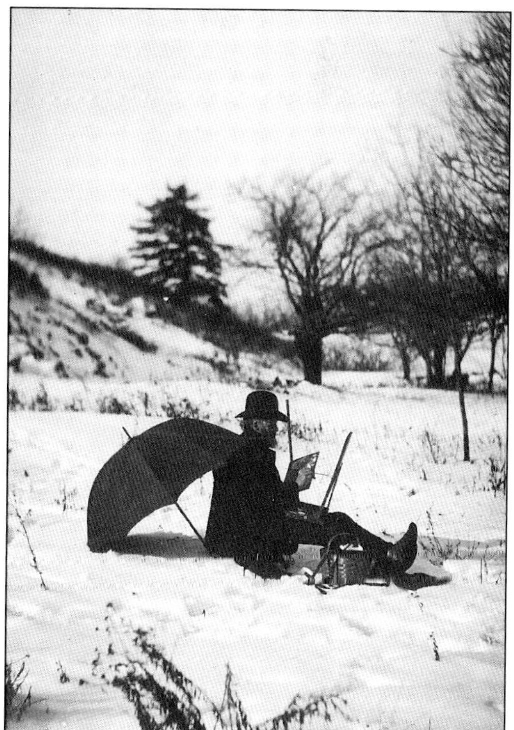

A MAN FOR ALL SEASONS. George F. Morse takes advantage of a late fall snowfall to create a winter landscape at Delano Park in Cape Elizabeth, c. 1892. (Robert Shuman family)

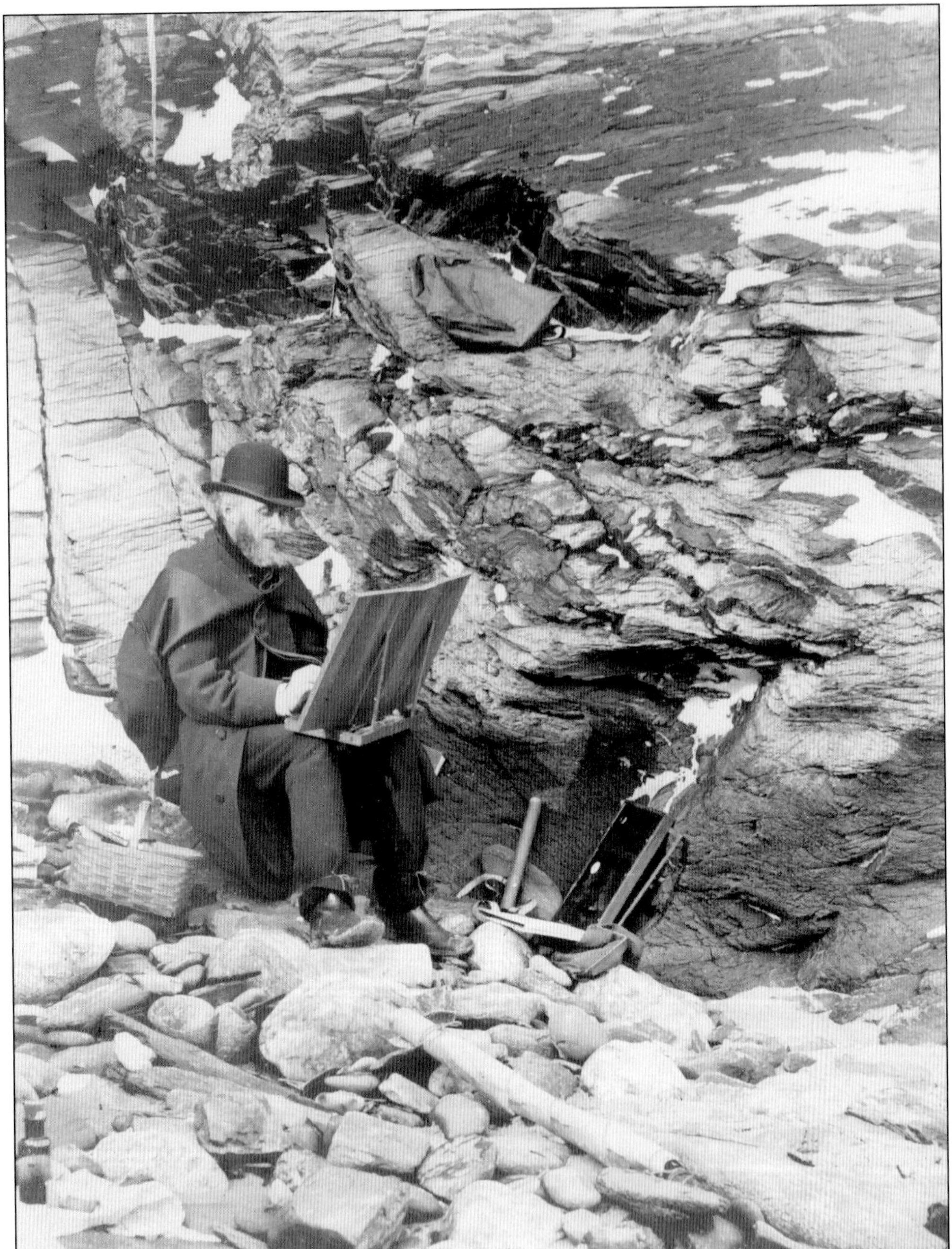

GEORGE F. MORSE. An accomplished landscape painter, George F. Morse pursued his love of oil painting and pencil sketching throughout his life, often focusing on the spectacular scenery around Delano Park. This is a *c.* 1890 photograph. (Robert Shuman family)

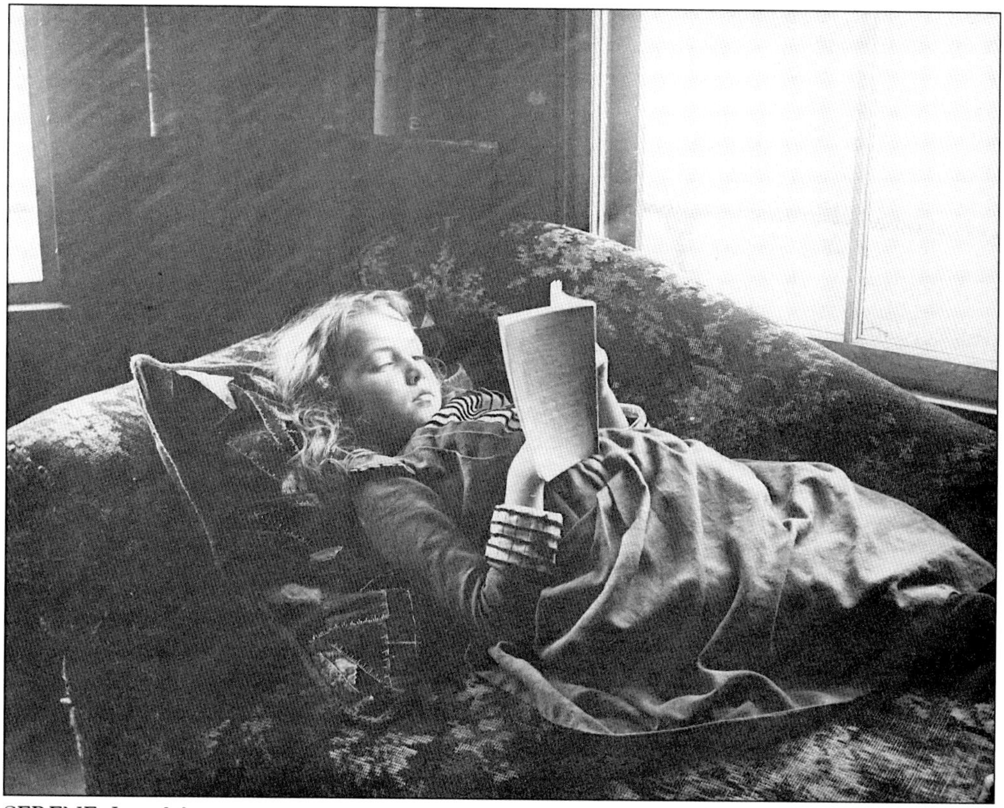

SERENE. Jane Morse relaxes with a book, *c*. 1890, in the living room of the family cottage at Delano Park overlooking the ocean. Jane was from a family of readers, and her sister Emma, who spent most of her latter years in the house, left hundreds of books behind when she died. (Robert Shuman family)

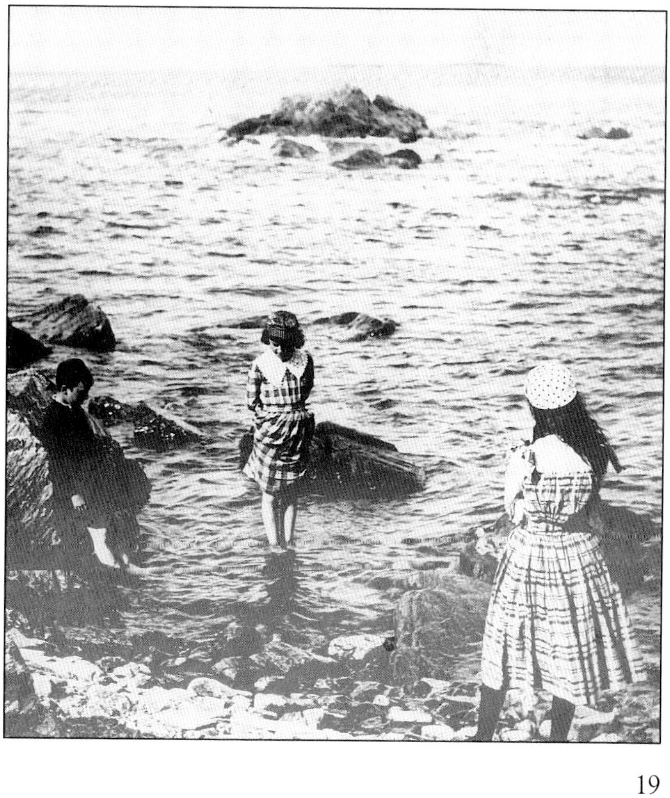

WADING. Living near the ocean provided its own entertainment for the children in Cape Elizabeth and South Portland. George G., Jane, and Emma Morse play in Delano Park around the turn of the century. (Robert Shuman family)

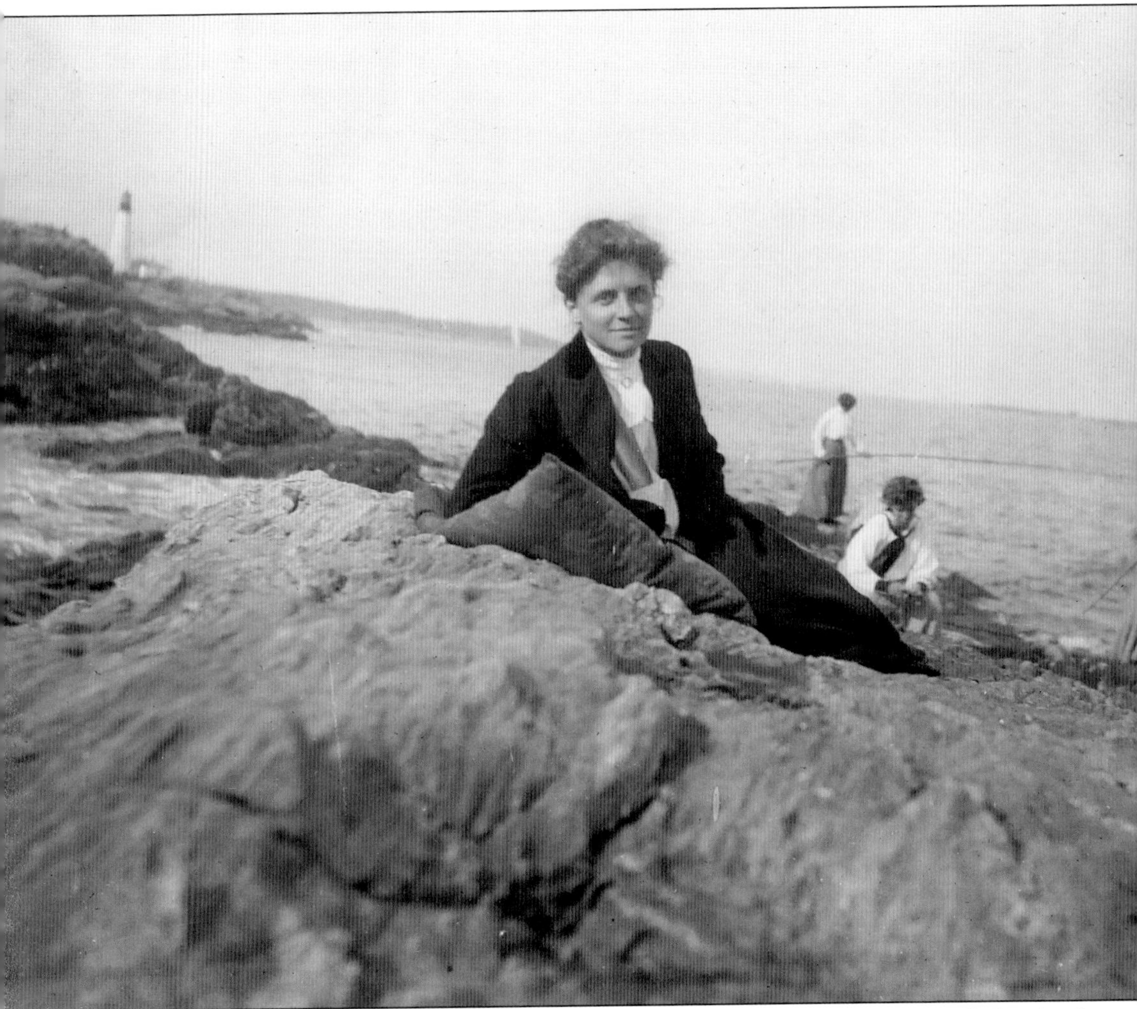

ON THE ROCKS. Jane Morse enjoys an afternoon on the Cape's rocky coast, with Portland Head Light to the left and women fishing for cunner with bamboo poles to the right. The small fish were once so plentiful off the Atlantic Coast that a gathering place for gentlemen called the Cunner Club was built at Staples Cove (now Hannaford Cove) in Cape Elizabeth. (Robert Shuman family)

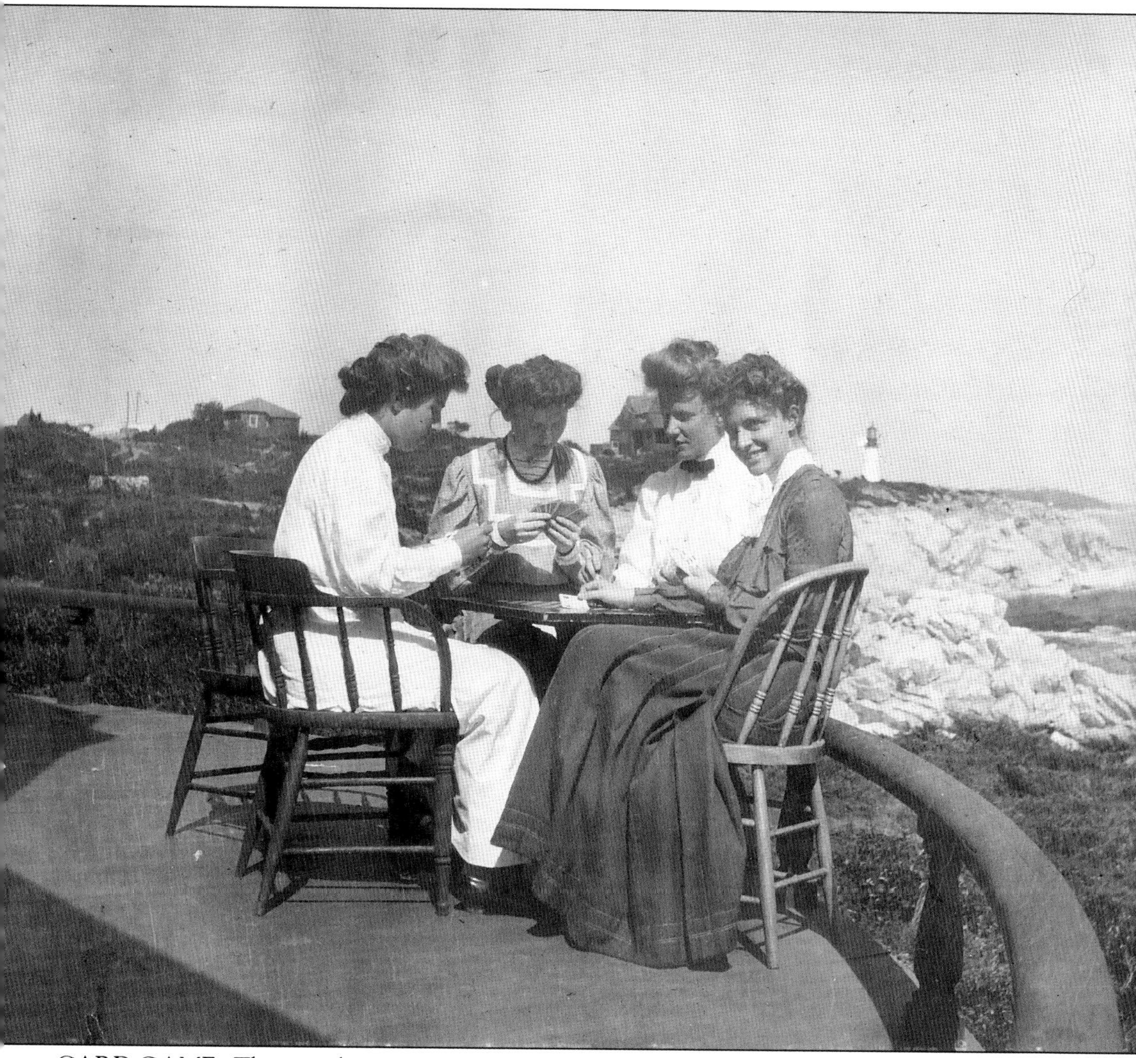

CARD GAME. The circular piazza surrounding the Morse cottage at Delano Park provides the perfect ocean perch for an afternoon card game. Popular games at the time were Whist and Authors. (Robert Shuman family)

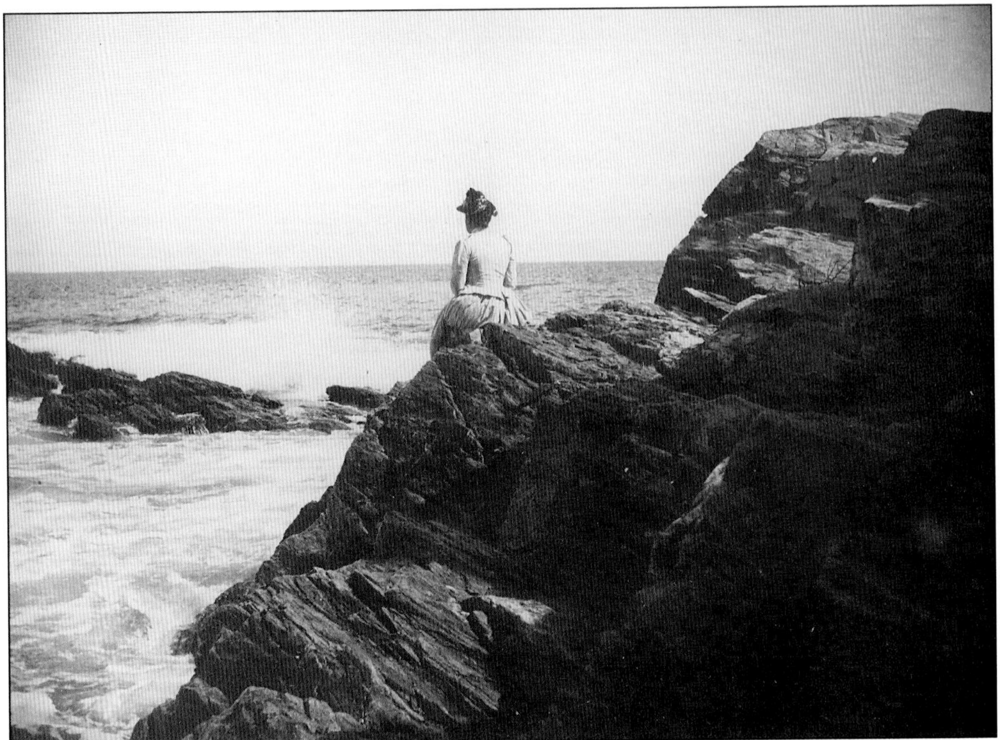

PICTURE PERFECT. A woman, thought to be Emma Morse, enjoys the ocean view off the rocks at Delano Park. The composition of the photograph suggests it may have been taken by her father's friend and fellow Brush'un, Charles Fuller, with his "photographic apparatus," c. 1910. (Robert Shuman family)

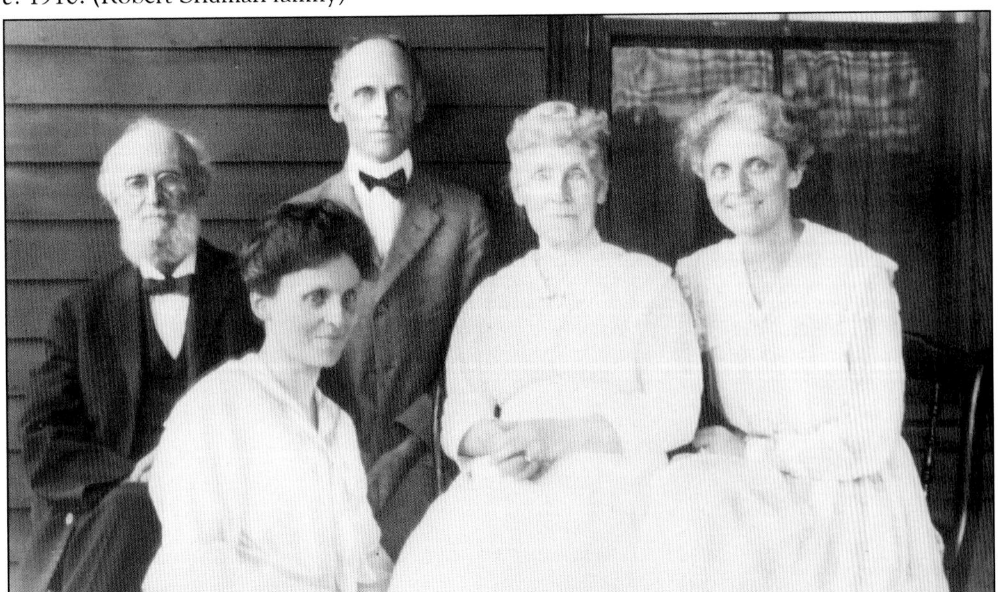

THE MORSE FAMILY. A *c.* 1910 photograph of the first summer residents of Delano Park, Cape Elizabeth. From left to right are George Fred Morse, daughter Emma, son George G., wife Rhobie, and daughter Jane. (Robert Shuman family)

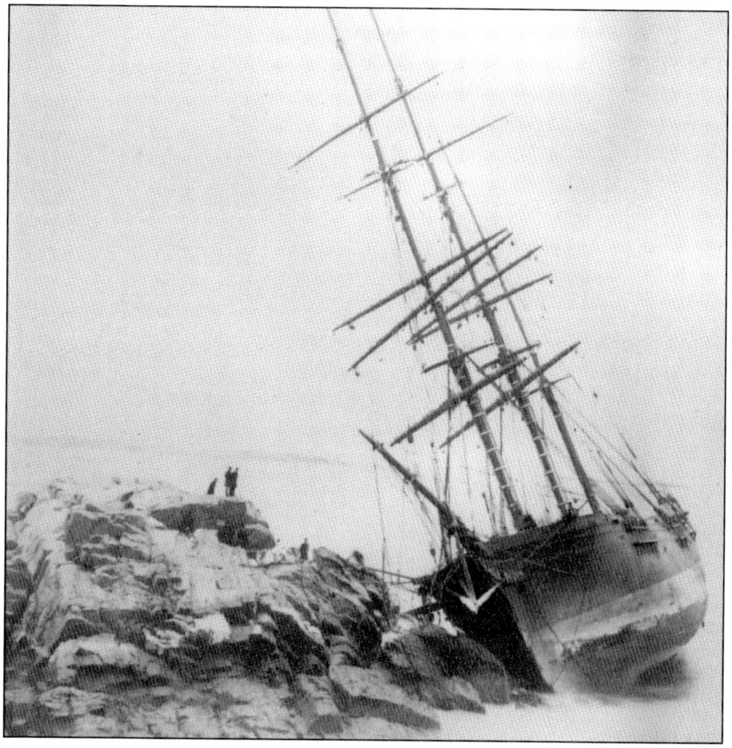

SHIPWRECK. The *Annie C. Maguire*, returning from its maiden voyage, comes to rest near Portland Head, Cape Elizabeth. It crashed on the rocks on Christmas Eve 1886. By New Year's Day, it had been broken up and carried out to sea by a heavy swell. (Robert Shuman family)

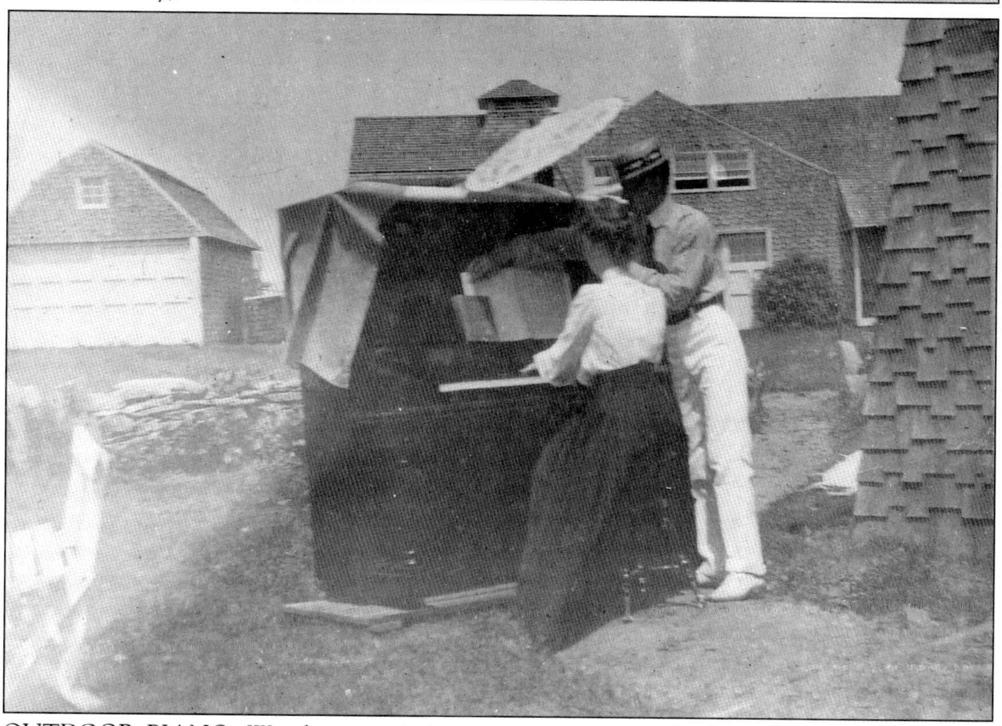

OUTDOOR PIANO. Weather permitting, entertainment took place out of doors on warm summer days at Delano Park. Here a piano is readied for an afternoon performance at the Brown estate. (Robert Shuman family)

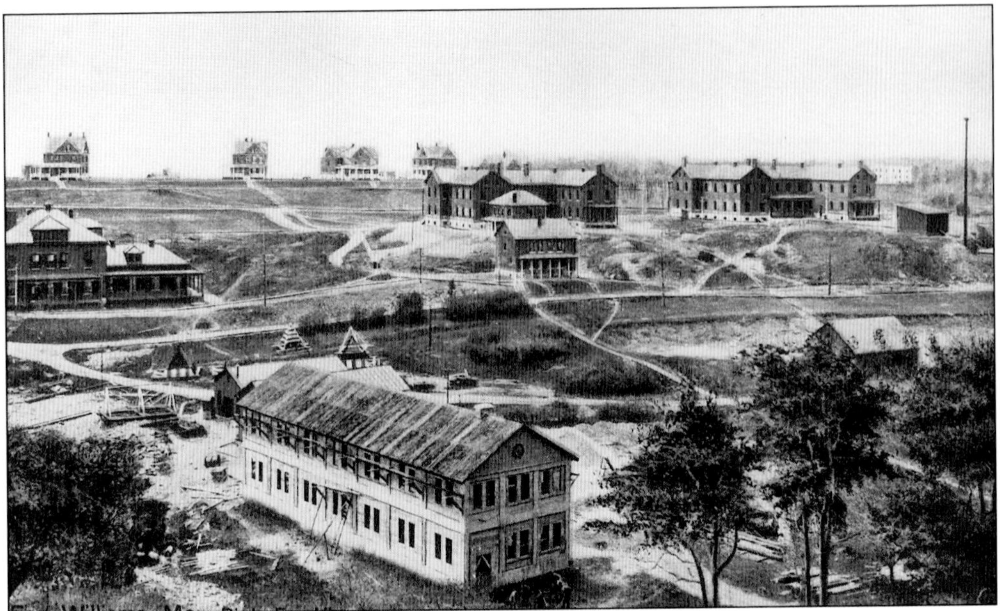

FORT WILLIAMS. Operational as a military base from 1899 through World War II, Fort Williams is located off Shore Road, Cape Elizabeth, near the South Portland line. Closed in 1963, the oceanfront site was purchased the next year by the Town of Cape Elizabeth for $200,000. Its scenic beauty and spectacular view attract hundreds of visitors a year. (Sullivan Photo Collection)

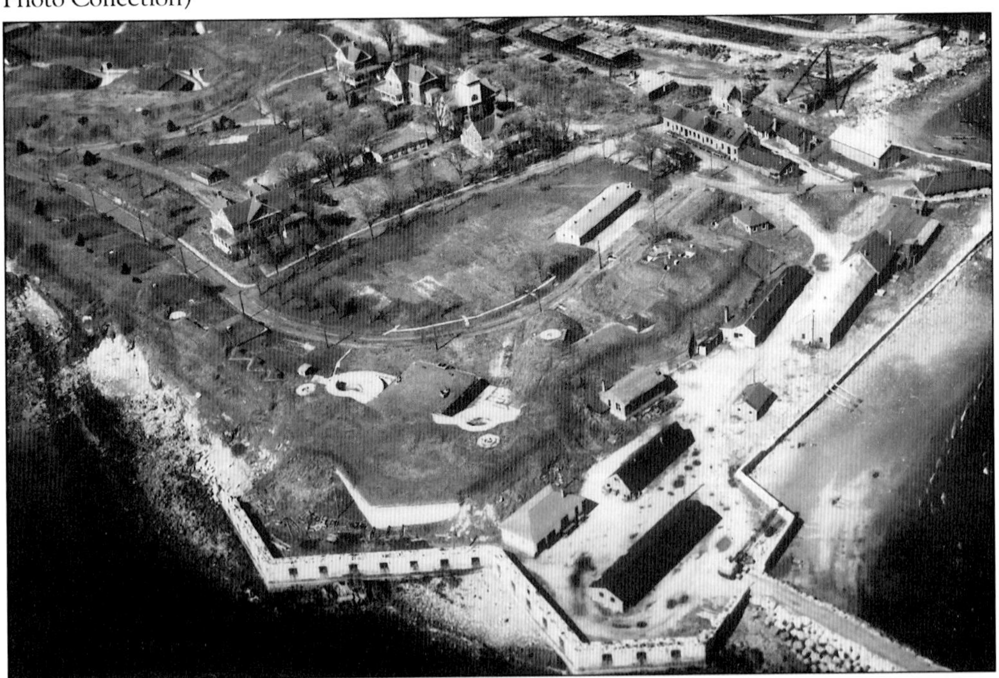

FORT PREBLE. Overlooking Casco Bay, Fort Preble served as a garrison at Spring Point from 1812 to 1950, encompassing an impressive parade ground, hospital, barracks, and blacksmith shop. Known as Fort Hancock during the Revolutionary War, it is now the home of Southern Maine Technical College. (Sullivan Photo Collection)

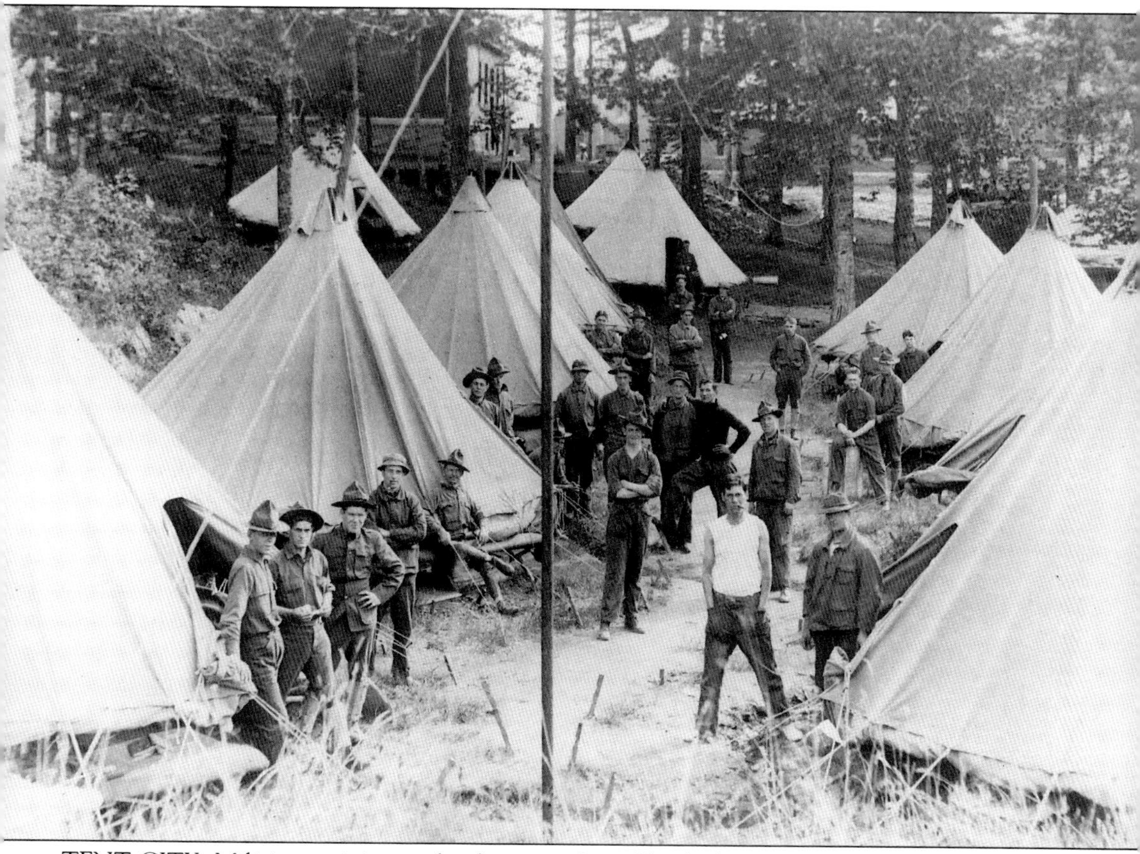

TENT CITY. Militiamen join regular forces at Cape Elizabeth in defense of the coast at the turn of the century. (Sullivan Photo Collection)

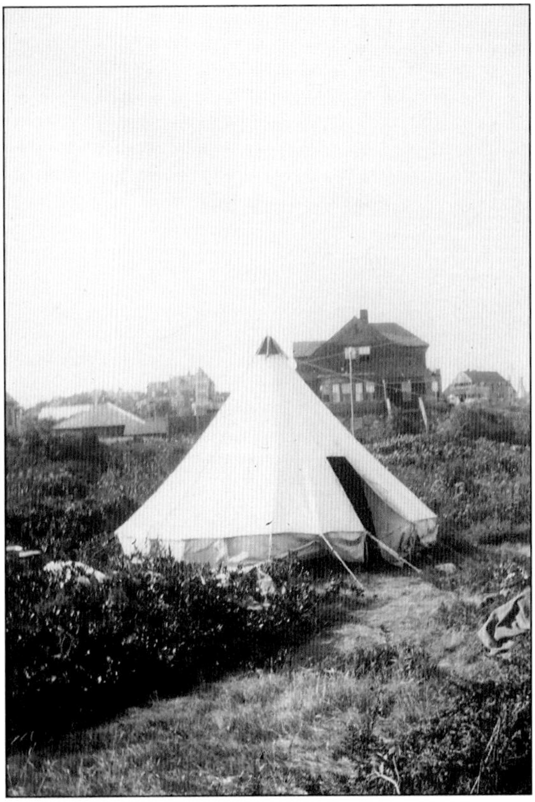

OUTPOST. This military tent was one of several located around Delano Park, Cape Elizabeth, c. 1903. (Robert Shuman family)

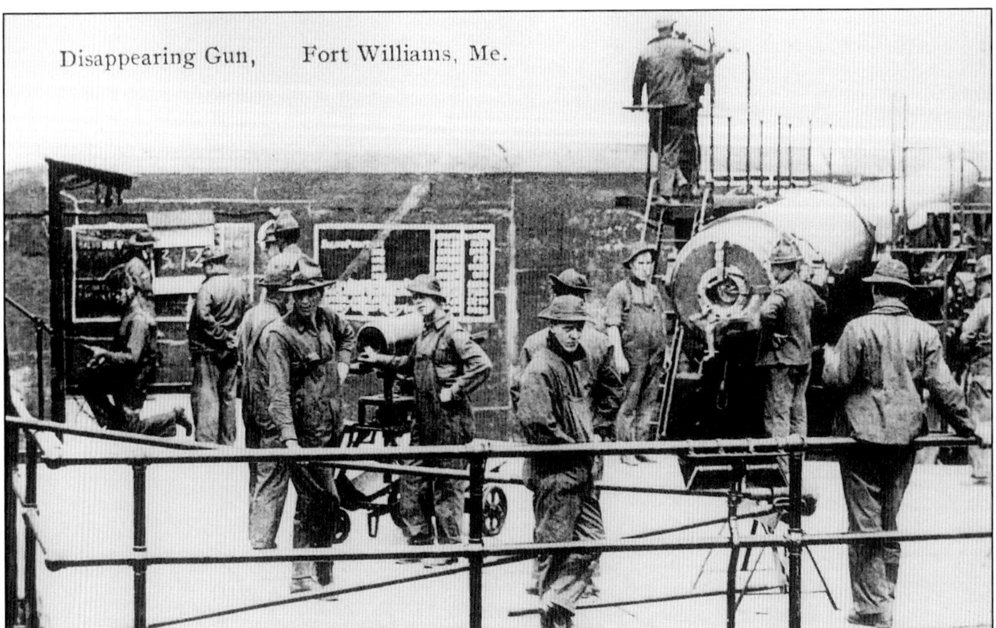

DISAPPEARING GUN. This gun at Fort Williams was designed to return to its undercover position after firing, c. 1900. (Sullivan Photo Collection)

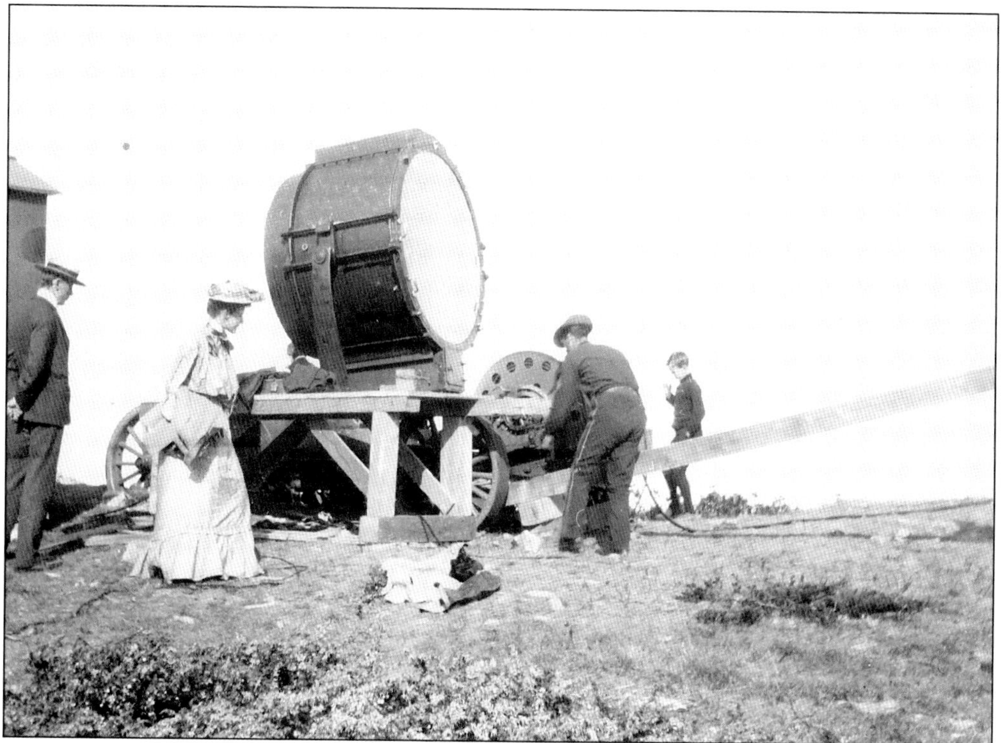

SEARCHLIGHT. One of the three largest search lights in the world is positioned at Delano Park, Cape Elizabeth, to illuminate enemy vessels that might try sneaking into the harbor after dark, c. 1898. (Robert Shuman family)

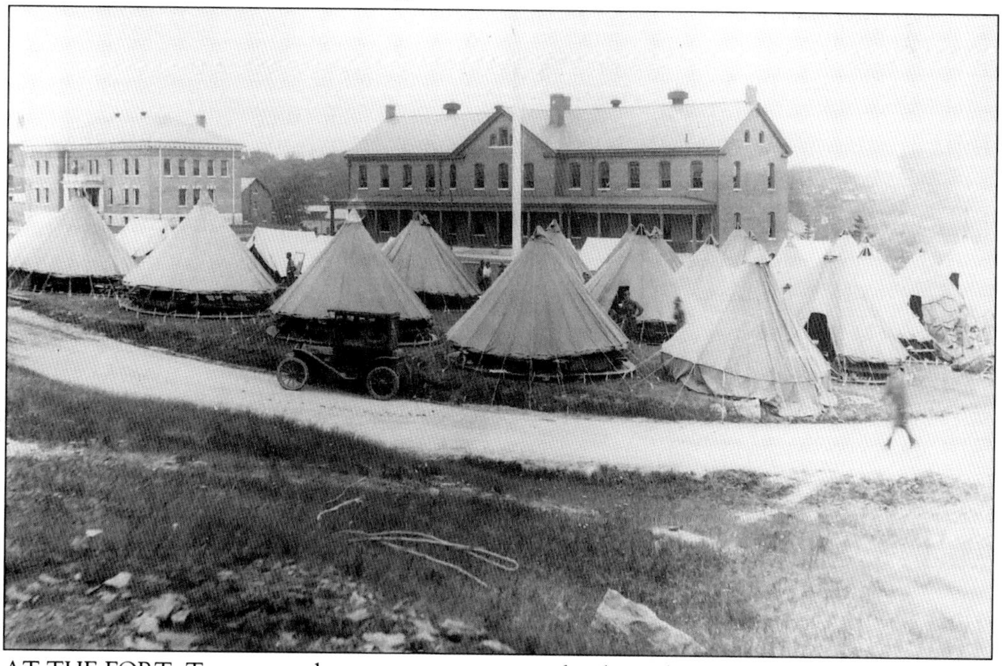

AT THE FORT. Tents served as temporary quarters for the militia stationed at Fort Williams, c. 1907. (Sullivan Photo Collection)

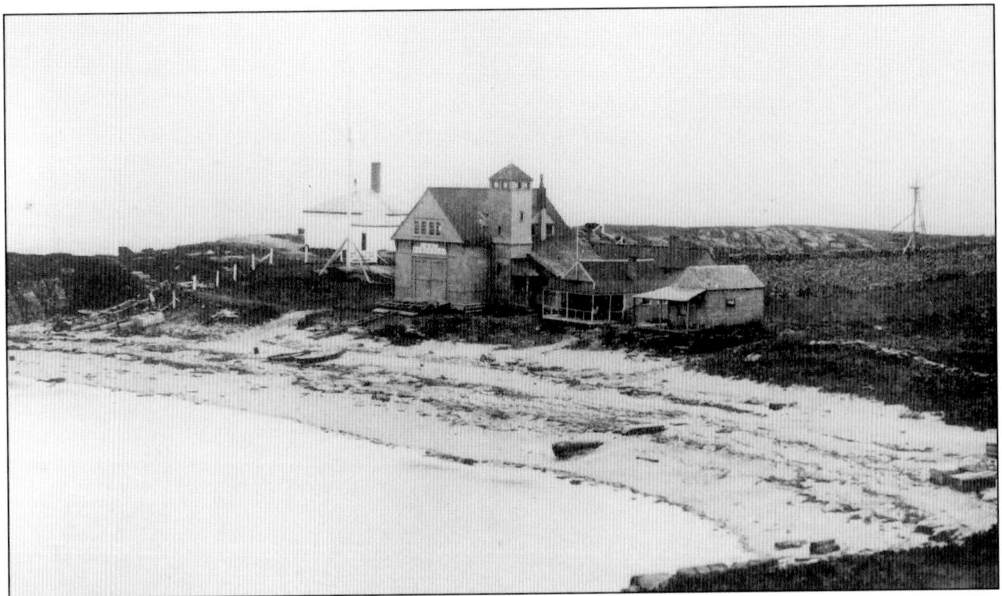

LIFE-SAVING STATION. Volunteers trained in seamanship provided rescue service from the station in Dyer Cove at Two Lights from the late 1890s to 1915, when the Coast Guard took over. The Coast Guard base is presently located at Ferry Village, South Portland. (Sullivan Photo Collection)

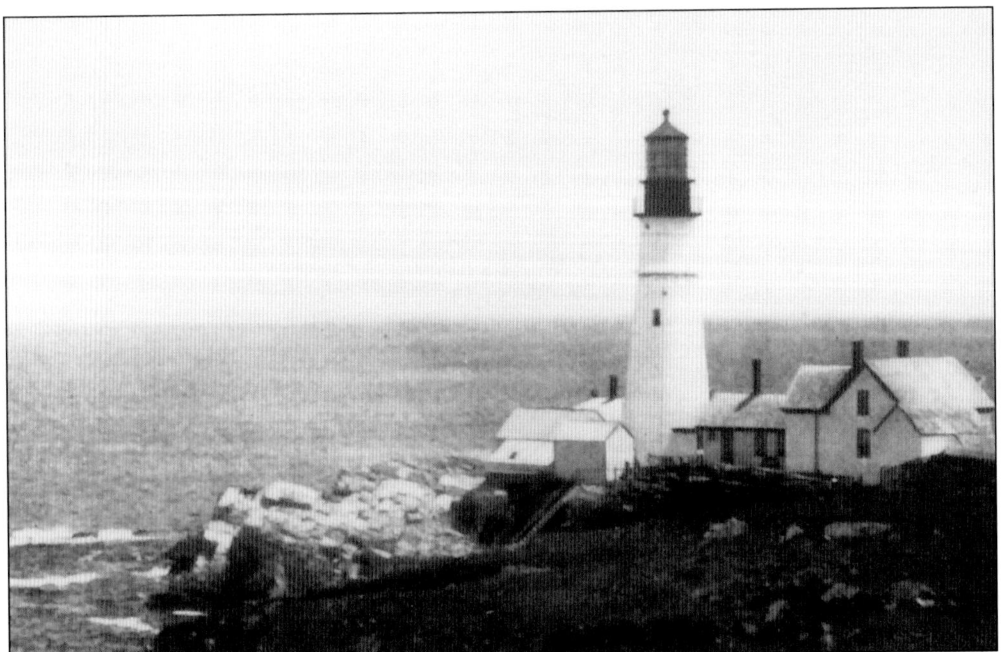

PORTLAND HEAD LIGHT. Operational from 1791 to 1989 and located at Cape Elizabeth, Portland Head Light has long been a favorite subject of photographers and artists. The first lighthouse in Maine, its beacon and fog bell warned many a sailor away from the rocky coast. (Sullivan Photo Collection)

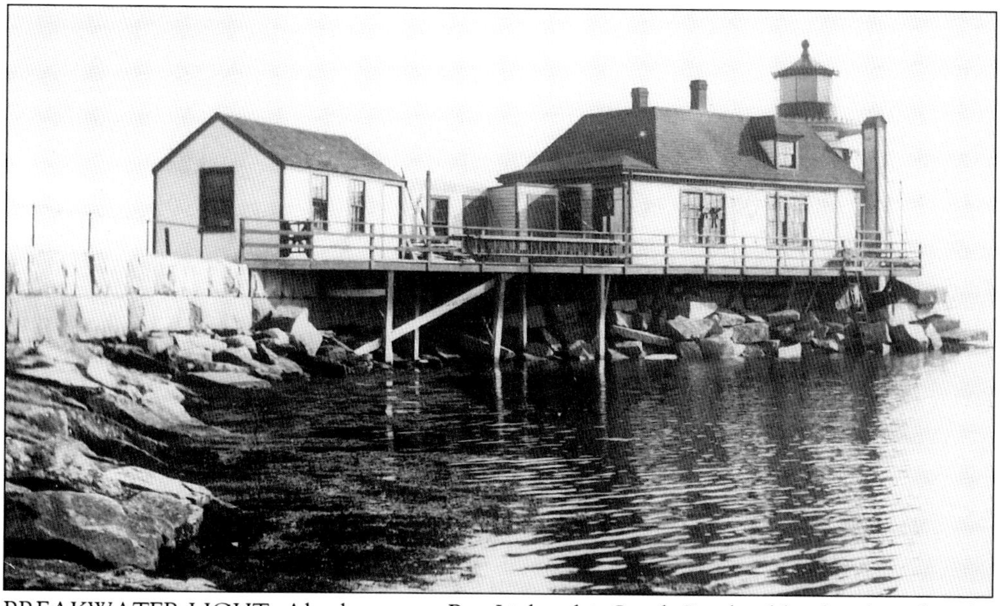

BREAKWATER LIGHT. Also known as Bug Light, this South Portland landmark replaced a wooden tower in 1875. The keeper's house was built in 1889. (Sullivan Photo Collection)

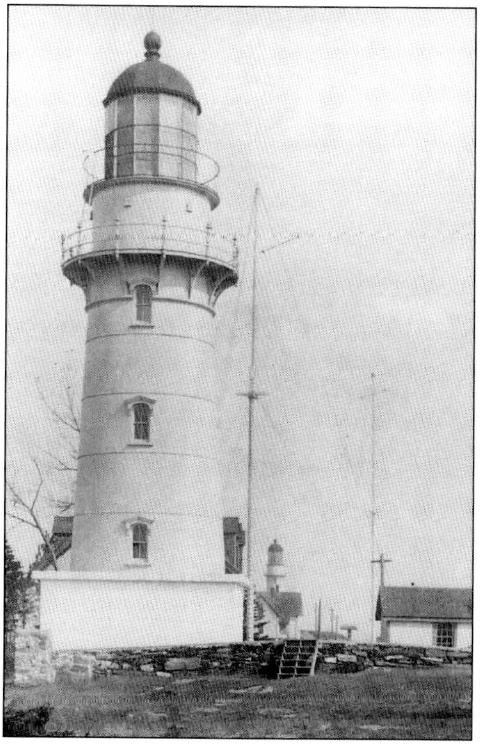

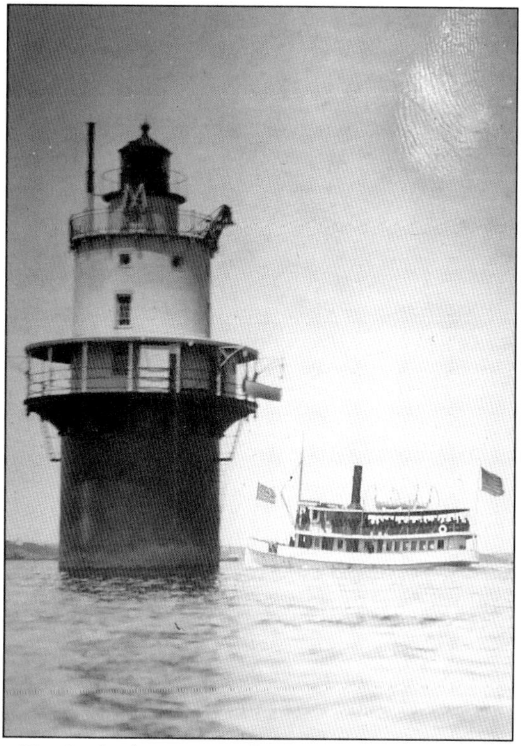

LEFT: TWO LIGHTS. Twin towers at Cape Elizabeth, known as the East and West lights, marked the navigational course for vessels entering Portland Harbor in the mid-1800s. (Sullivan Photo Collection)

RIGHT: SPRING POINT LIGHT. Operational in 1897, this light is now connected by a breakwater to the South Portland shore. (Robert Shuman family)

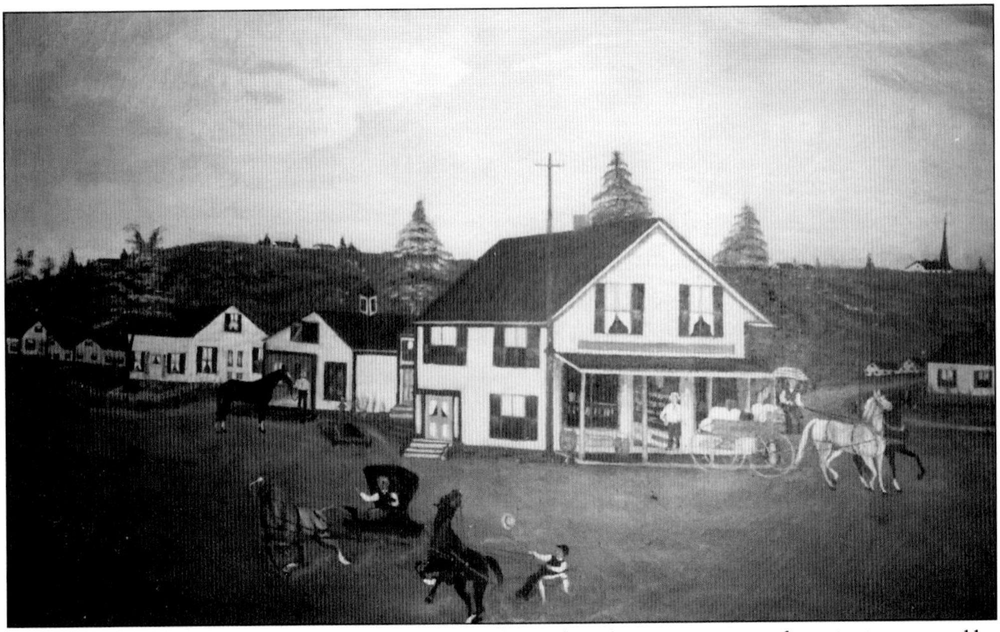

HOW TIMES CHANGE. The above photograph is taken from a painting of a painting owned by Dr. Carl Murphy of South Portland. It is said to be the intersection of Main Street and Broadway at Cash Corner around the turn of the century. The photograph below is the same spot in the 1920s occupied by an Amoco station with a "hot house" in the back. (George Thompson)

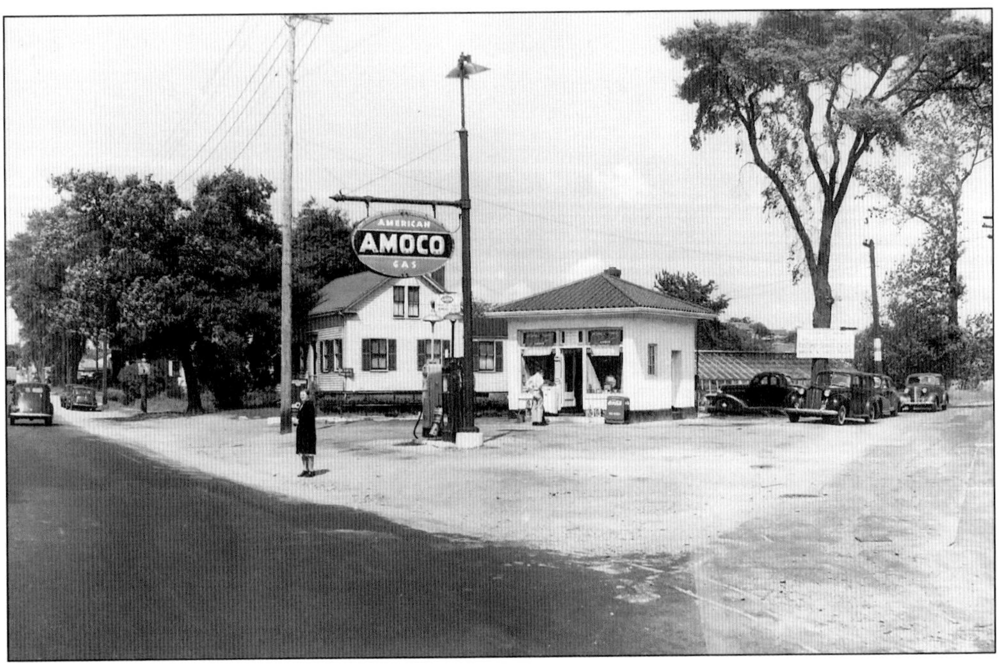

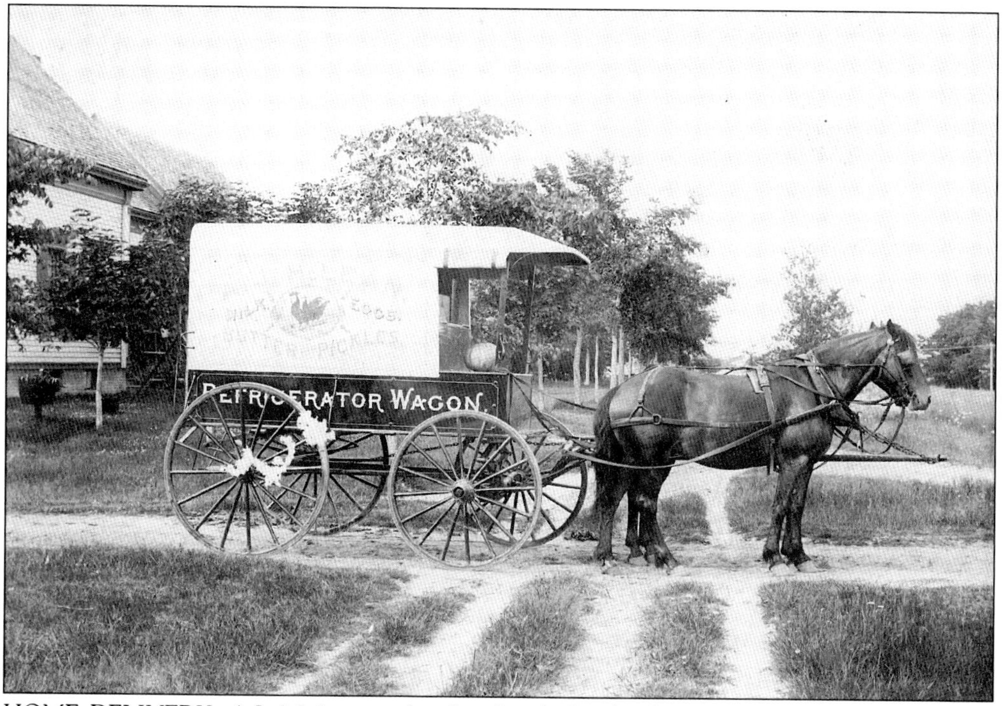

HOME DELIVERY. A.J. McLean makes his South Portland rounds delivering milk, butter, pickles, and other perishables in his refrigerated wagon. This c. 1900 photograph is believed to be in the Parrott Street area. (Dorothy M. Wilkes)

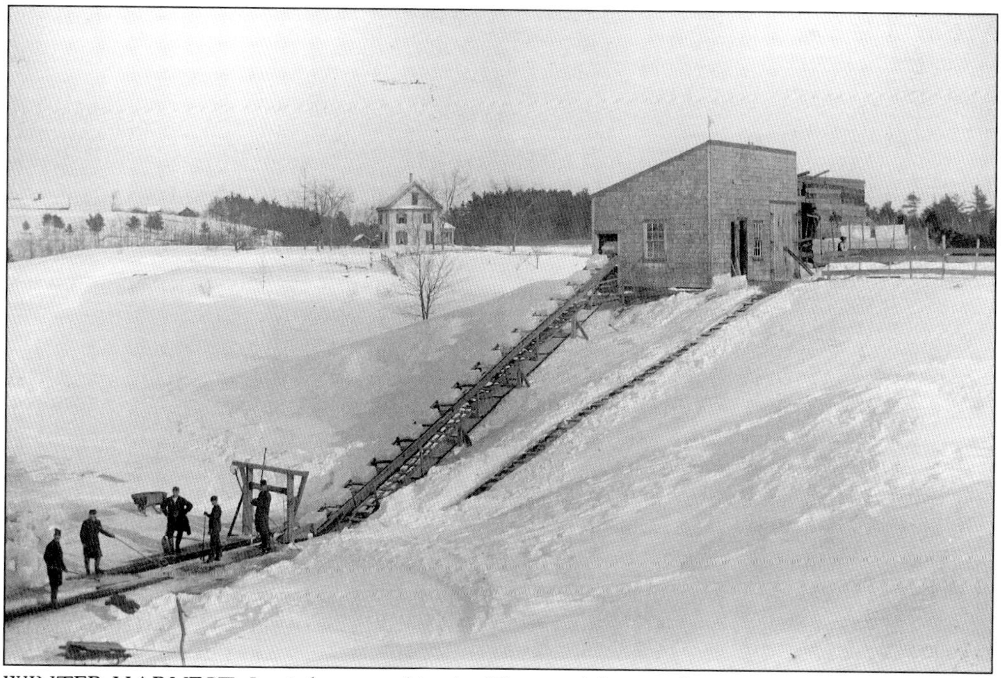

WINTER HARVEST. Ice is harvested in the Pleasantdale area for storage in D.W. Clark's ice house, c. 1900. Another ice house was located at Clark's Pond at Long Creek. In 1946 the pond was stocked with fish and the city's first fishing derby was held there. (Ray Taylor)

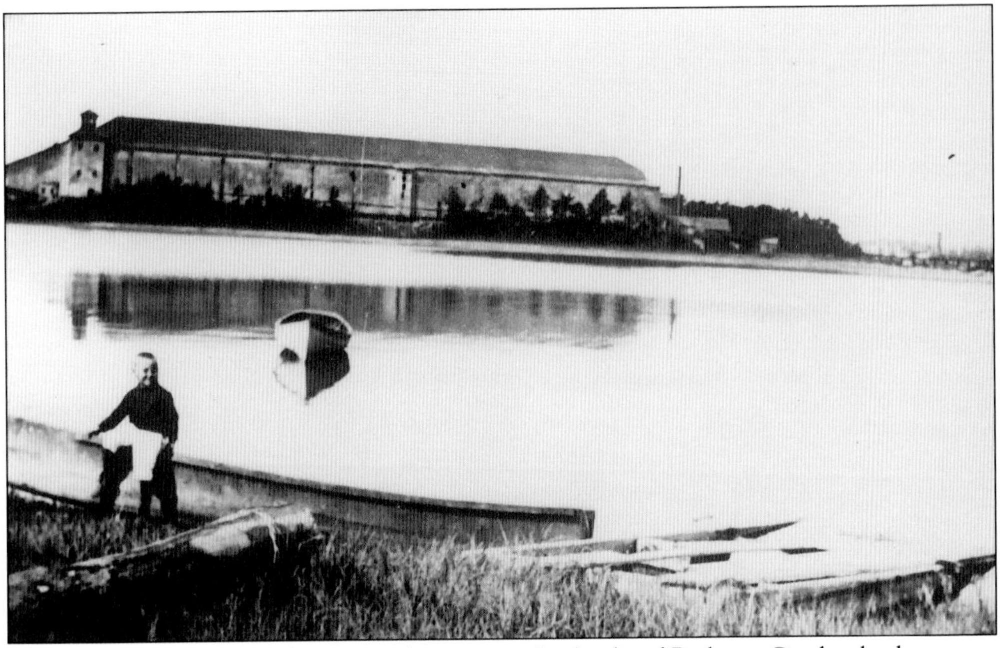

IN SUMMER. Clark's ice house can be seen on the banks of Barberry Creek, also known as Taylor's Brook, in Pleasantdale. It was a favorite boating and swimming spot in the early 1900s. (Ray Taylor)

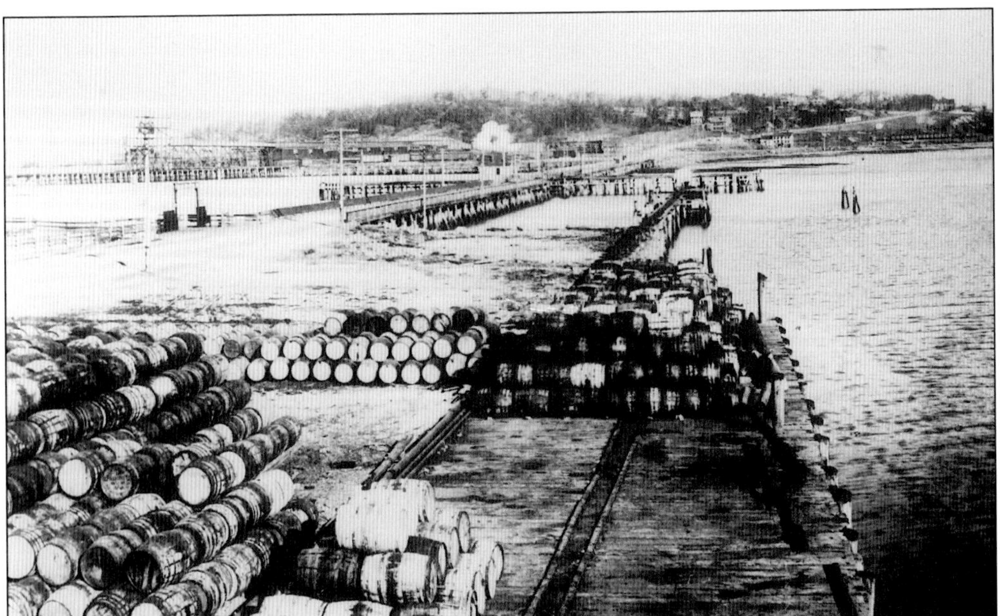

VAUGHAN'S BRIDGE. This toll bridge connected the Ligonia section of South Portland, called Kerosene Corner, to the Danforth Street area of Portland. The bridge was torn down in 1955 and replaced by the Veteran's Bridge. (Sullivan Photo Collection)

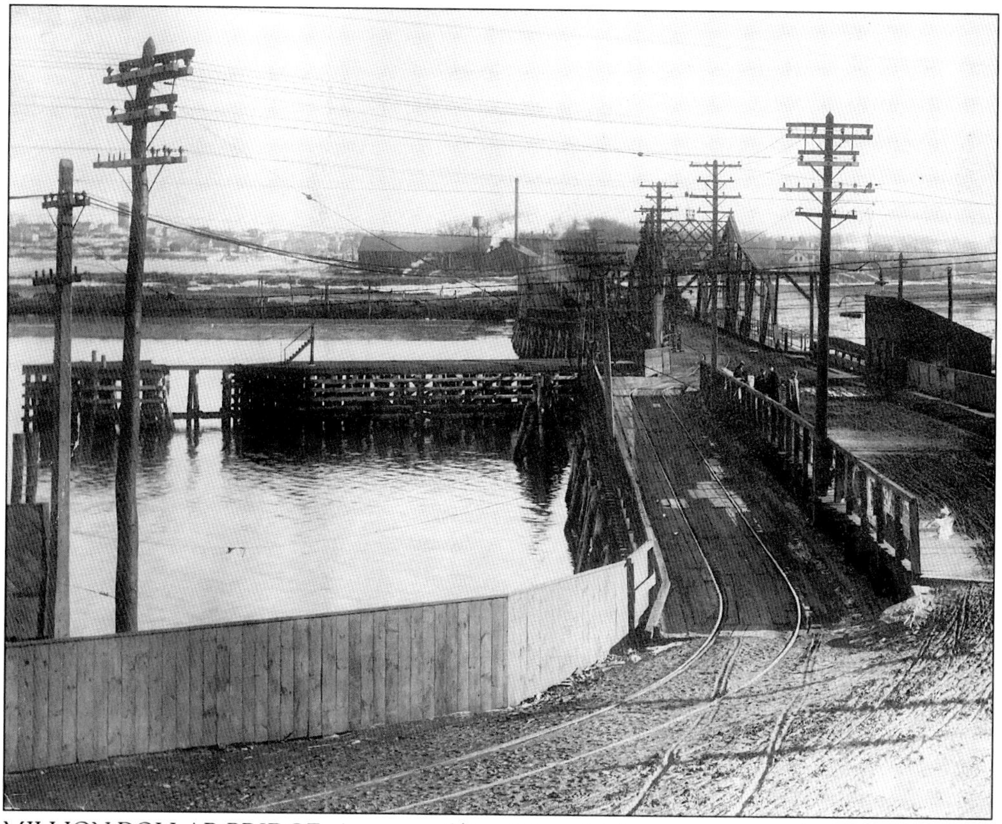

MILLION DOLLAR BRIDGE. At a cost of $1 million, this bridge spanning the Fore River from Portland to South Portland was opened in 1916. Construction is underway for its replacement. (Ray Taylor)

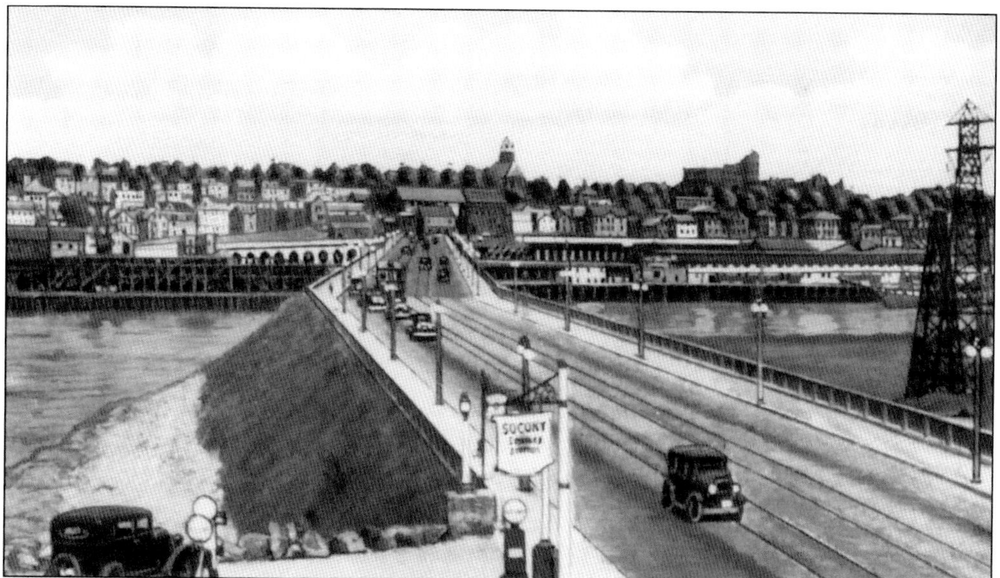

OTHER SIDE. This is the Portland skyline looking from South Portland over the Million Dollar Bridge in the 1920s and '30s. (Sullivan Photo Collection)

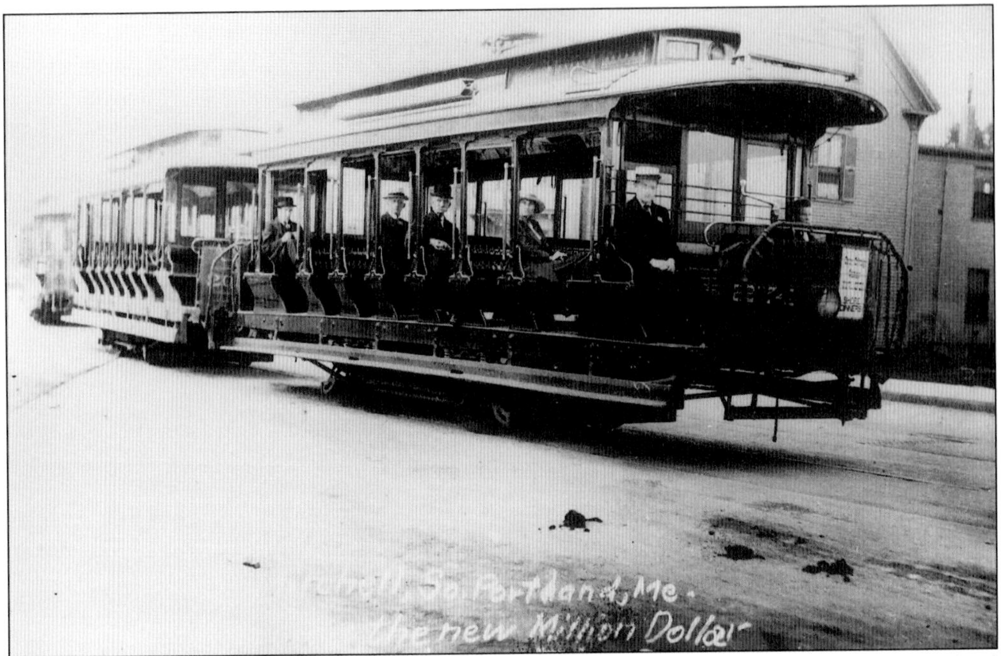

FIRST TROLLEY. The first electric car crosses the new Million Dollar Bridge to South Portland in July 1916. This travel convenience brought new development and recreational opportunities to the area. Trolley service was discontinued in 1940. (Sullivan Photo Collection)

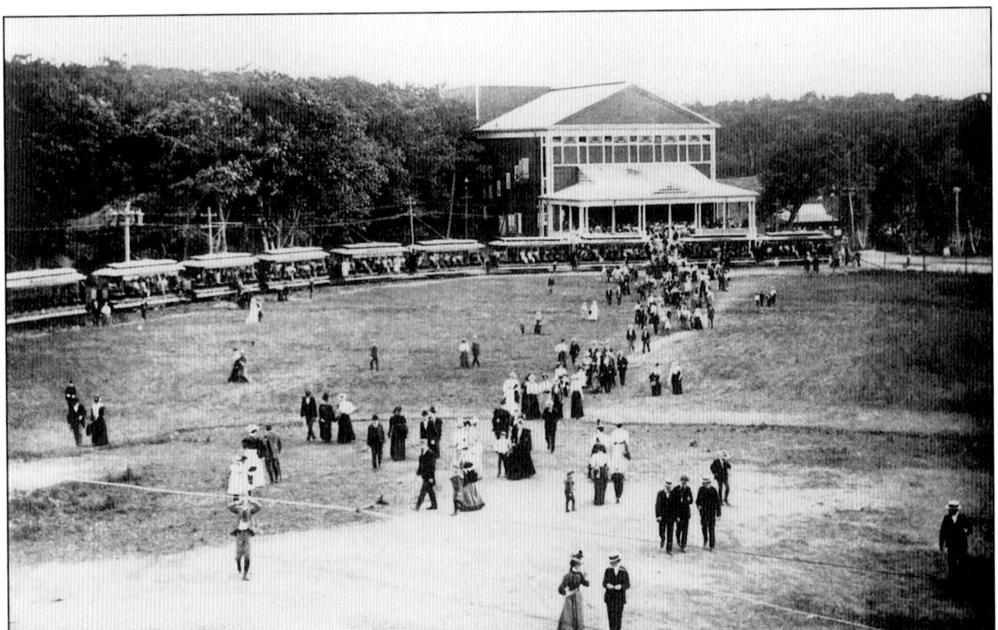

CAPE COTTAGE THEATRE. This 1,000-seat summer theater in Cape Elizabeth, dismantled in 1921, featured light opera and shore dinners. Trolleys serviced the area from Monument Square, Portland, leaving every ten minutes, c. 1904. (Sullivan Photo Collection)

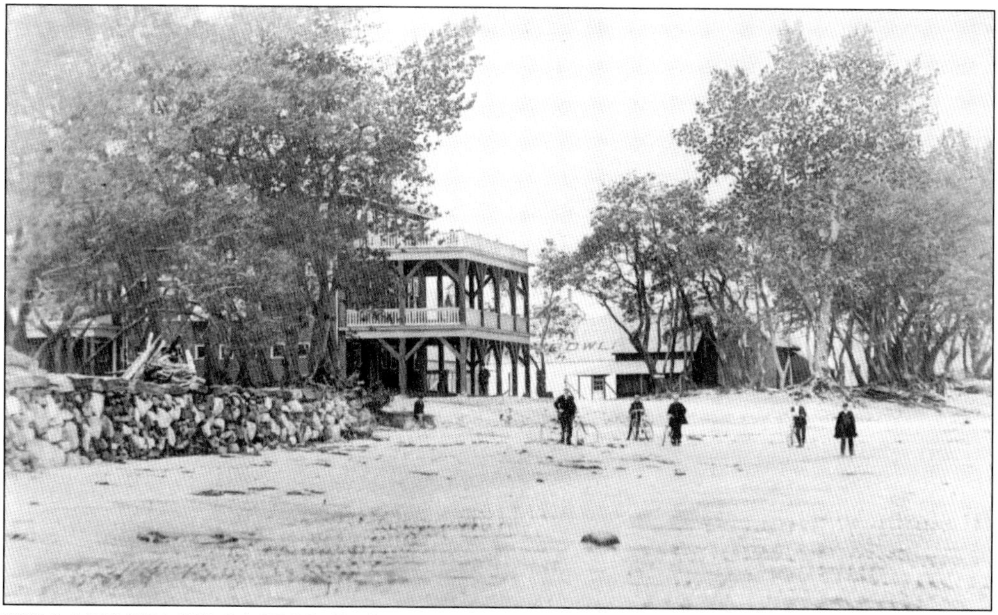

WILLARD BEACH CASINO. Built in 1896 at Willard Beach, South Portland (then Simonton Cove), this two-story structure offered the best in recreation: a spectacular oceanfront view, bathing, dining, dancing, and a bowling alley next door. Built by the Cape Shore Railroad Co. at a cost of $30,000, it burned down in 1898. (Rosella Loveitt)

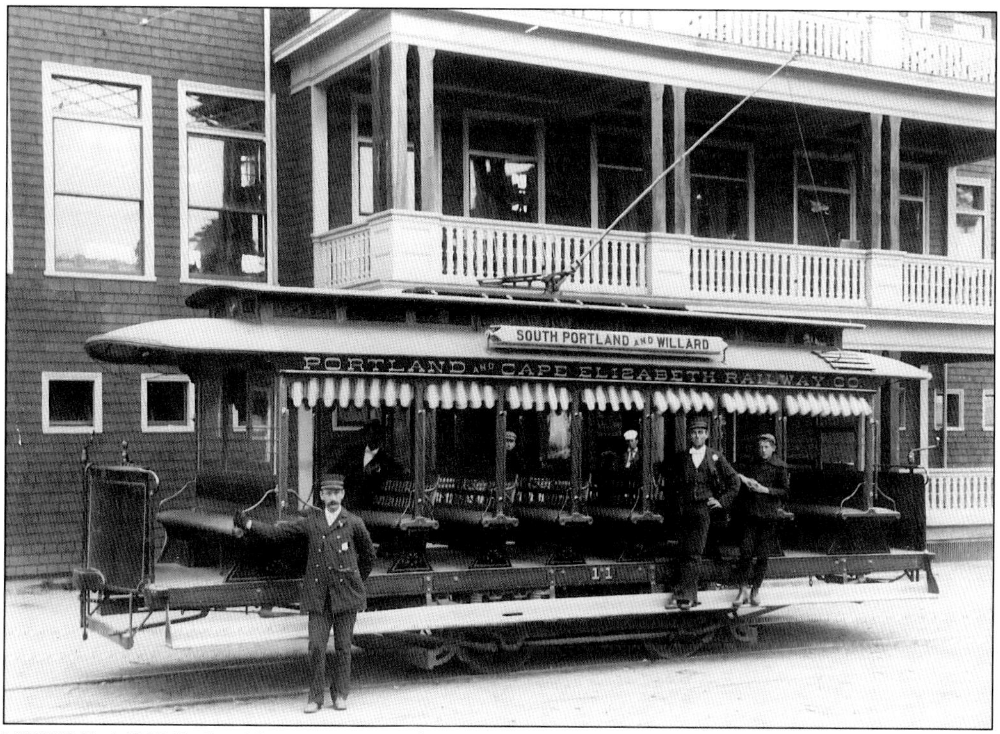

NICKLE A RIDE. Car No. 11 stops at the Willard Beach Casino in South Portland at the turn of the century. Tracks for this route ran from Monument Square in Portland, to Broadway in South Portland, to Willard Beach. Travel time was twenty minutes. (Rosella Loveitt)

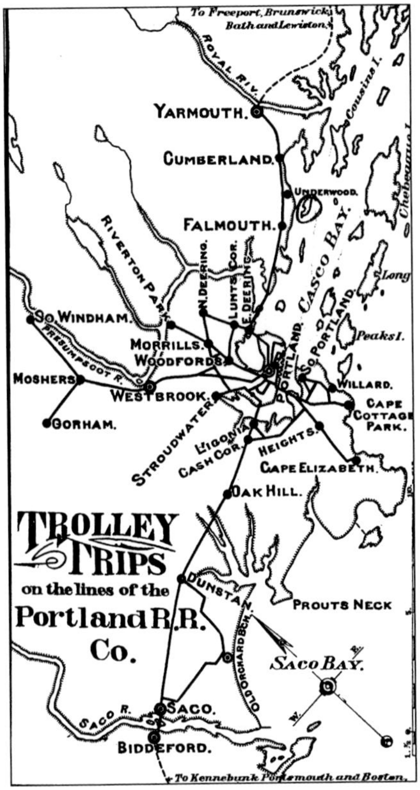

TROLLEY ROUTE. The South Portland/Cape Elizabeth trolley map. (Ellen Knight)

CAPE CASINO. This playing card is from a souvenir pack once published by Chisholm Bros. in Portland. Each card in the deck features landmarks in the Greater Portland/White Mountains areas. The Casino at Cape Cottage enjoyed great popularity in the early 1900s. It later became the Cape Shore Inn. (Ellen Knight)

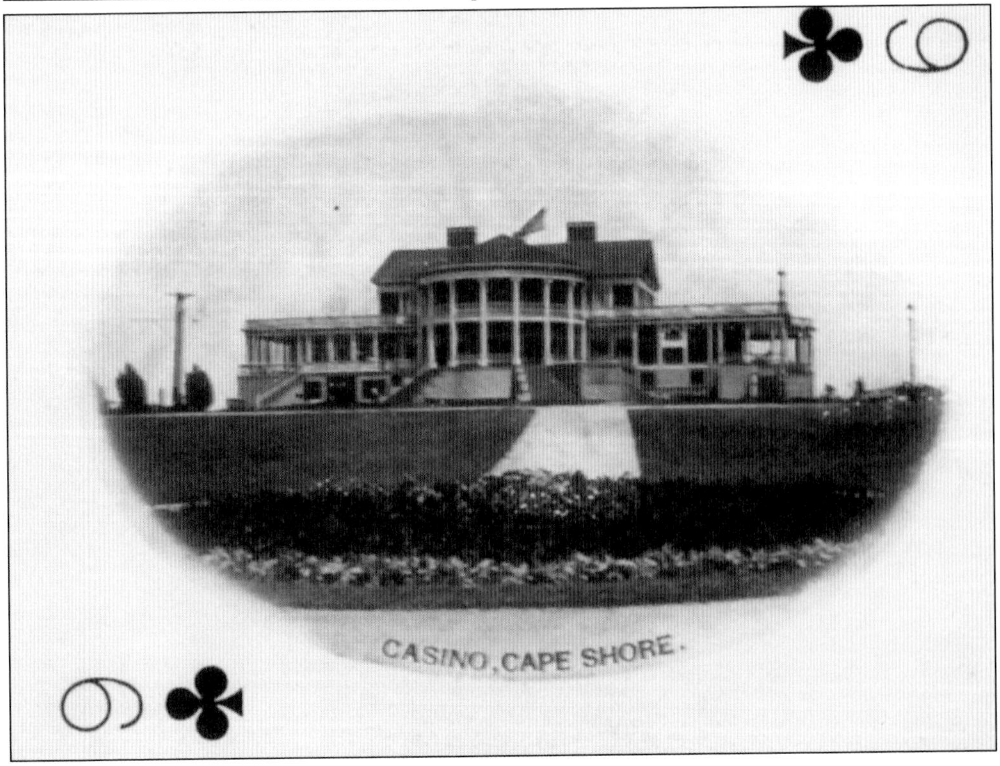

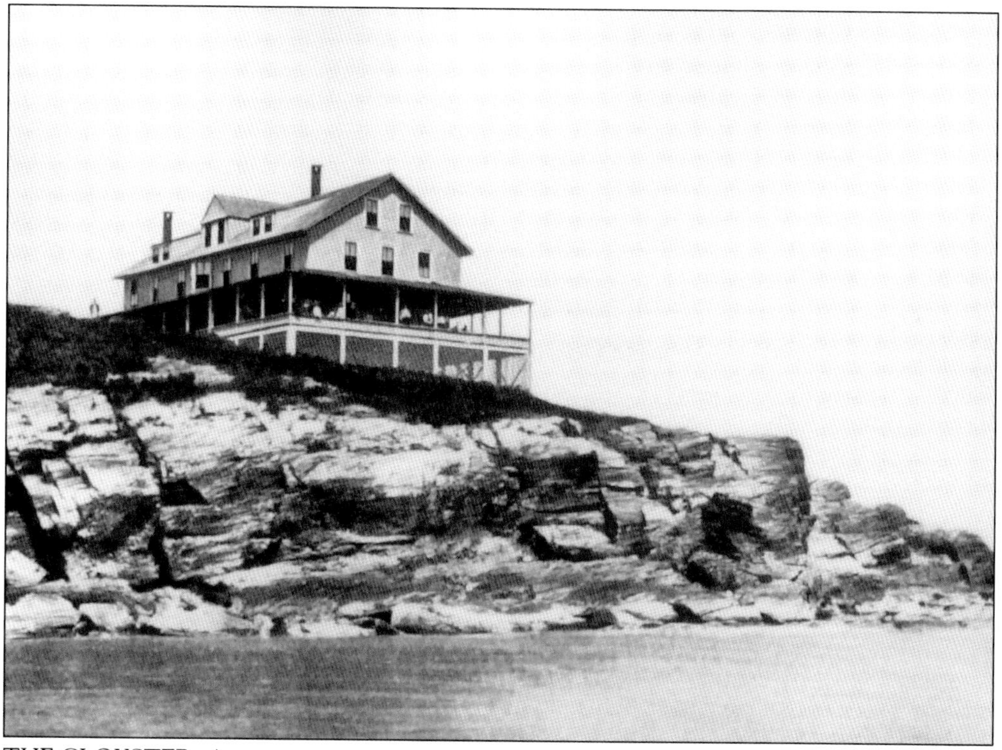

THE CLOYSTER. A summer hotel at the end of Cloyster Road, South Portland, the Cloyster was a favorite vacation spot for tourists from Canada at the turn of the century. (Sullivan Photo Collection)

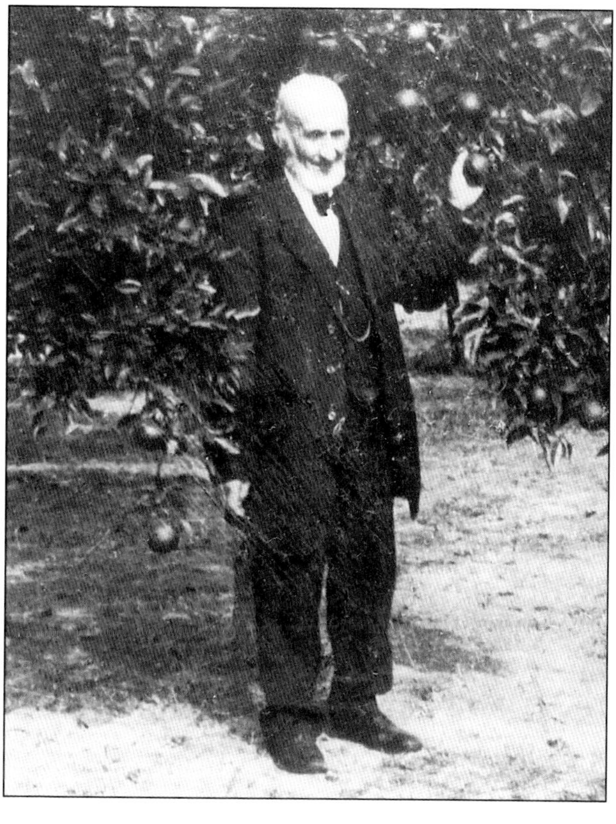

NATHANIEL DYER. Born in 1830, Nathaniel was the son of Jonah and grandson of Nathaniel, born in 1771, whose house is one of the oldest in Cape Elizabeth. The younger Nathaniel lived on Wells Road. (Norman Jordan)

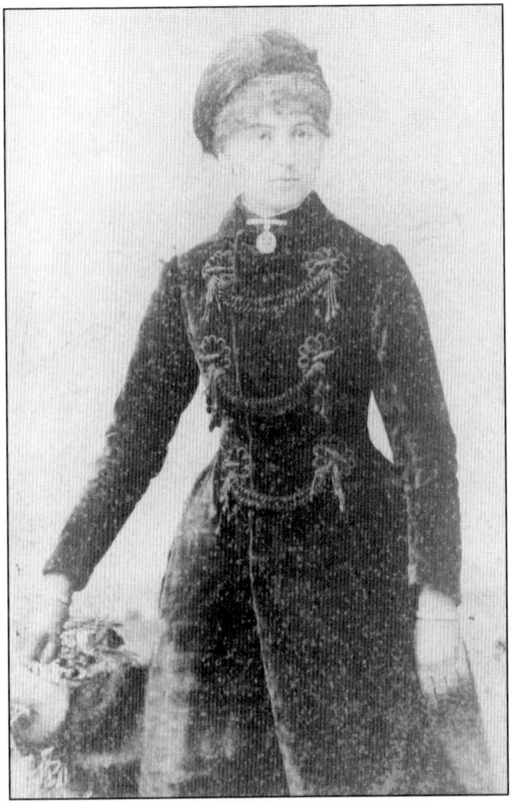

MARY ELIZABETH JORDAN. Born in 1848, Mary, shown here at age twenty-four, grew up in Cape Elizabeth with siblings Clementine, Emma W., and Pomeroy Jordan. (Norman Jordan)

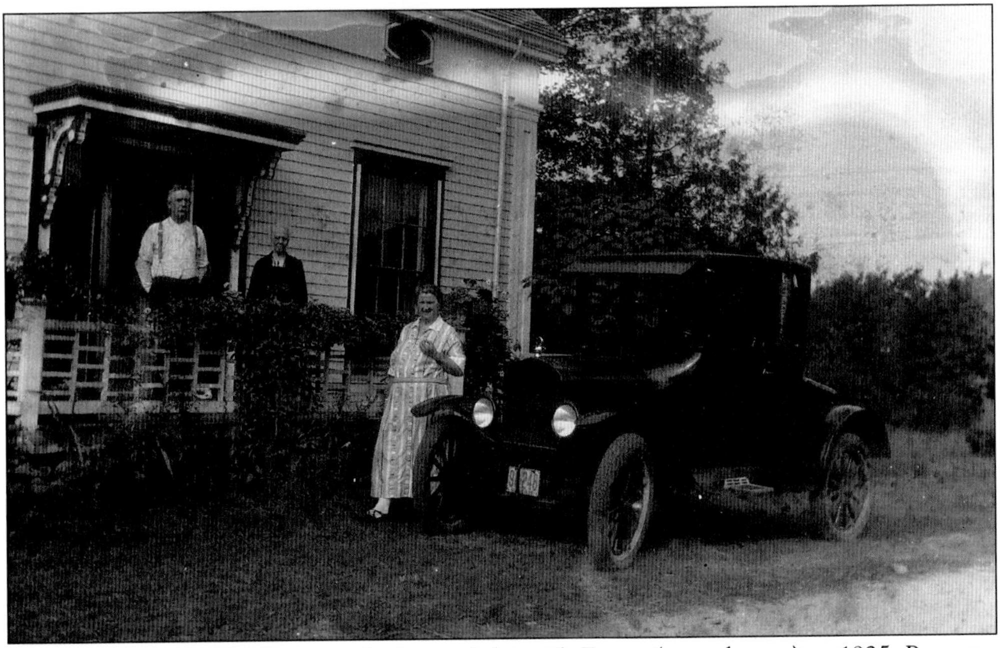

THE JORDAN FARM. Pomeroy Jordan with his wife Emma (near the car), c. 1925. Pomeroy was born in 1862 and was the proud owner of the first Dodge automobile sold in New England in 1914. He was active in state and local politics and the Grange. (Norman Jordan)

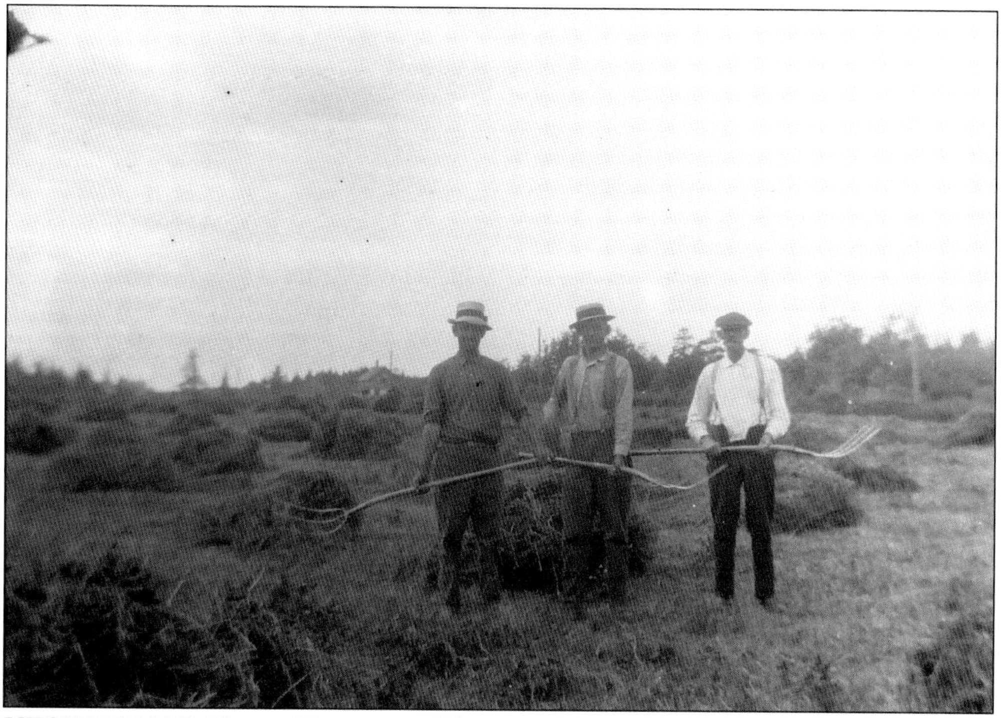

PITCHING HAY. Three of Pomeroy and Emma Jordan's eight sons lend a hand on the family farm in Cape Elizabeth, *c.* 1920. (Norman Jordan)

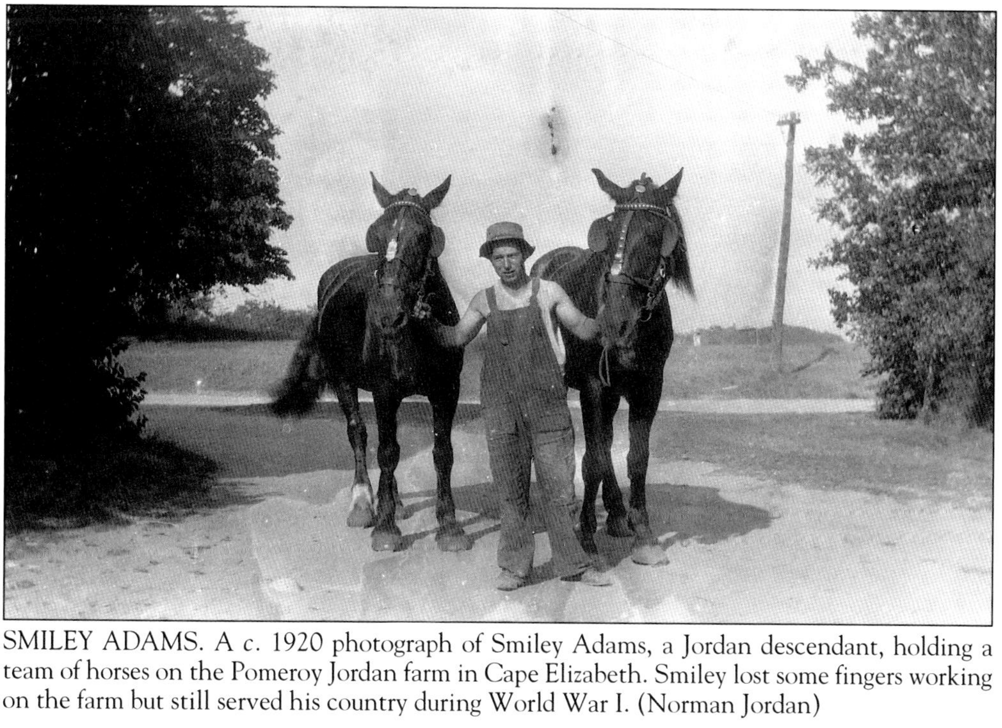

SMILEY ADAMS. A *c.* 1920 photograph of Smiley Adams, a Jordan descendant, holding a team of horses on the Pomeroy Jordan farm in Cape Elizabeth. Smiley lost some fingers working on the farm but still served his country during World War I. (Norman Jordan)

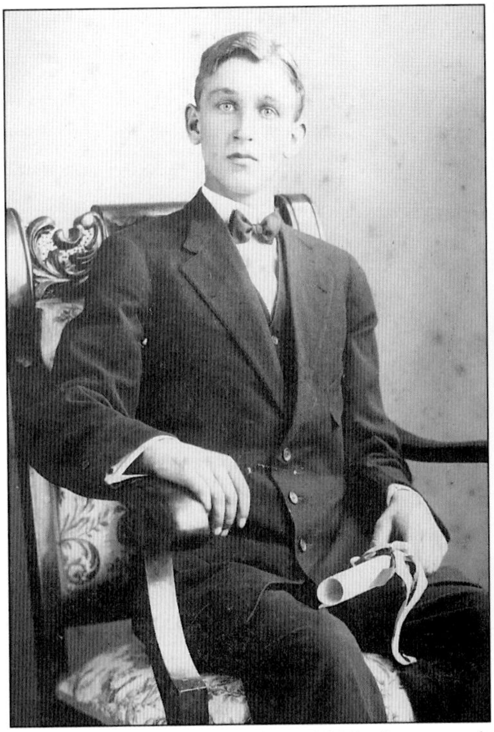

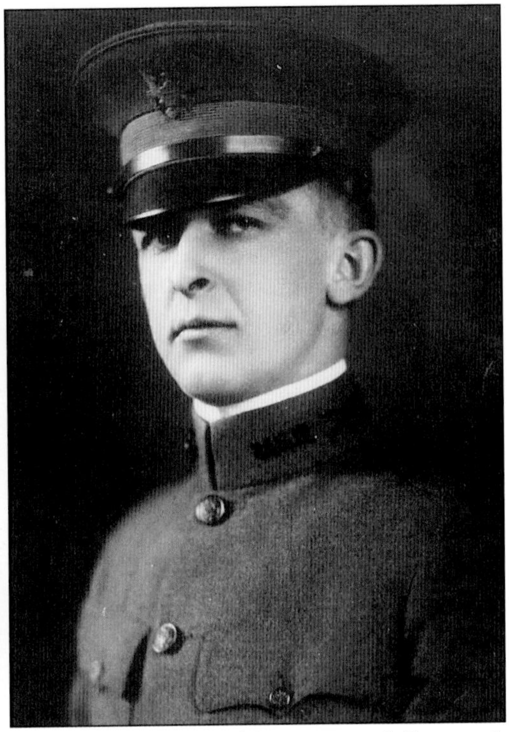

LEFT: SELECTMAN. A c. 1920 photograph of Phil Jordan, son of Pomeroy and Emma. A 1910 graduate of Cape Elizabeth High School, Phil served in World War I and was a three-time selectman. (Norman Jordan)

RIGHT: SHERIFF JORDAN. Shown in his World War I uniform, Lloyd W. Jordan of Cape Elizabeth was a Portland businessman and the sheriff of Cumberland County. Born in 1894, he was accidentally shot in a hunting accident, developed gangrene, and died in 1933. (Norman Jordan)

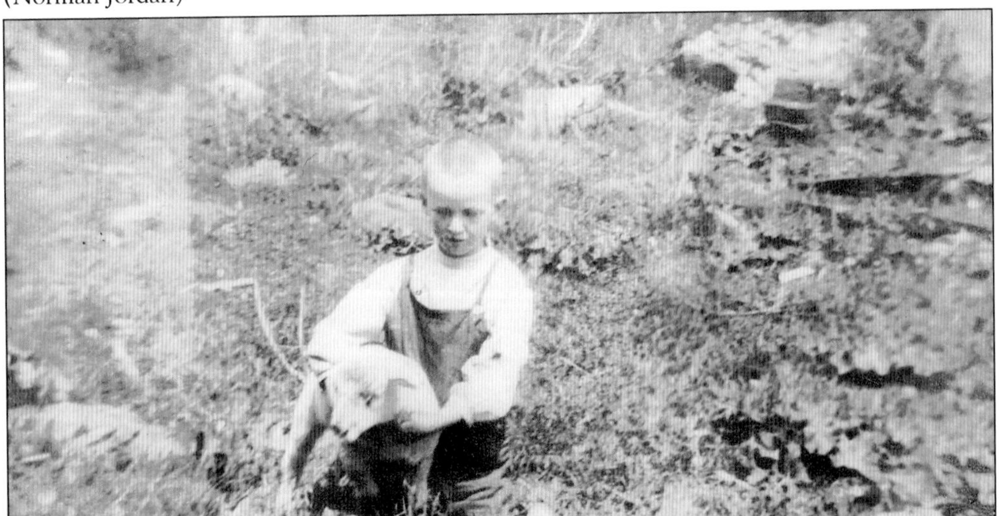

PIGLET. A c. 1916 photograph of Norman Jordan Sr. of Cape Elizabeth holding a red pig given to the family to raise as part of the war effort in World War I. The family traveled to Portland to pick up the pig, and his sister Gladys chose this one. (Norman Jordan)

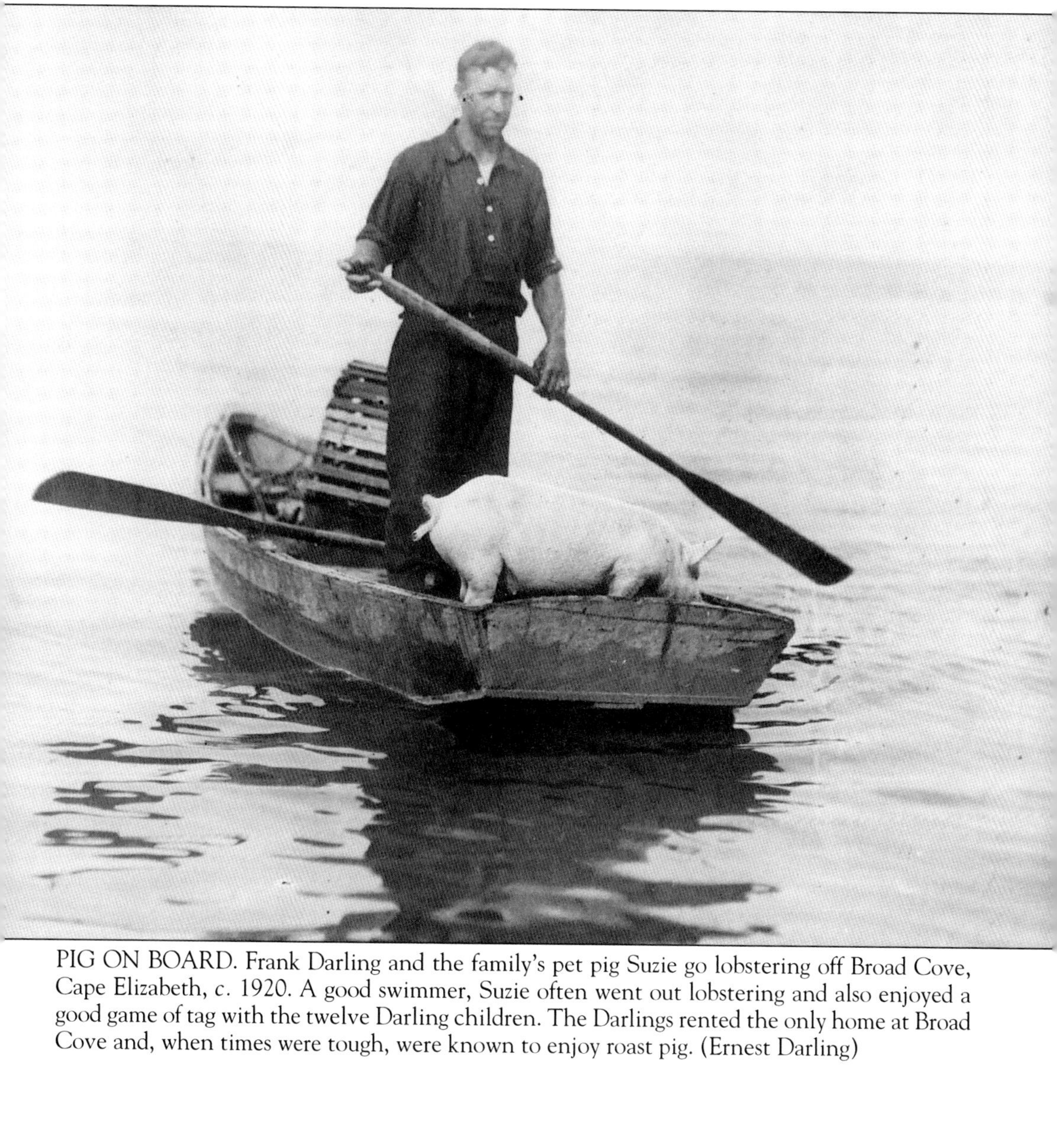

PIG ON BOARD. Frank Darling and the family's pet pig Suzie go lobstering off Broad Cove, Cape Elizabeth, *c.* 1920. A good swimmer, Suzie often went out lobstering and also enjoyed a good game of tag with the twelve Darling children. The Darlings rented the only home at Broad Cove and, when times were tough, were known to enjoy roast pig. (Ernest Darling)

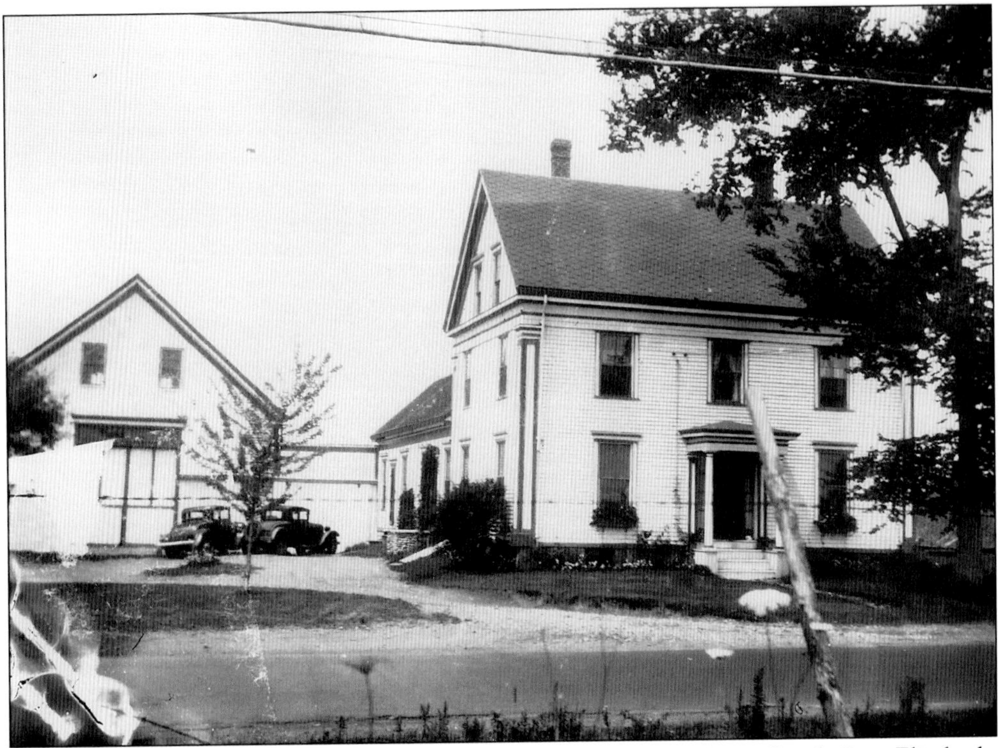

HANNAFORD BUILT. Emma Dyer Jordan lived here on Ocean House Road, Cape Elizabeth, from about 1929 to 1944. (Norman Jordan)

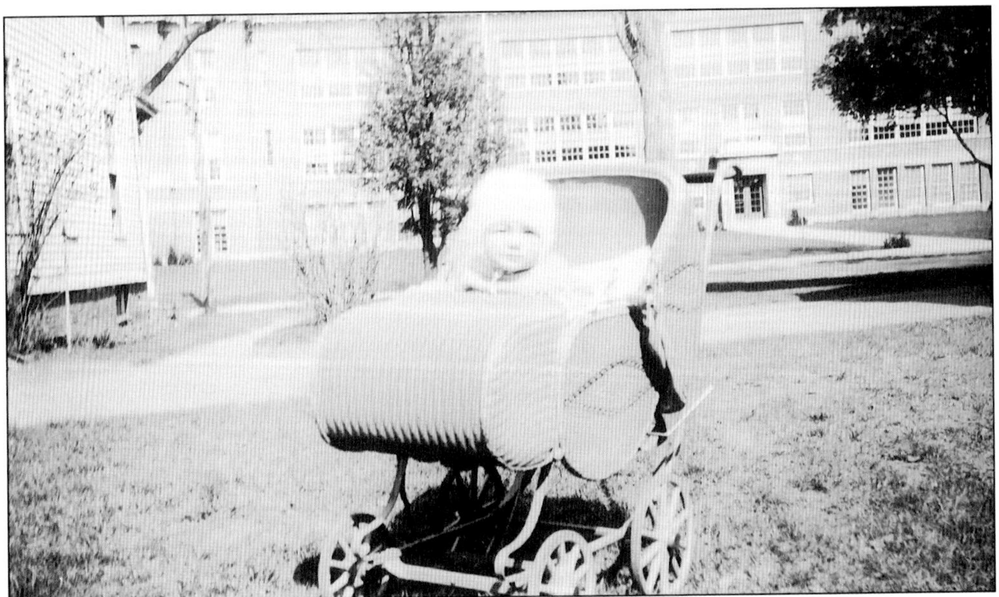

OUT FOR A STROLL. Norman Jordan Jr. enjoys an outing in his wicker carriage, with South Portland High School on Ocean Street in the background, c. 1935. The house at left is where the Pizza Joint is now. (Norman Jordan)

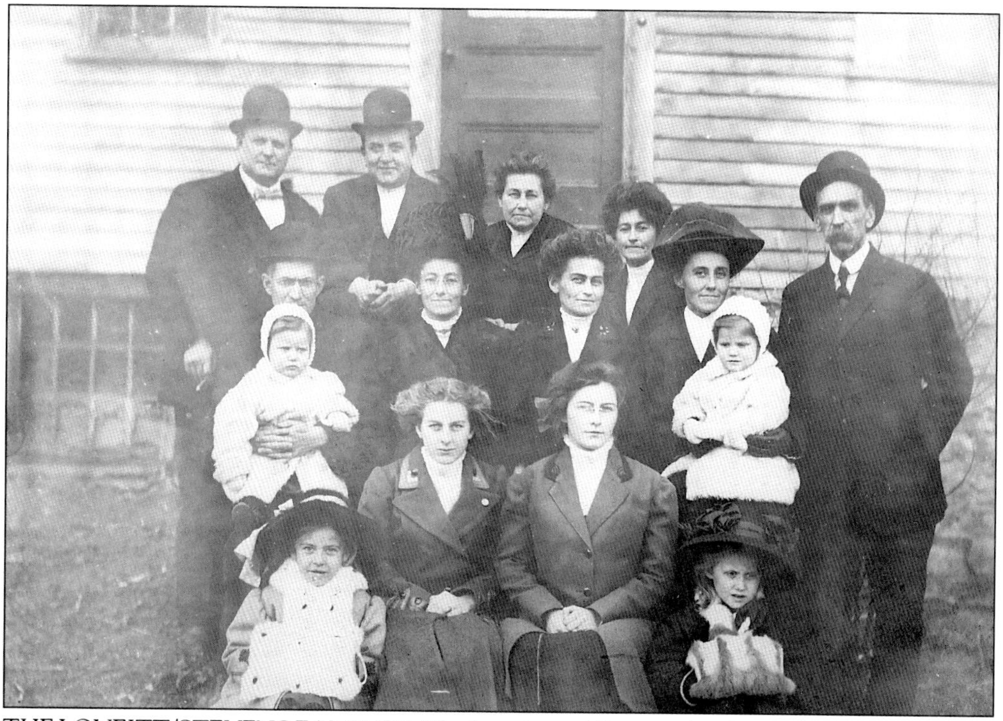

THE LOVEITT/STEVENS FAMILIES. The Loveitt and Stevens families gather in 1908 outside the William Stevens home on Myrtle Street, South Portland, formerly the Old Blockhouse. From left to right are: (front row) Phyllis Bangert, Hazel Stevens, Eleanor Dickenson, and Lauretta Loveitt; (middle row) George Loveitt (holding daughter Rosella), mother Ella Loveitt (holding Rosella's twin Lillian), Addie Dickenson, Lillian Stevens, and William Stevens; (back row) Edwin Dickenson, Francis Bangert, Hattie Stevens, and Hattie Bangert. (Rosella Loveitt)

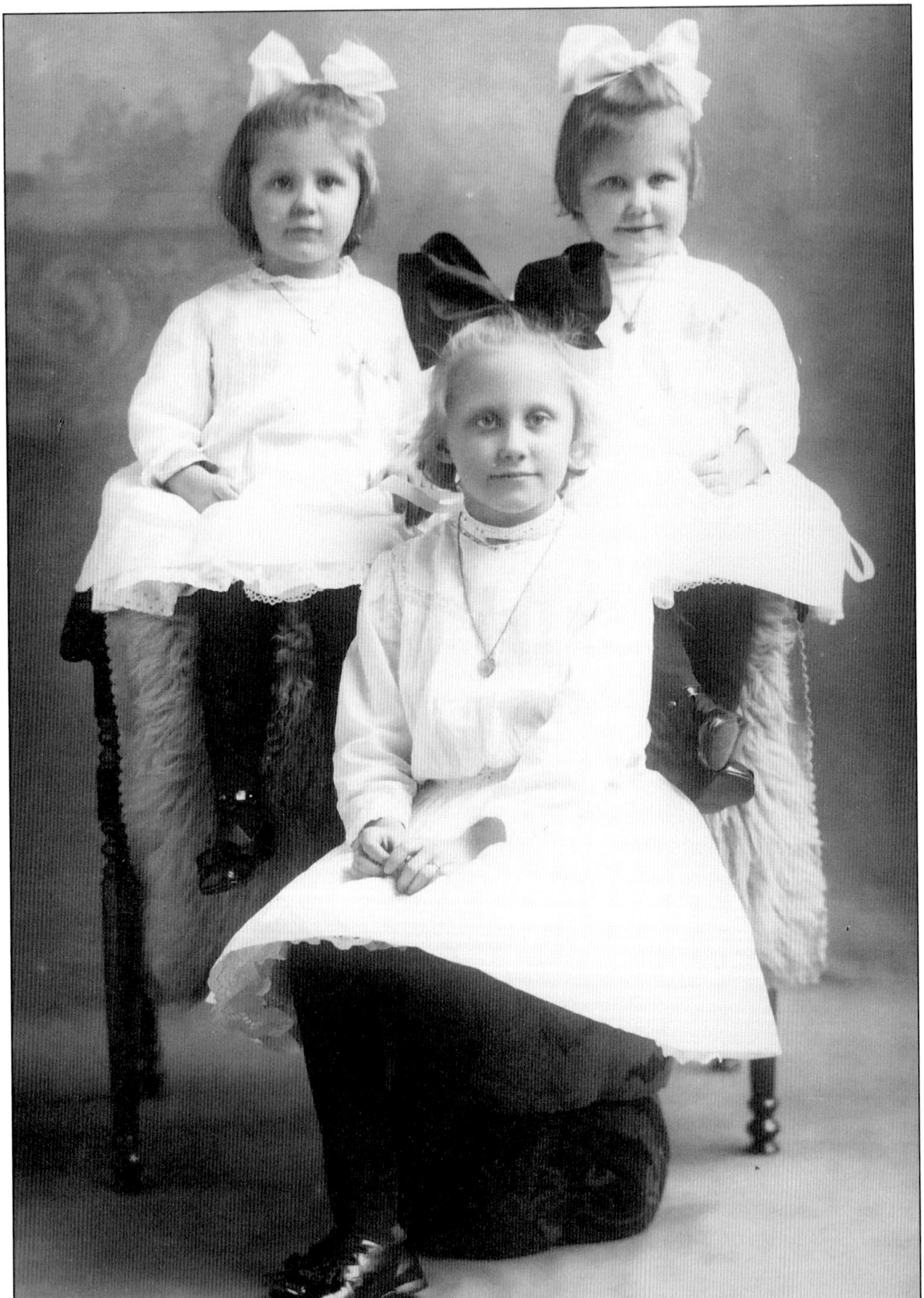

THE LOVEITT SISTERS. Twins Lillian and Rosella Loveitt, in back, pose with big sister Lauretta in 1911. They grew up on Preble Street, South Portland. (Rosella Loveitt)

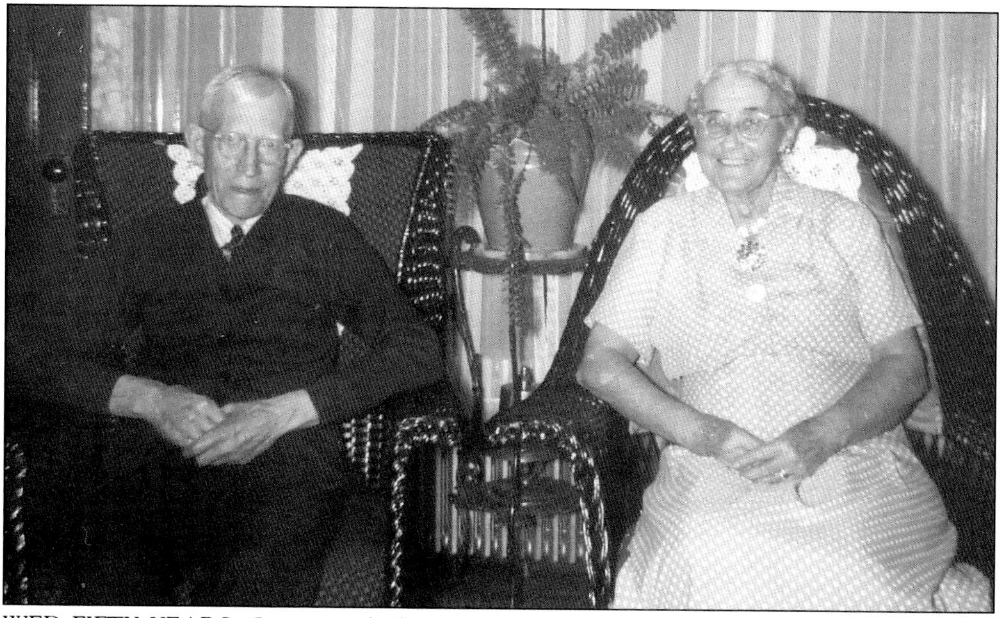

WED FIFTY YEARS. George and Ella Loveitt celebrate their 50th wedding anniversary at a party given by their three daughters in 1951. They lived on Preble Street, South Portland, in the home they moved into on their wedding night, now the residence of their daughters Lauretta and Rosella. The Loveitts descend from Enoch Loveitt who, in 1836, purchased more than 29 acres at Simonton's Cove for taxes owed the town of Cape Elizabeth. The area is now known as Loveitt's Field, South Portland. (Rosella Loveitt)

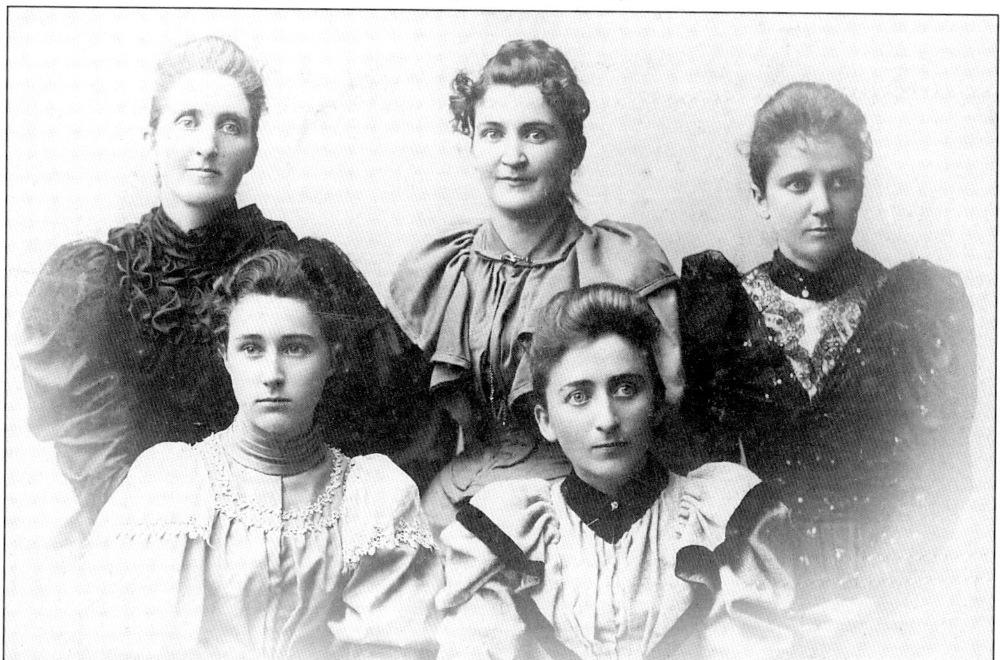

THE DYER SISTERS. Elizabeth Toby (front left) was a cousin of the Nathaniel Dyer family and was raised with his daughters. From left to right are: (front) Alice Dyer; (back) Frances, Emmaline, and Clara Dyer. This is a *c.* 1905 photograph. (Norman Jordan)

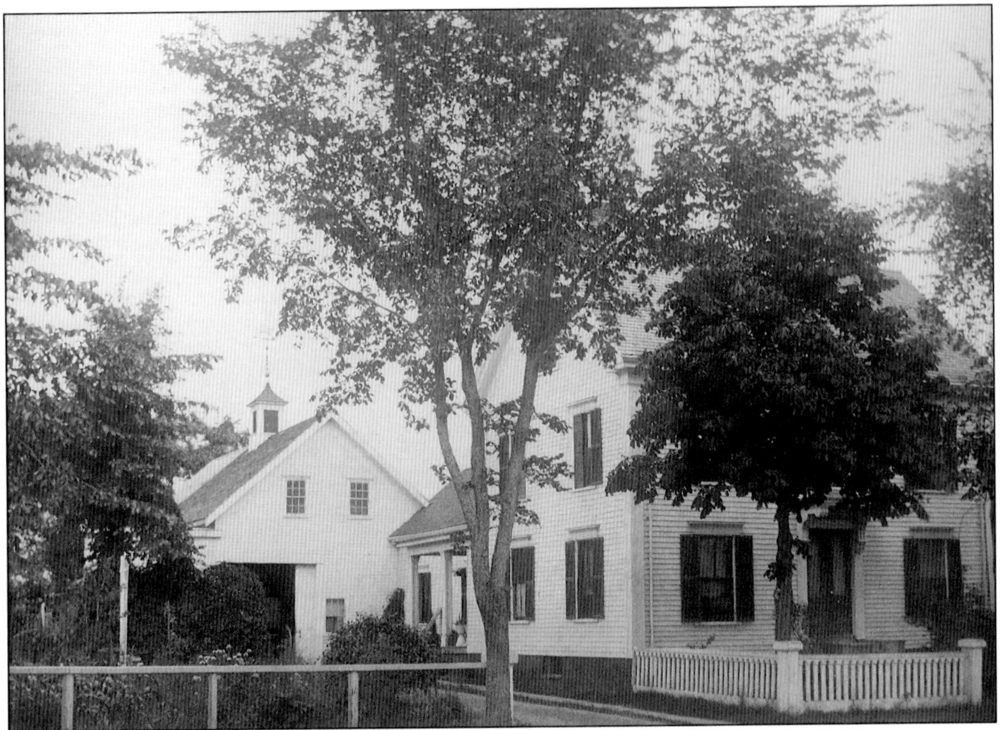

THE JESSIE DYER HOUSE. Shown on Evans Street prior to 1918 is the Jesse Dyer house. In 1869 Jessie Dyer purchased the Brown's Hill Church chapel, now part of the Elm Street Methodist Church. One of the first of the Dyers to settle in the area was Henry, who came from Cape Cod in the 1700s. (Ray Taylor)

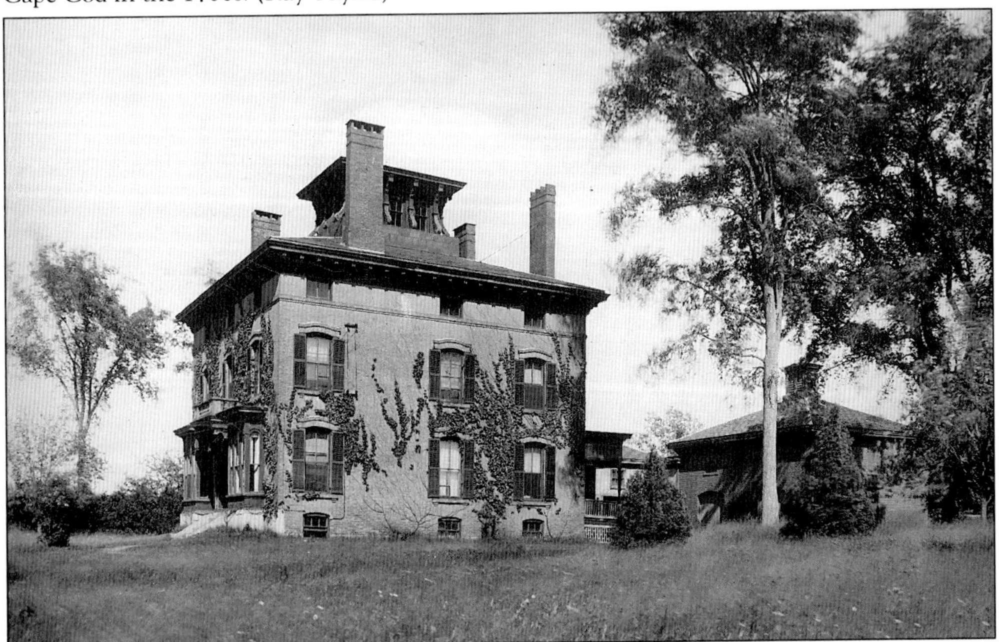

THE NUTTER HOUSE. This stately 1850s home in the Pleasantdale area was built by brothers Eben and Irving Nutter and was the scene of much social activity. (Ray Taylor)

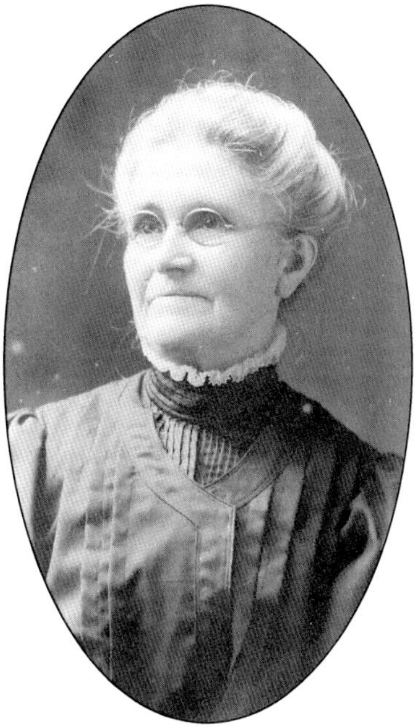
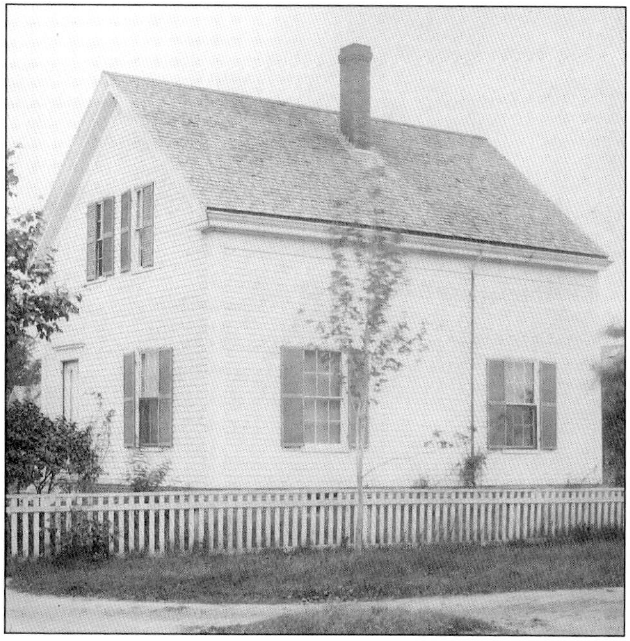

THE AMES HOUSE. William and Mahalia Ames lived in this house on the corner of Elm and Chestnut Streets, South Portland. Mahalia (left) was the sister of James Taylor, who lived on Broadway, *c.* 1900. (Ray Taylor)

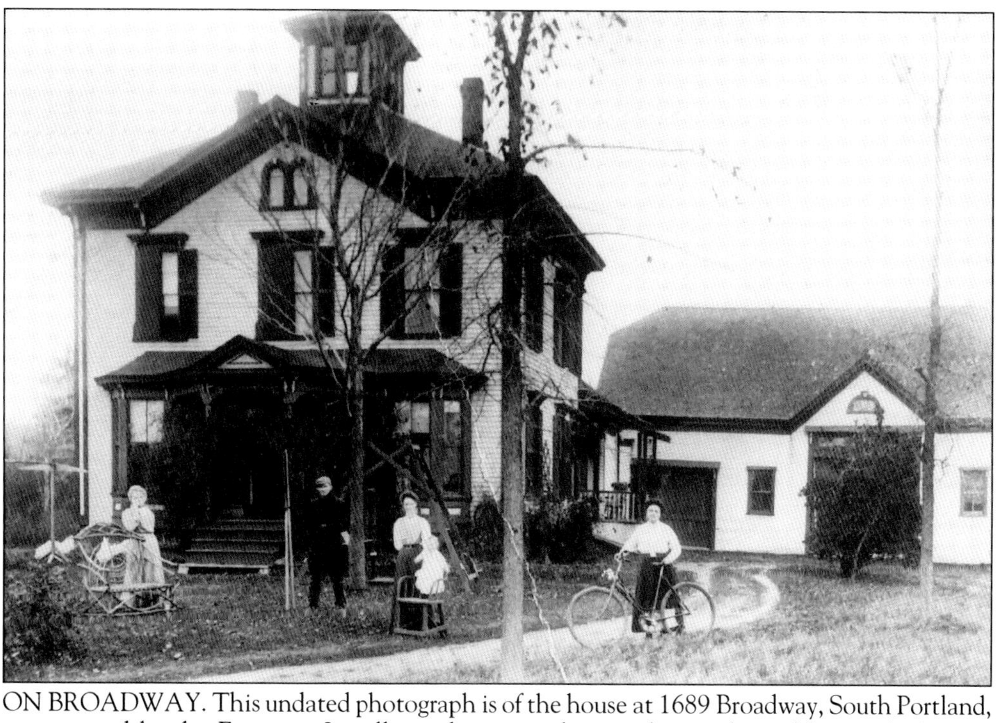

ON BROADWAY. This undated photograph is of the house at 1689 Broadway, South Portland, once owned by the Farnums. It still stands, minus the cupola, porch, and barn, which were destroyed by fire. (George Thompson)

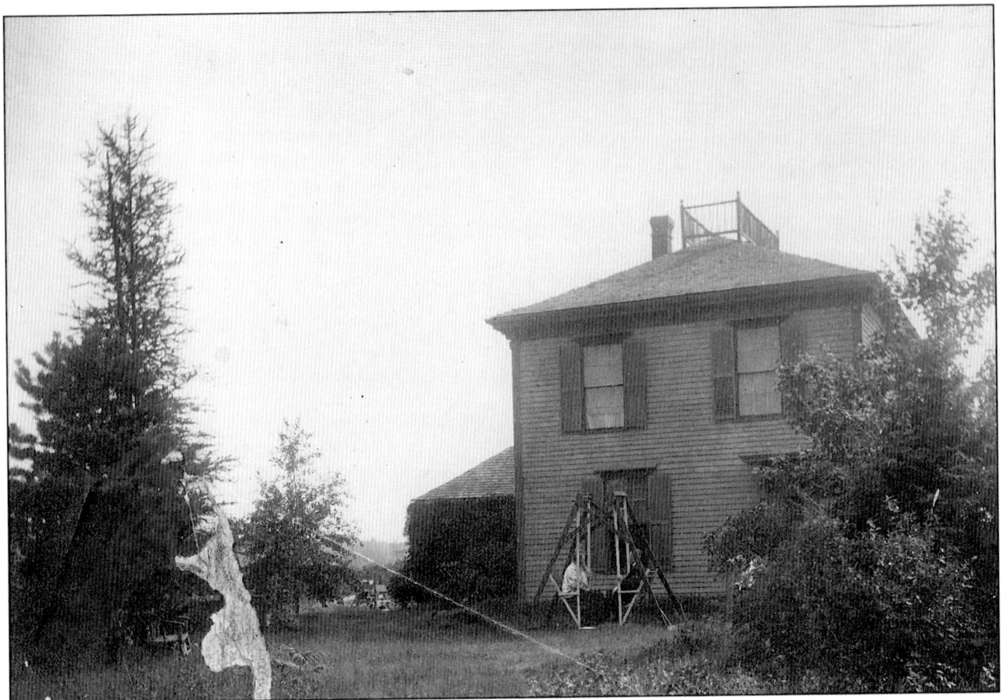

THE TAYLOR HOUSE. A c. 1914 photograph of the house located at 13 Evans Street (now Taylor Lane), South Portland. This house was built in the 1880s by James H. and Alice Taylor after their marriage in 1877. Jane was a teacher in the local schools; James, a Civil War veteran, was a journalist. (Ray Taylor)

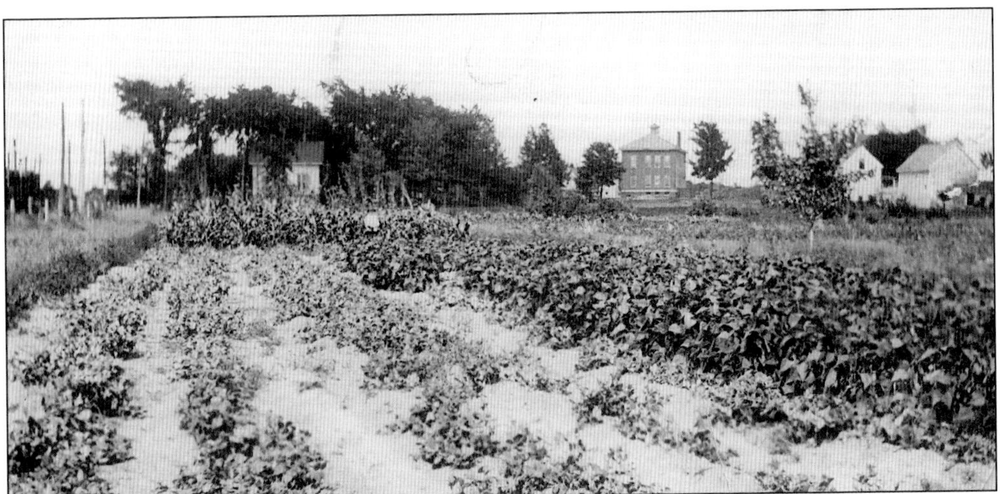

GARDEN GIVEAWAY. The Taylors allowed employees of the J.L. Libby Department Store in Portland to plant their own gardens on this land bordering the Taylor house. In the background, from left to right, are the Frank C. Sawyer house (later the Peary residence), the Summer Street School, and the David Jones house, c. 1900. (Ray Taylor)

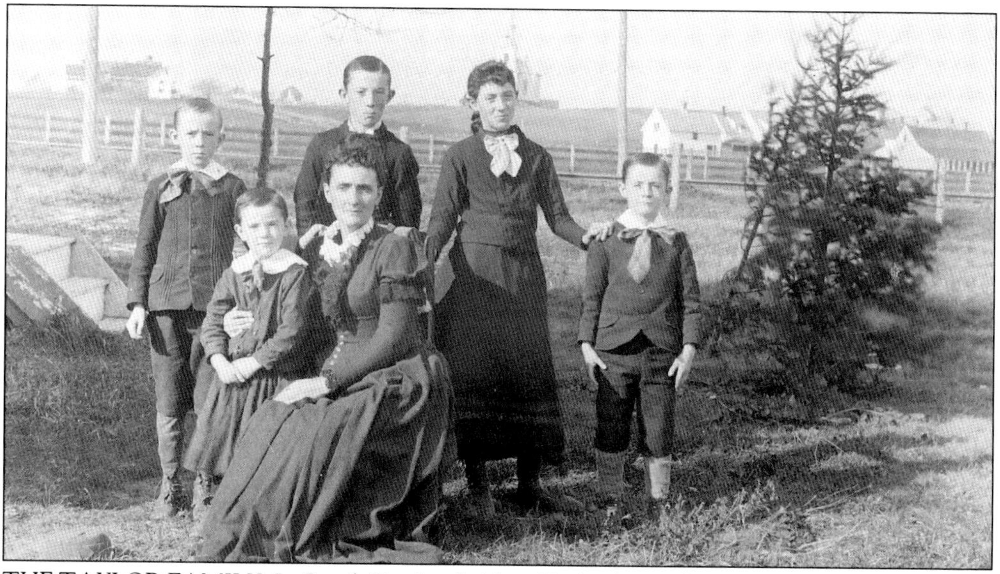

THE TAYLOR FAMILY. In South Portland, Alice Taylor (seated), the wife of James H. Taylor, gathers with the family at 13 Evans Street in the 1880s. From left to right are Frank, Will, Charlie H., Elizabeth, and Harry. The Brown's Hill Church is in the background. Its tower once served as a beacon for ships at sea and stories are told of Indians camping nearby to watch for ships coming into port. (Ray Taylor)

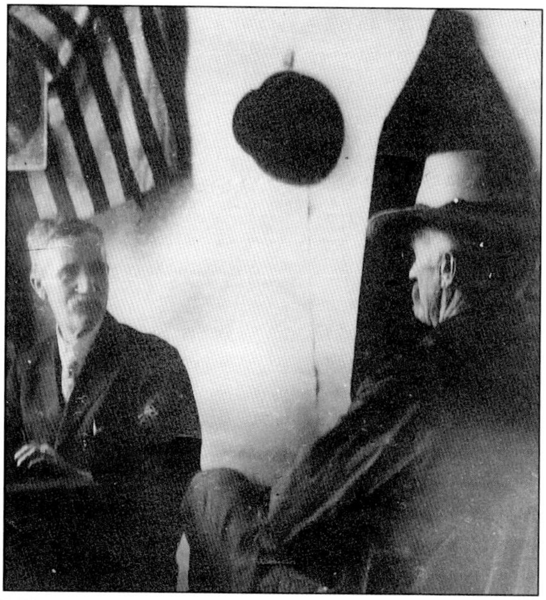

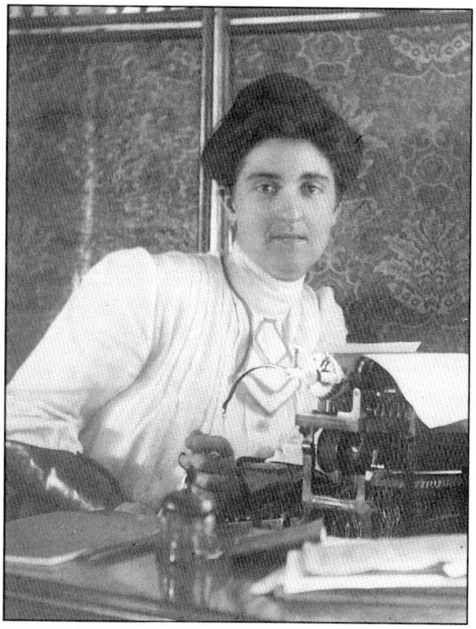

LEFT: JAMES H. TAYLOR. A reporter with the *Portland Evening Express* until 1914, James H. Taylor of Evans Street, South Portland, conducts an interview in the newspaper's Portland office. He also was an editor of the *Cape Elizabeth Sentinel*, a weekly newspaper published at Ferry Village from 1881 to 1912 by Fred and James Hartford. (Ray Taylor)
RIGHT: ELIZABETH I. TAYLOR. Following in her father's footsteps, Elizabeth I. Taylor types up her column as the South Portland correspondent for the *Portland Evening Express*, c. 1917. Born in 1878, Elizabeth was the only daughter among James and Alice Sawyer's five children. (Ray Taylor)

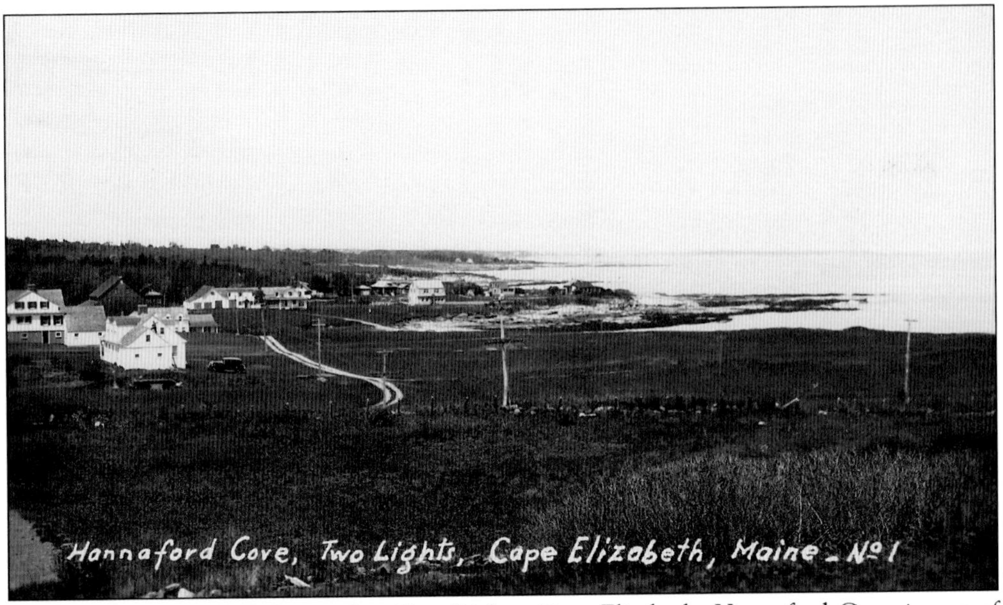

HANNAFORD COVE. Located at Two Lights, Cape Elizabeth, Hannaford Cove is one of many picturesque coves snuggled into the Cape shoreline. (Ted & Norma Wainwright)

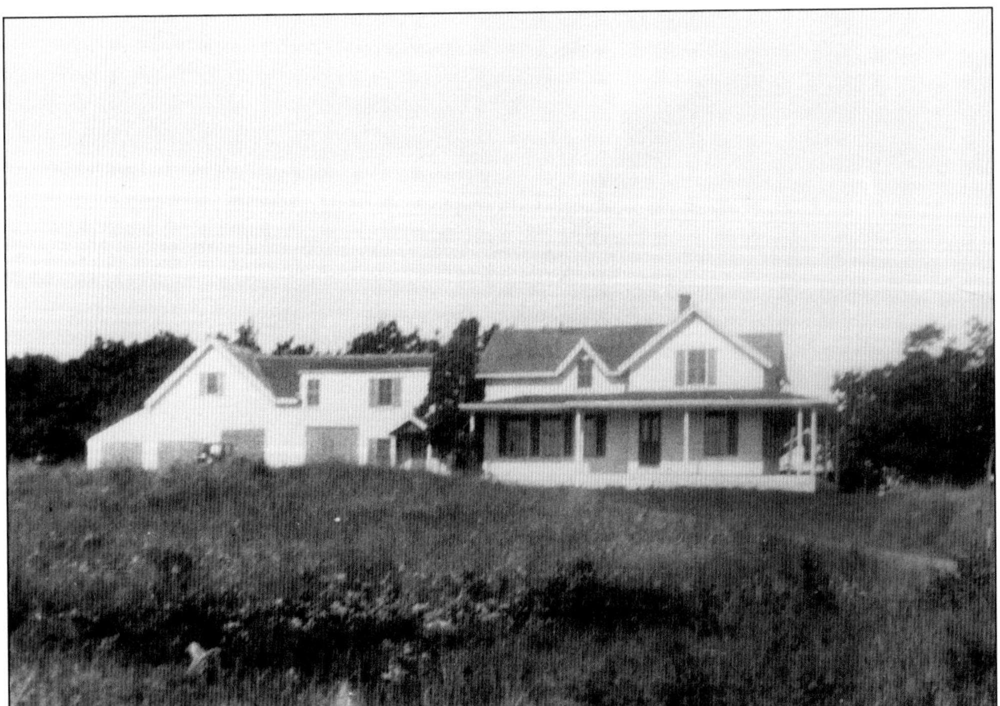

HANNAFORD FARM. A typical vacation home, this "summer cottage" was owned by Harrison and Gertrude Rodick in the 1930s. (Nancy Wainwright Woodward)

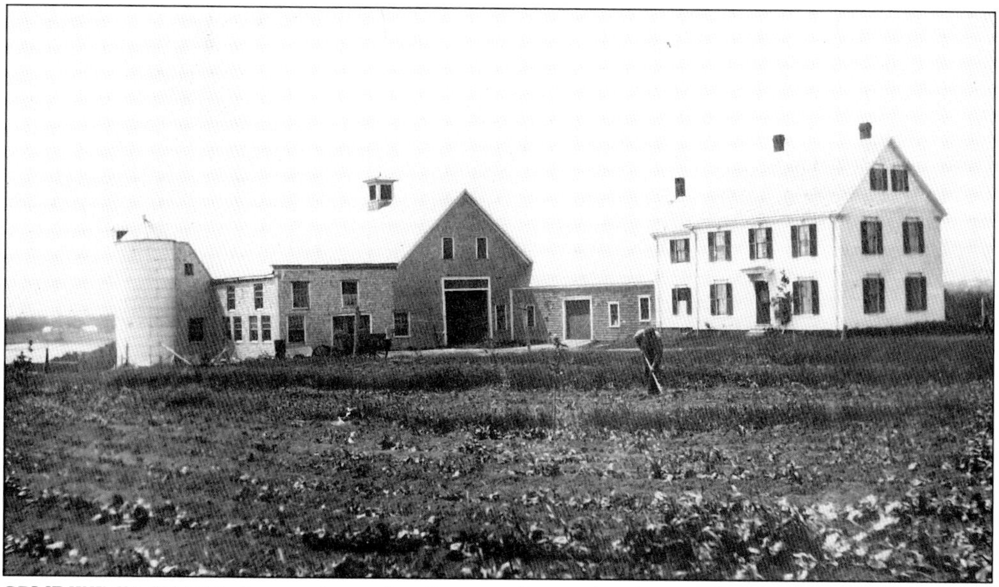

SPURWINK FARM. Located on the Sprague Estate bordering the Spurwink River, Cape Elizabeth, this farm was once a dairy. Ted and Norma Wainwright raised four children here from 1942 to the early 1980s. (Ted & Norma Wainwright)

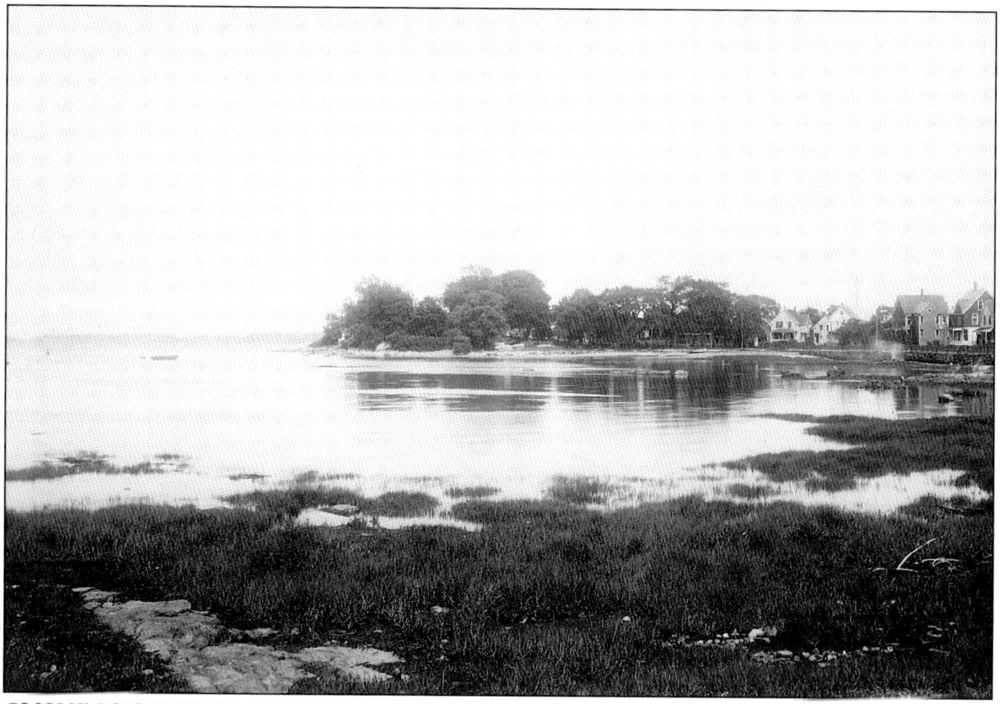

CUSHING'S POINT. A *c.* 1900 photograph of the public beach on the tip of Cushing's Point (in the background). This was a favorite bathing and picknicking spot for area residents. The point was named for Ezekiel Cushing, who, in the mid-1700s, engaged in lucrative West India trading from his wharf and warehouse built there. This shoreline, from Cushing's Point to Ferry Village, was forever altered with the construction of the World War II shipyards. (Eugene Swiger)

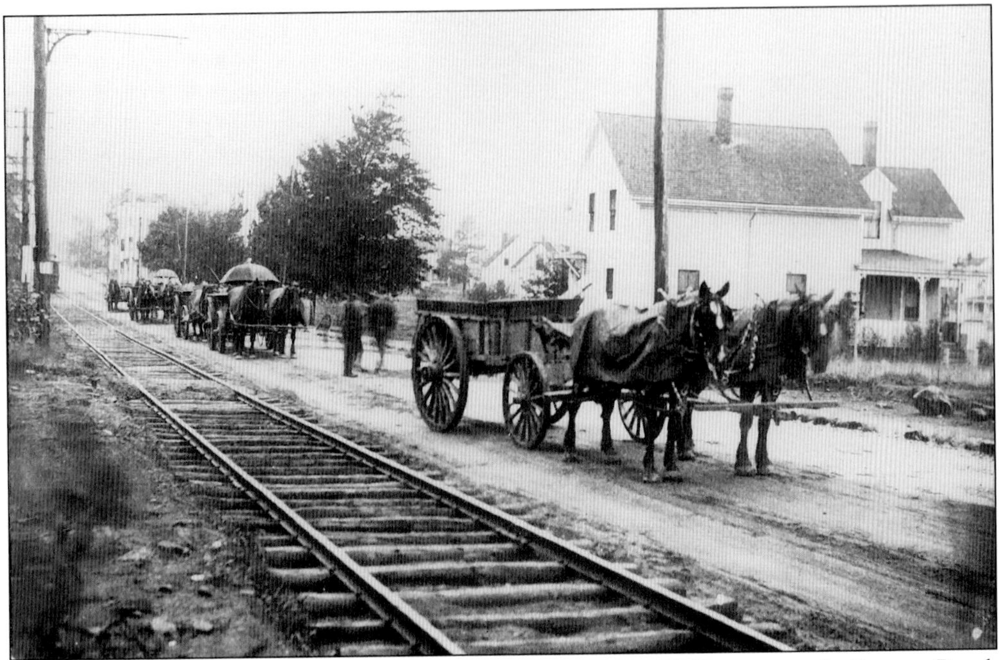

COTTAGE ROAD. A procession, perhaps heading for Fort Williams, travels Cottage Road, South Portland, at the turn of the century. The large, three-story building (at the left rear) was a house and store on Angell property. (Sullivan Photo Collection)

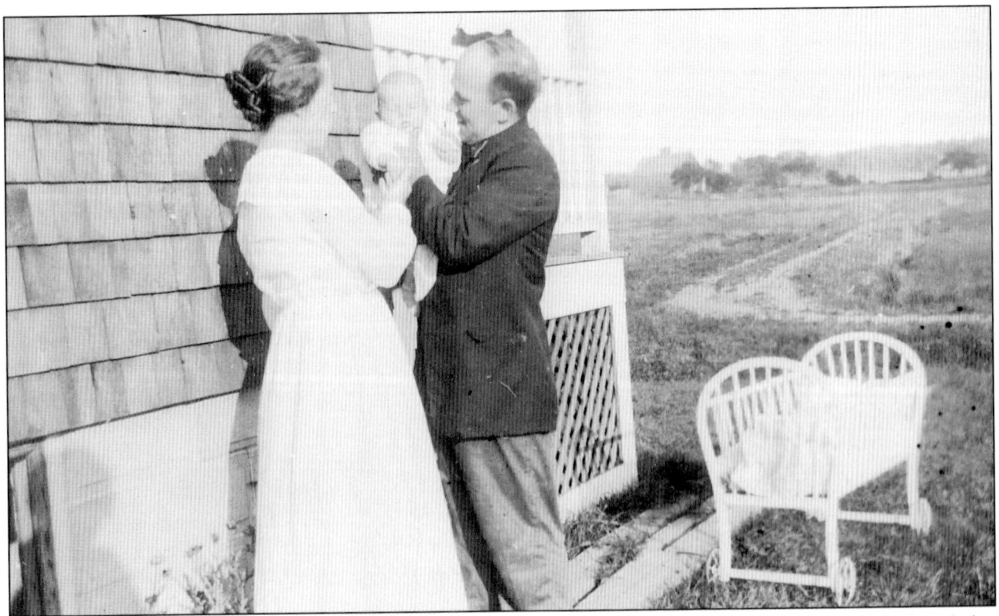

PLEASANTDALE. A *c.* 1918 view of Evans Street, South Portland. This street ran behind the Olssen residence on George Street, where John and Mary Olssen, and their son Joseph, lived. (Mary Olssen)

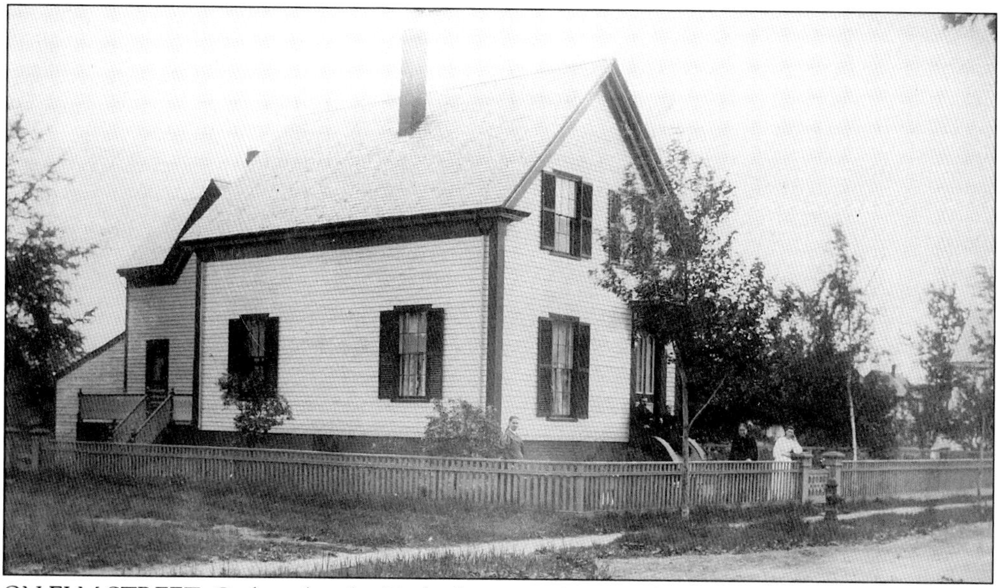

ON ELM STREET. Gathered at the Taylor home are Jane Taylor Milliken, Clara Rogers, Frank Rogers, and Halie Ames, *c*. 1900. (Ray Taylor)

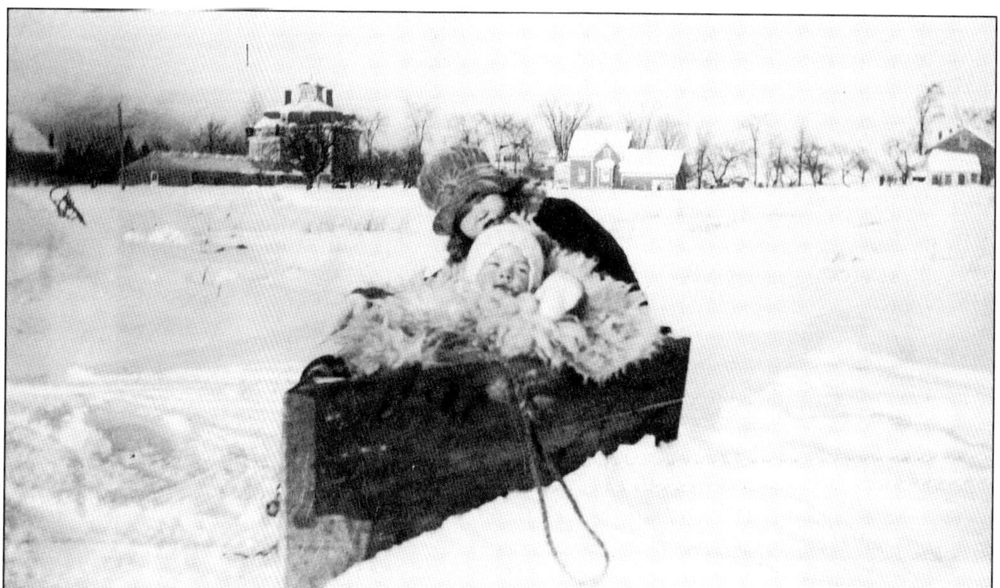

OPEN FIELD. This vintage 1920s sled carries Joseph and Mary Olssen through a field in the Evans Street area of South Portland. (Mary Olssen)

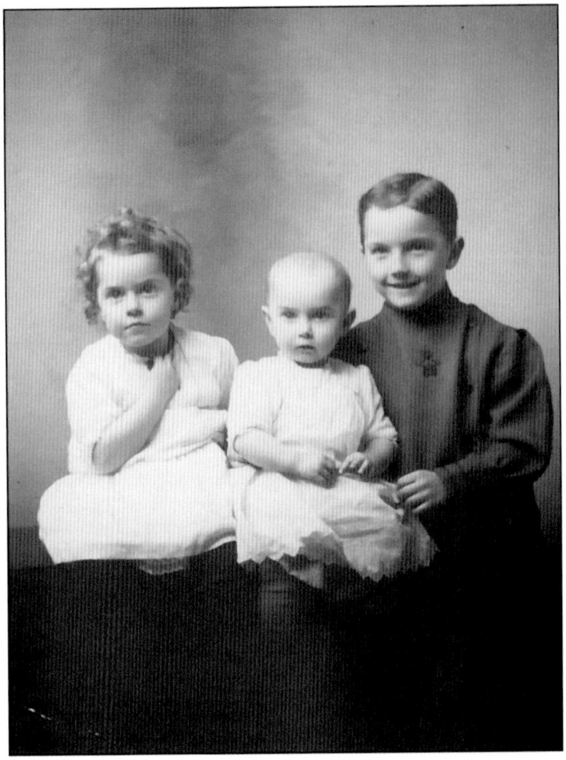

VICKERSON TRIO. A *c.* 1918 photograph of Dorothy, Florence, and Charles Vickerson, who grew up at the family home on Edgewood Road, South Portland. They are the children of Frank and Florence Vickerson. (Dot Hodgkins)

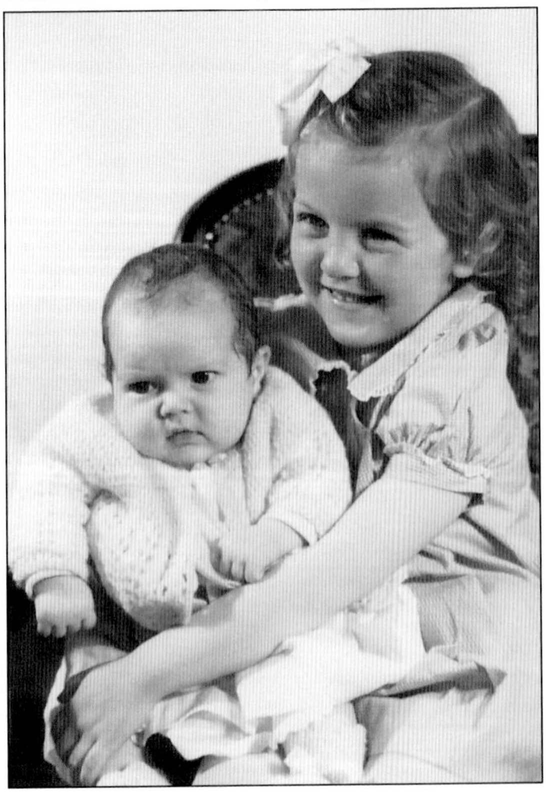

NEXT GENERATION. Big sister Janice holds her sister Sylvia at the Hodgkins' home on Pine Street, South Portland, in 1940. They are the daughters of George and Dot Vickerson Hodgkins. Janice now lives in Otisfield and Sylvia in Scarborough. (Dot Hodgkins)

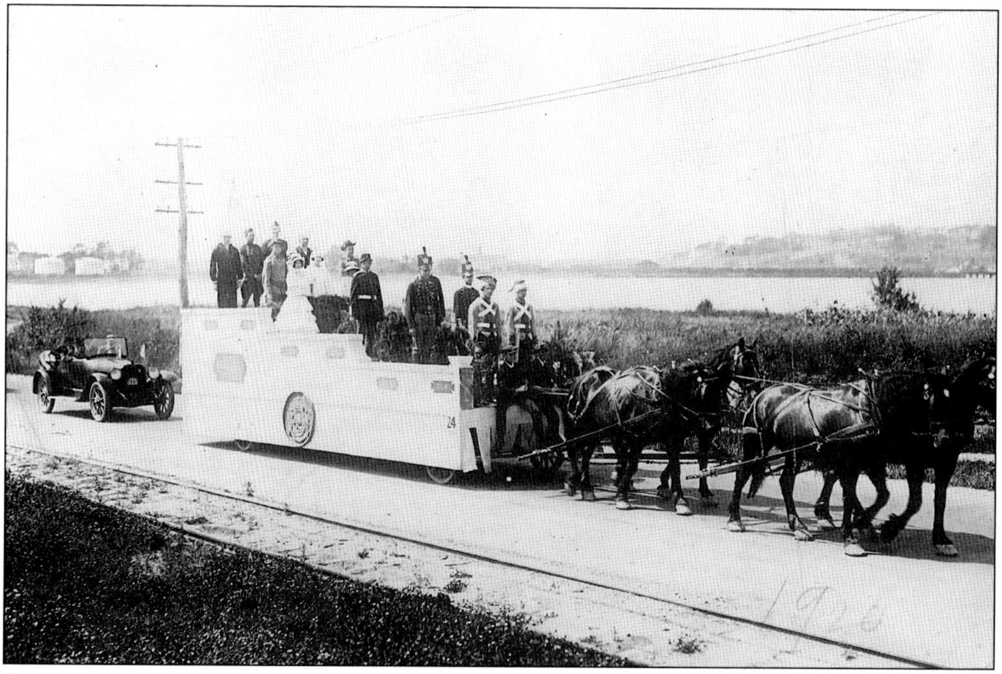

OLD HOME DAY. South Portland celebrated the 100th anniversary of the State of Maine in 1920 with a decorated float and men in military uniforms. They are traveling on Broadway, about where the Armory is now located. Contests of the day included nail driving, ladies baseball throwing, pie eating, and the greased pole. (Ray Taylor)

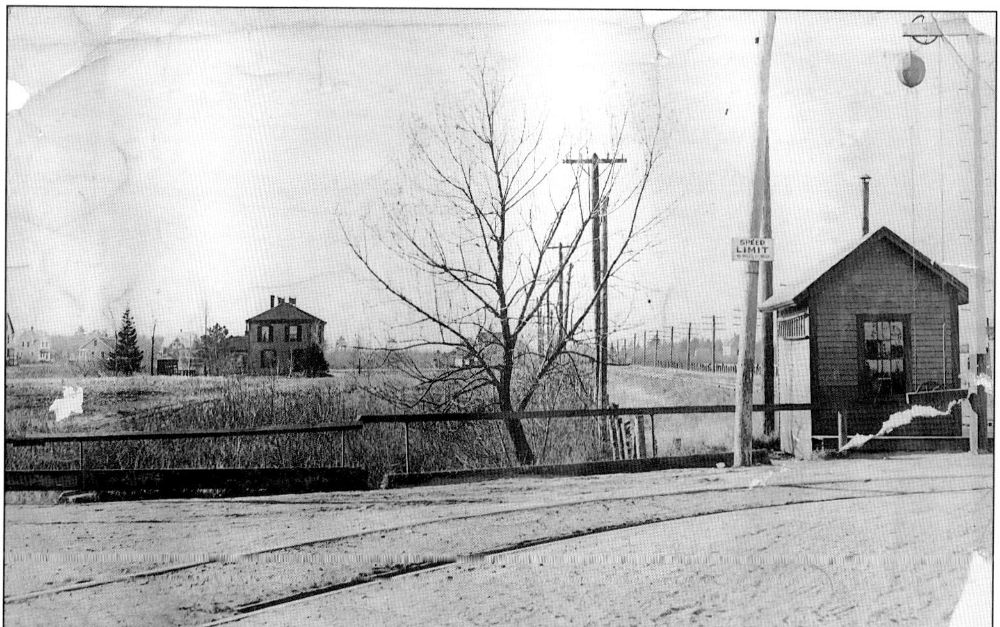

PLEASANTDALE CROSSING. Barberry Creek, also known as Taylor Brook, runs under the tracks here at Pleasantdale Crossing in the early 1900s, the present site of Michael's Variety store in South Portland. A red "signal ball" can be seen in its raised position above the tender's station, meaning the track is clear. The Taylor house is in the background. (Ray Taylor)

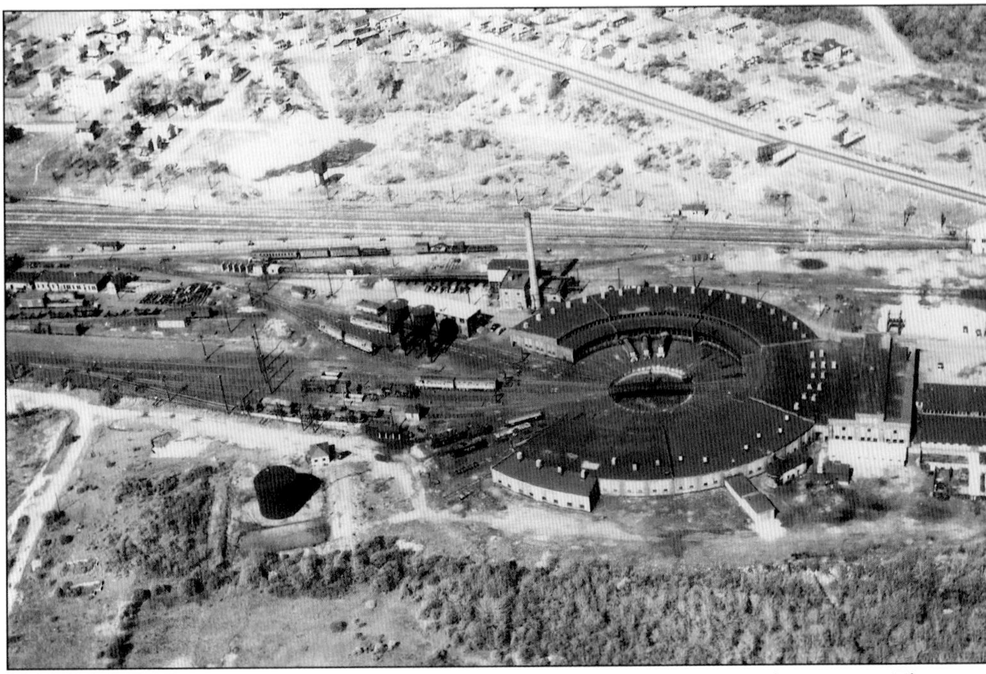

THE ROUNDHOUSE. In 1923 Maine Central Railroad took over the site in Thornton Heights that, in the 1890s, was home to Rigby Park, one of the country's fastest horse racing tracks. Located off Rigby Hill, the roundhouse consisted of about forty train bays. (Sullivan Photo Collection)

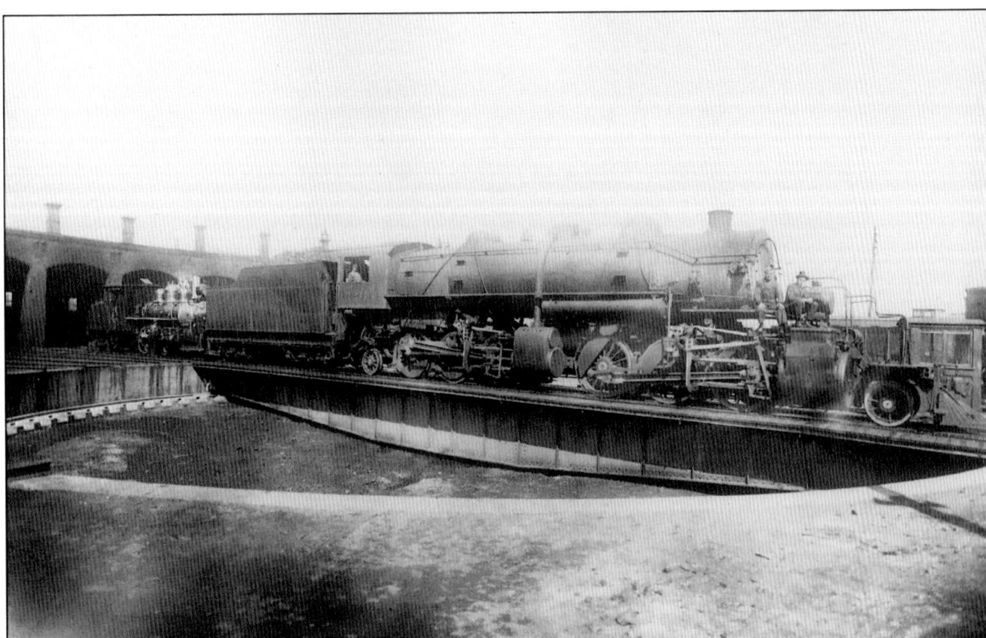

ON ITS WAY. A steam-powered train emerges from one of the bays at the Rigby Railway Yard roundhouse in the early 1950s. (Sullivan Photo Collection)

SPURWINK CHURCH. The Spurwink Meetinghouse was built in 1802, and is in the National Historic Register. This Cape Elizabeth landmark was rebuilt in 1834 and is a coveted spot for summer weddings. (Janet Hannigan)

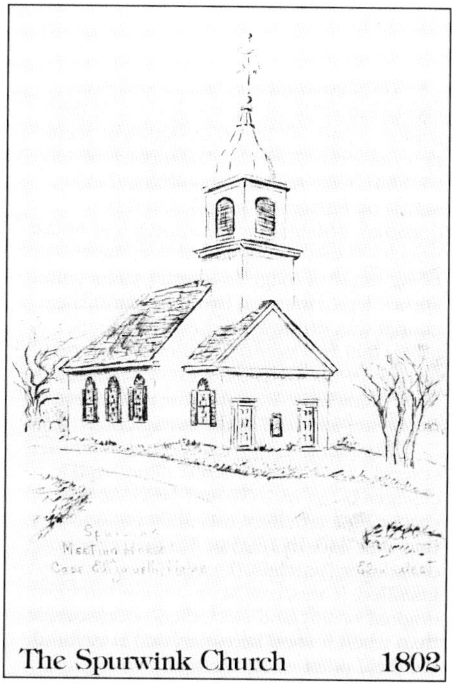

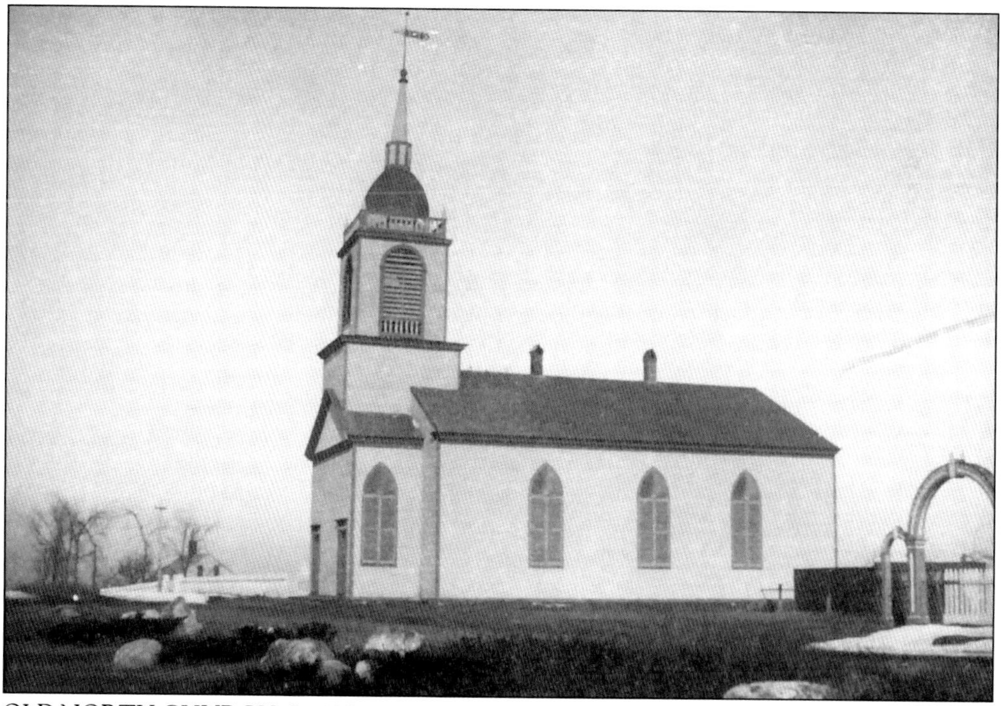

OLD NORTH CHURCH. In 1834 a meetinghouse, which was located for one hundred years in a corner of the Mt. Pleasant Cemetery, South Portland (then Cape Elizabeth), was torn down and replaced by this new church, known as the Old North Church. In 1891 a team of oxen moved it from the cemetery, across the street to the corner of Cottage and Mitchell Roads, where it was rededicated as the North Congregational Church on Meeting House Hill.

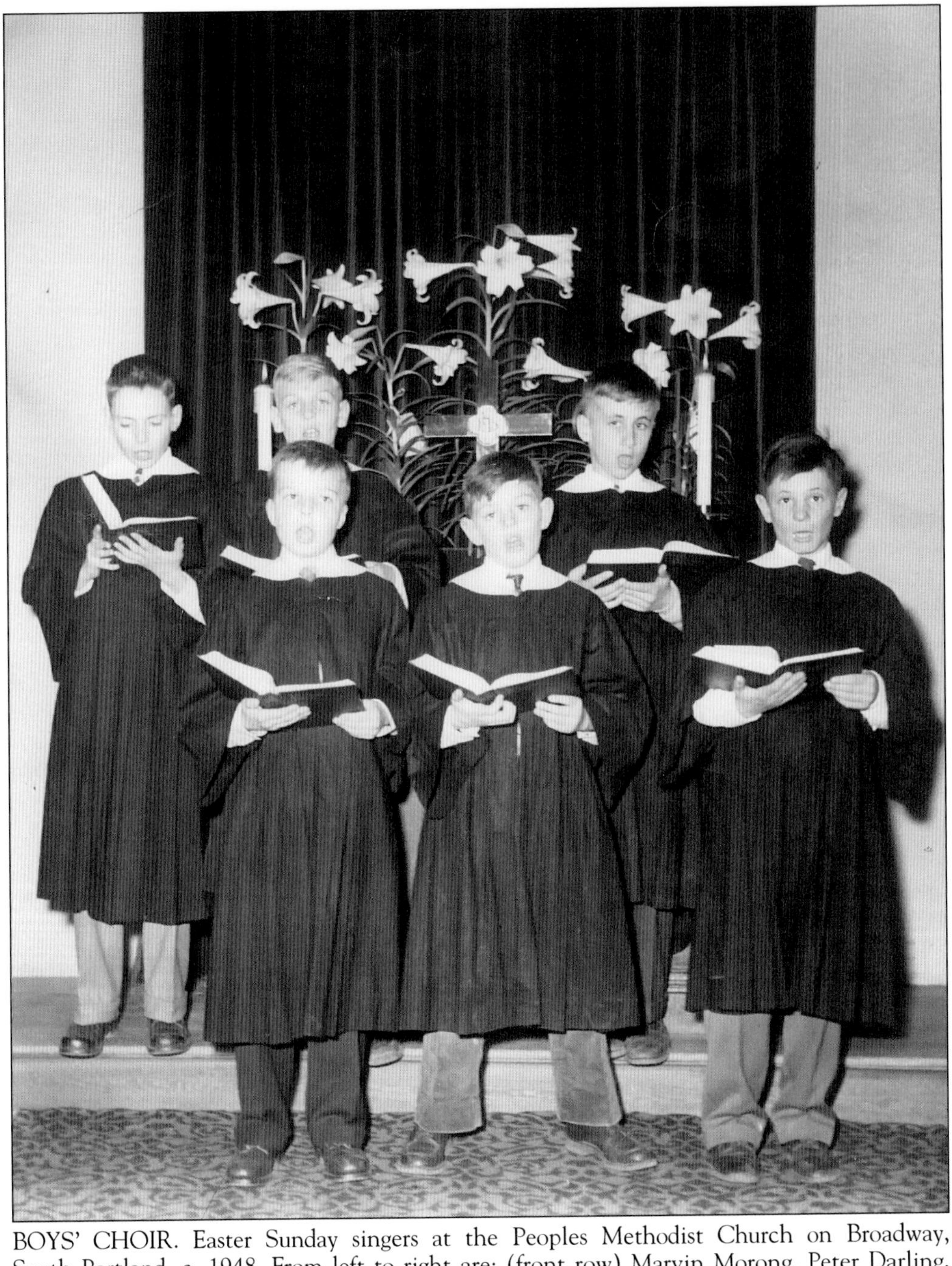

BOYS' CHOIR. Easter Sunday singers at the Peoples Methodist Church on Broadway, South Portland, c. 1948. From left to right are: (front row) Marvin Morong, Peter Darling, and Robert Upton; (back row) Joel Craven, George Darling, and Ronald Tripp. (Loretta Dobson Coughlin)

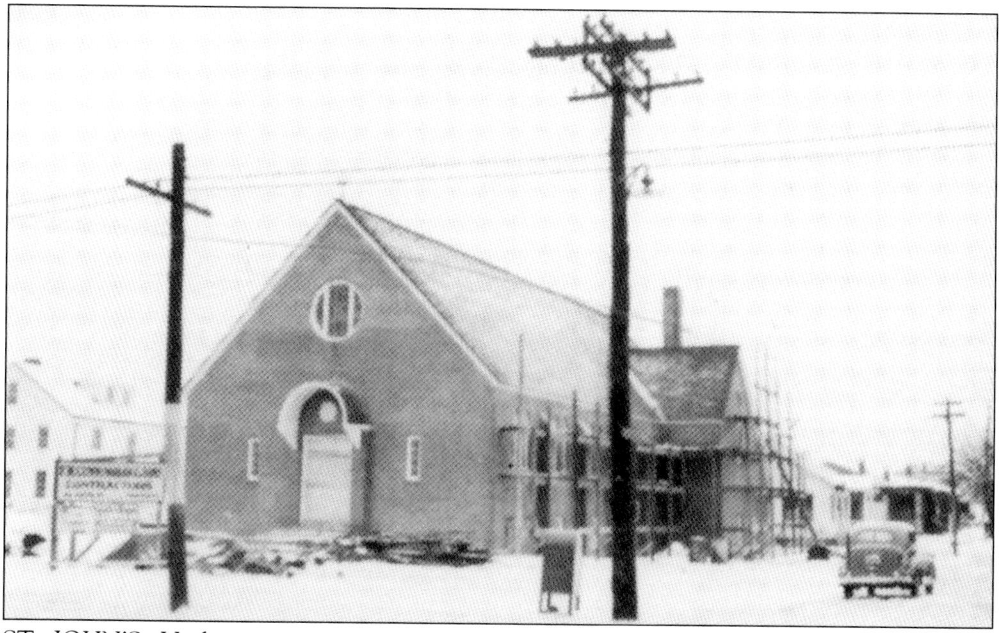

ST. JOHN'S. Under construction in 1938, the St. John the Evangelist Roman Catholic Church on Main Street, Thornton Heights, was founded by the late Reverend John R. Ryan, who remained pastor for thirty-three years. The new rectory can be seen at left. The first two houses in back of the church were razed in the 1970s for a parking lot. (The St. John Commemorative Booklet)

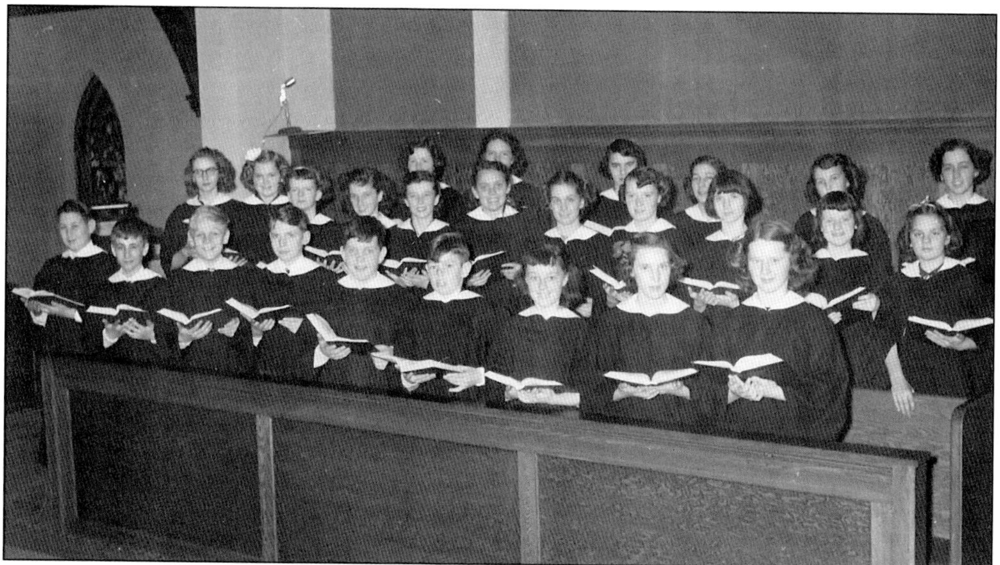

JUNIOR CHOIR. Members of the Junior Choir at the Peoples Methodist Church on Broadway, South Portland. From left to right are: (front row) Stanley Nickerson, Ronald Tripp, George Darling, Joel Craven, unknown, Peter Darling, Laurel Hoyt, unknown, and Sandra Barnes; (middle row) unknown, Carol Darling, Karen Seabury, Marlene Dobson, Loretta Dobson, Carolyn Day, Eleanor Willey, Evelyn McKenney, unknown, unknown, and unknown; (back row) unknown, unknown, unknown, Joanne Lowell, unknown, and Margaret Darling. (Loretta Dobson Coughlin)

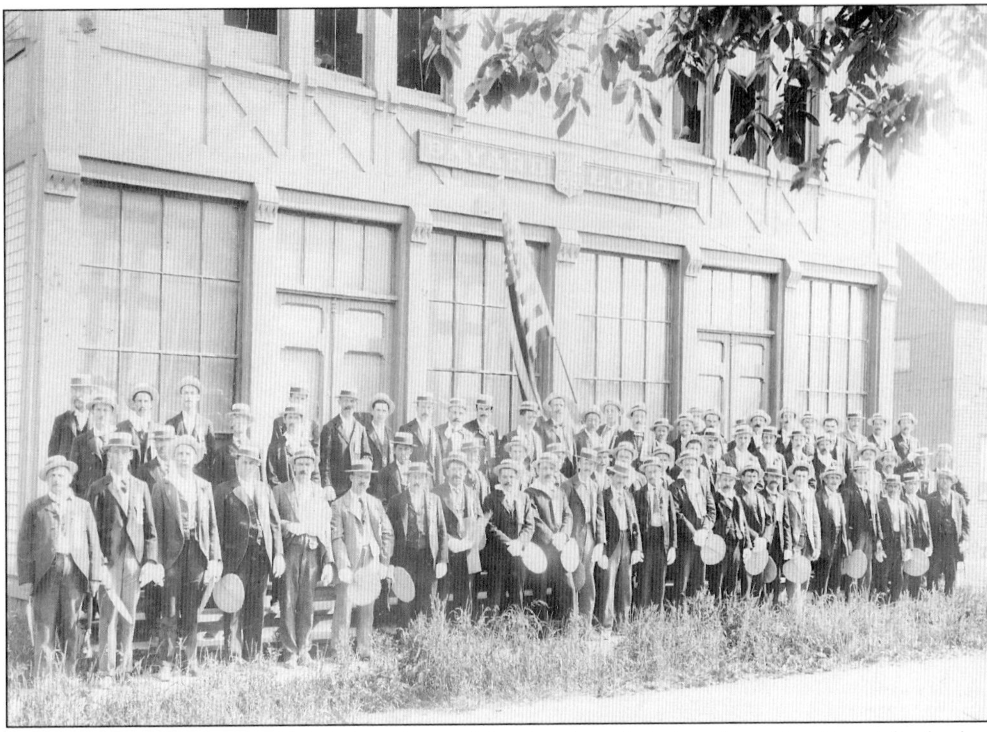

THE KNIGHTS OF PYTHIAS. Members of the Knights of Pythias from the Cape Elizabeth-South Portland area, established in 1884, gather at Bayard Lodge in Ferry Village in the early 1900s. (Herbert Pray)

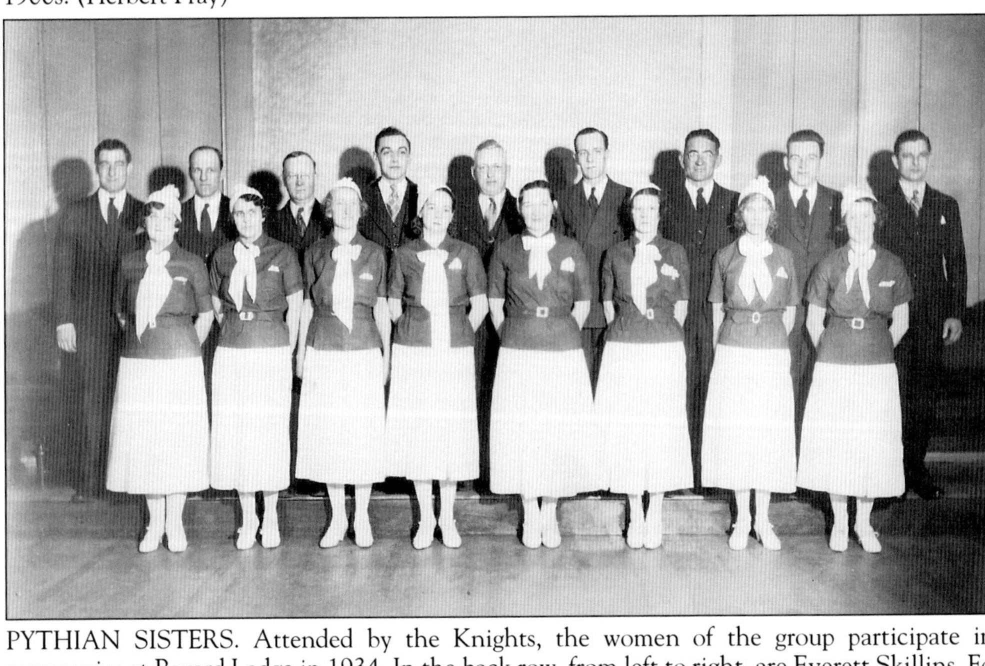

PYTHIAN SISTERS. Attended by the Knights, the women of the group participate in ceremonies at Bayard Lodge in 1934. In the back row, from left to right, are Everett Skillins, Ed Woodsum, unknown, Herbert Pray, Robert Abbott, Jim Loring, Julius Hertz, Charles Seaford, and Winfield Scott. (Herbert Pray)

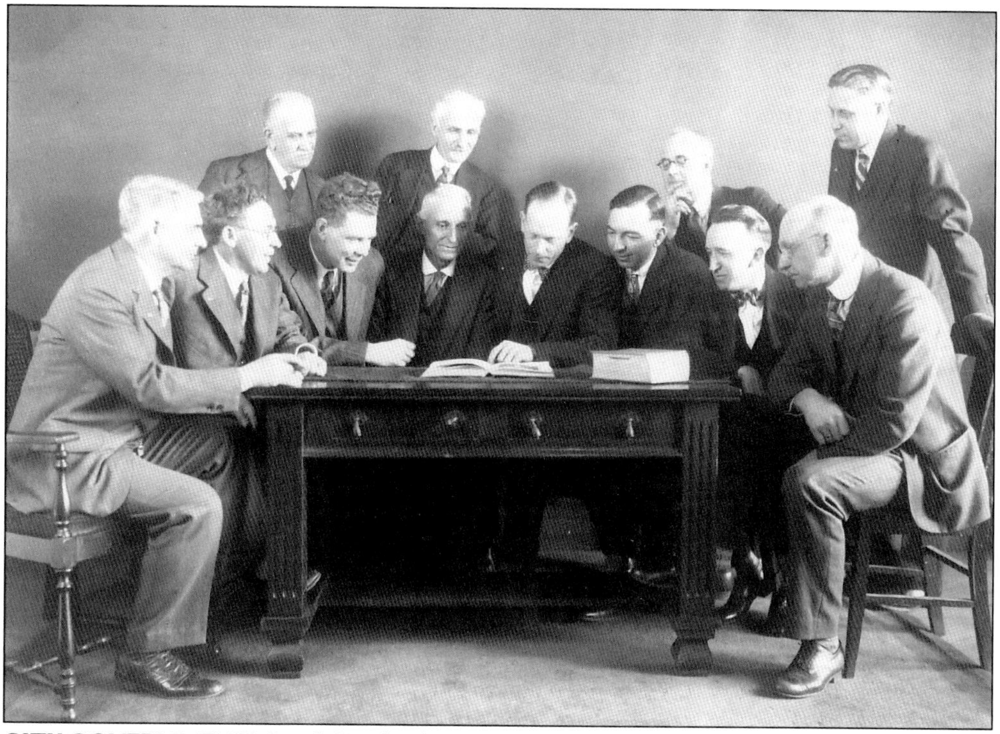

CITY GOVERNMENT. South Portland city leaders in 1929 included, from left to right: (front row) Breen, Jones, Mayor E. Perley Bullock, Carmichael, George Minott, Clinton Wallace, Leland Cole, and Cobb; (back row) Woodruff, Brown, Cory, and George Hinckley. (Harris Hinckley, M.D.)

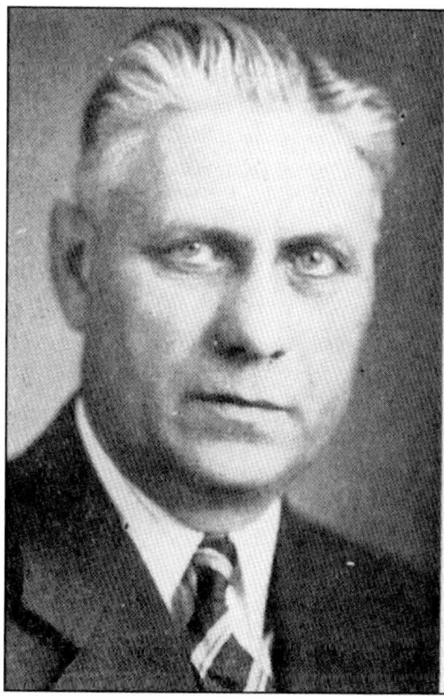

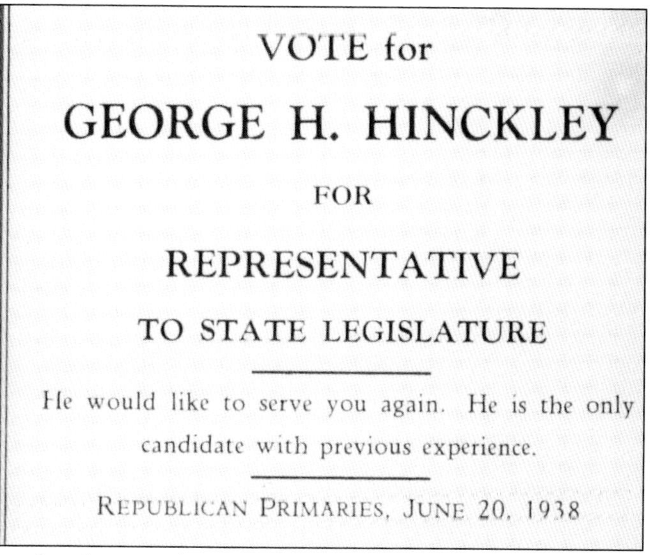

VOTE for

GEORGE H. HINCKLEY

FOR

REPRESENTATIVE

TO STATE LEGISLATURE

He would like to serve you again. He is the only candidate with previous experience.

REPUBLICAN PRIMARIES, JUNE 20, 1938

JUDGE HINCKLEY. Active in local and state politics, George H. Hinckley was a law partner with his brother Frederick in the early 1920s. Hinckley Pond is named after Frederick, a former state senator and mayor of South Portland. Hinckley Drive was named after George, a former state legislator and municipal court judge. His son Harris was a physician in South Portland for many years and lives in Cape Elizabeth with his wife Sally. (Harris Hinckley, M.D.)

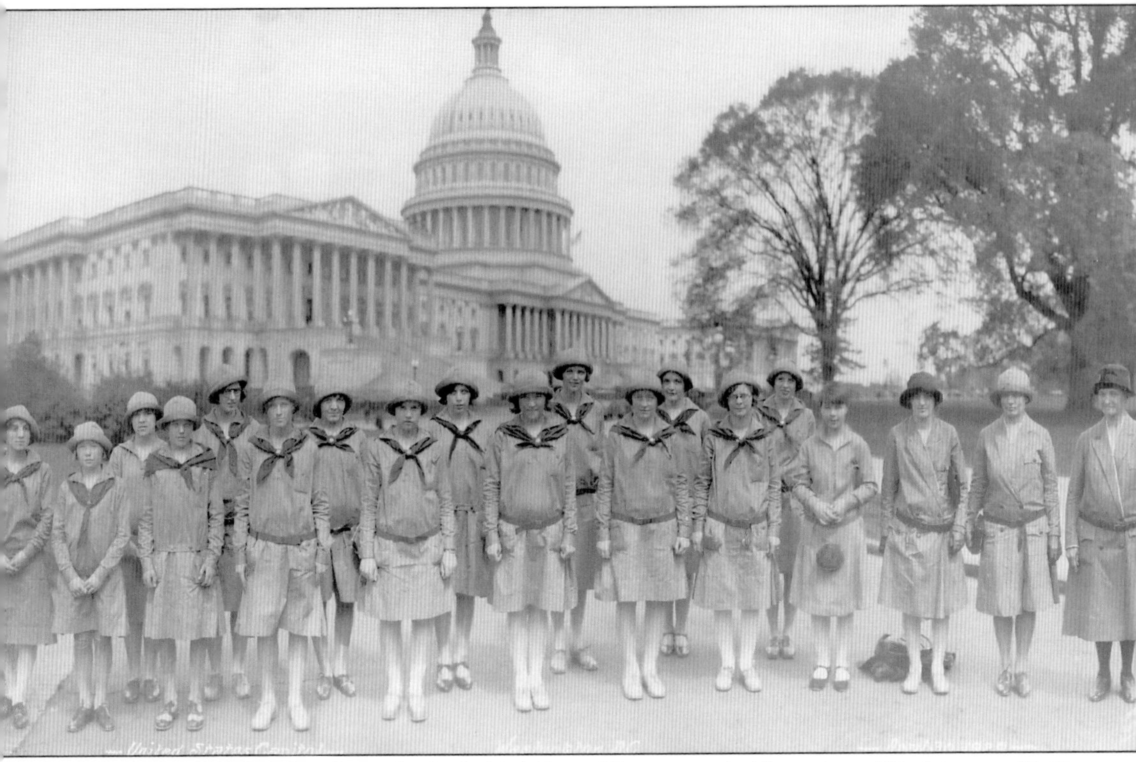

GIRL SCOUTS. This Cape Elizabeth Girl Scout Troop traveled by train to Washington, D.C., in April 1929. From left to right are: (front row) Edith Libby, Doris Hutchinson, Elva Murray, Cecelia Sweetsir, Margaret Jordan, Grace Lombard, Constance Murray, Dorothy Foss, Christine Cheeney, Lt. Dorothy Wing, Lt. Orissa Jordan, and Capt. E. Gertrude Copeland; (back row) Lillian McCullough, Janet Brown, Elizabeth Bishop, Charlotte Stanford, Maville Jordan, Bethia? Jordan, and Virginia Clark. (Kennebec Girl Scout Council Historical Committee)

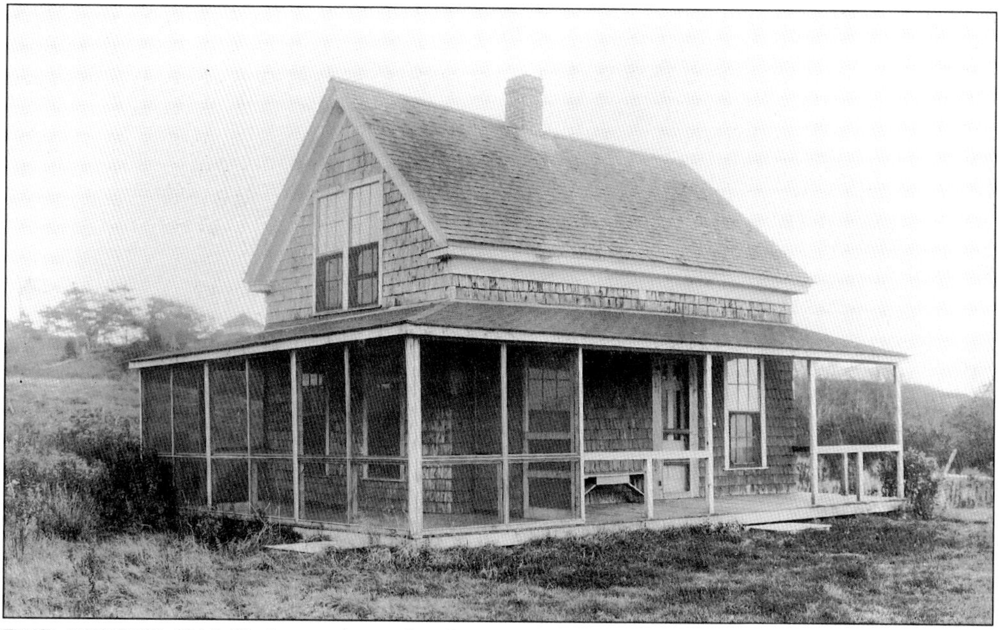

THE SOKOKI CAMP. Located on the Sprague Estate in Cape Elizabeth, overlooking the Scarborough Marsh, Sokoki was the site of many Girl Scout outings in the 1920s, led by E. Gertrude Copeland. Called Buena Vista, it was the first overnight camp in the Sokokis area. This is a *c.* 1930 photograph. (Kennebec Girl Scout Council Historical Committee)

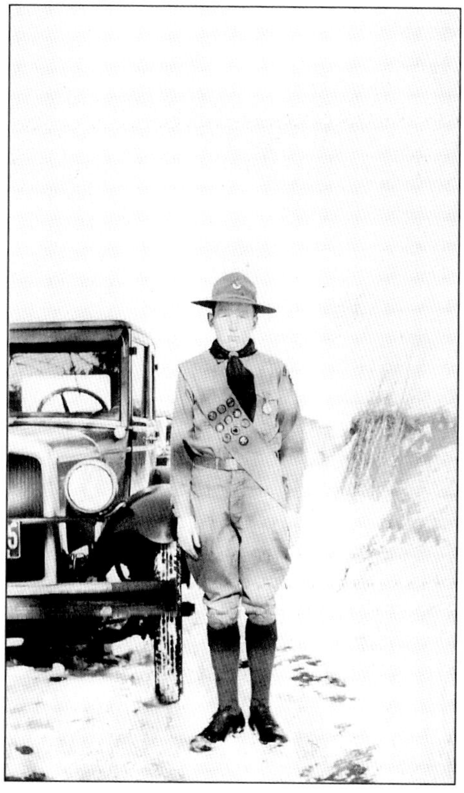

GOOD SCOUT. Ted Wainwright of Cape Elizabeth proudly displays his Boy Scout badges earned in the mid-1930s. (Ted & Norma Wainwright)

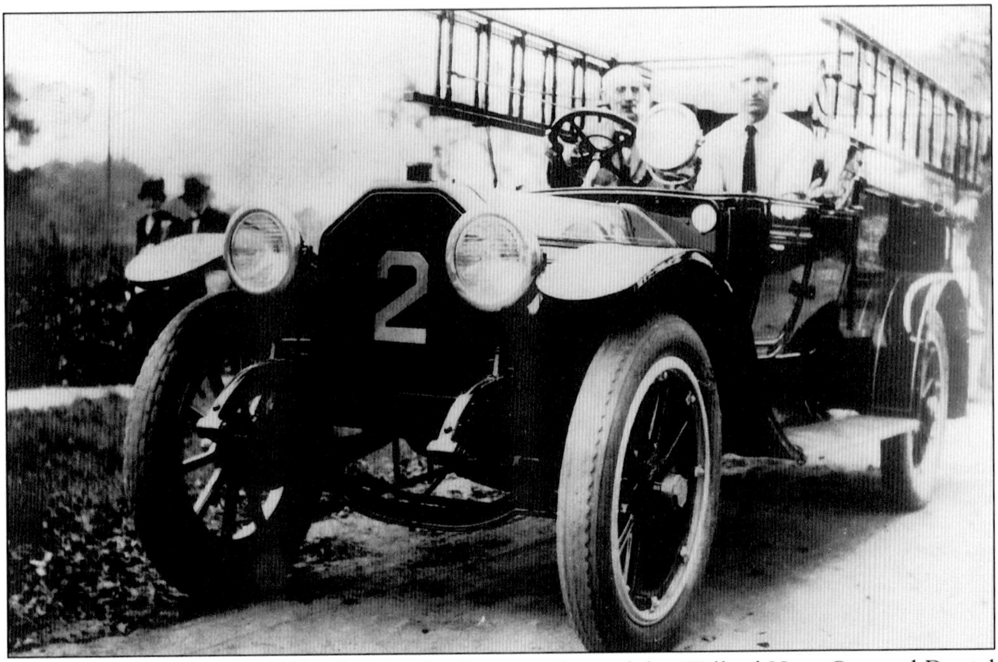

HOSE NO. 2. In 1923, Willlis Strout, the first president of the Willard Hose Co., and Daniel Strout rode in one of the company's first motorized fire trucks, a converted Peerless sedan. Willard's Hose No. 2 was organized in October 1892, and was preceded by Ferry Village's Hose No. 1 in September. Cape Elizabeth's first municipal fire department was established in the 1920s. (Tom Heseltine)

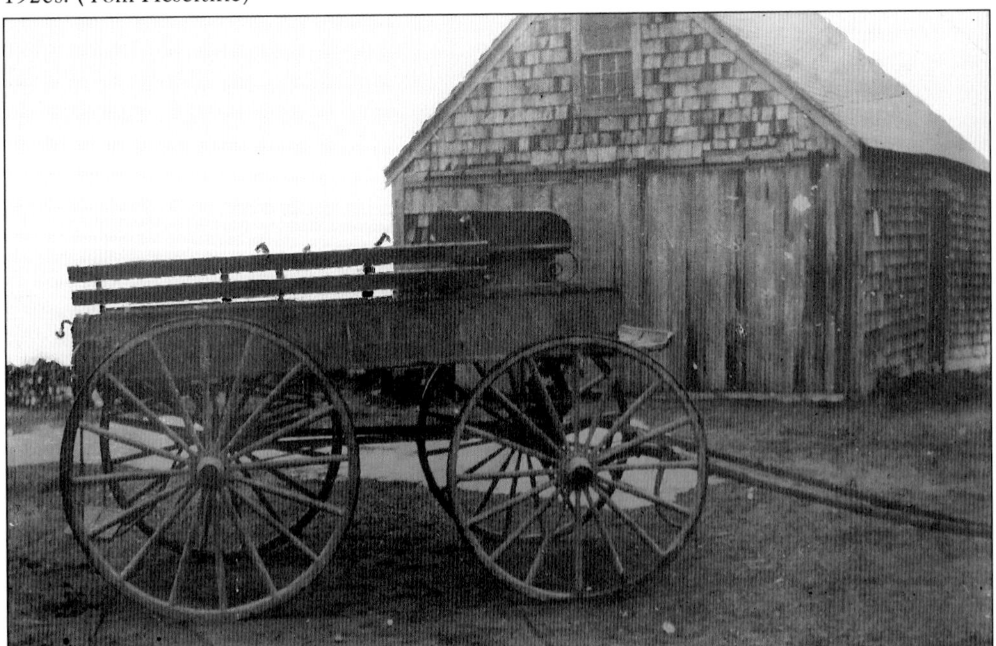

OLD HOSE NO. 3. This one-horse wagon, along with a later purchase of 700 feet of hose, served Hose No. 3 at the former Elm Street School in South Portland at the turn of the century. (Ray Taylor)

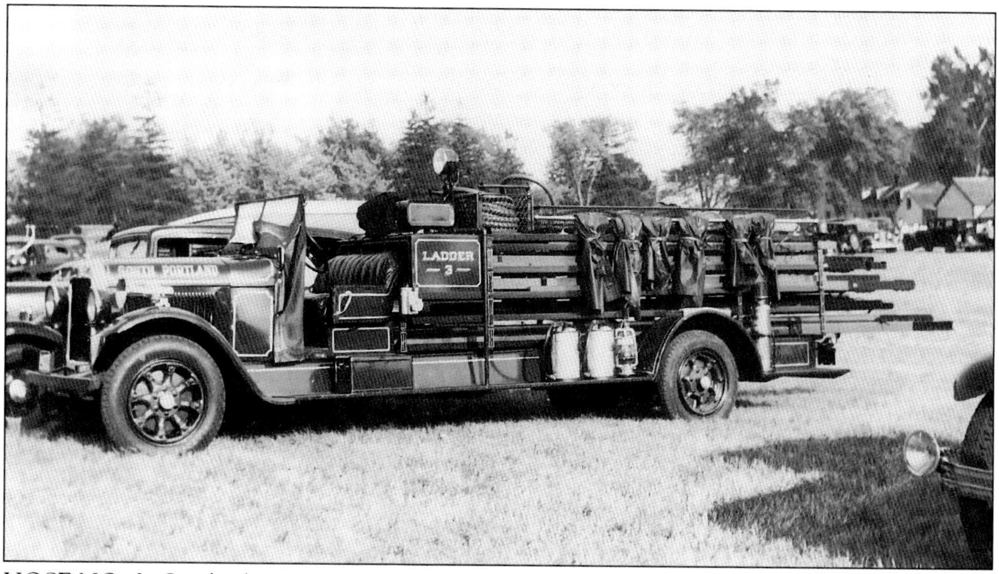

HOSE NO. 3. On display at a South Portland field day in the late 1920s is Pleasantdale Hose Co.'s new Dodge chassis truck. Hose No. 3 was organized in 1893. (Tom Heseltine)

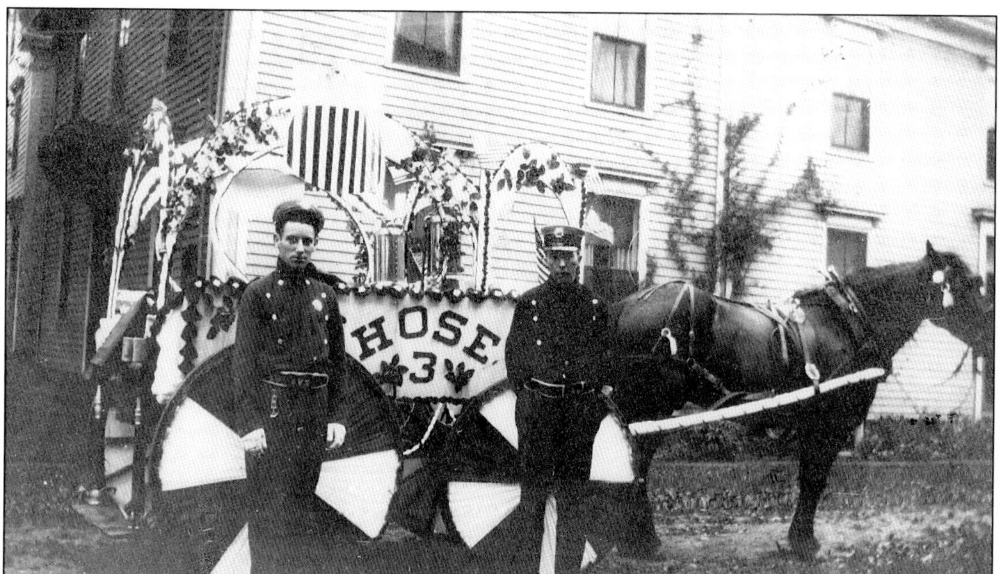

ON PARADE. Sparky Coolbroth (left) and Harry E. Taylor, firefighters from Hose No. 3, prepare for a parade in 1920. (Ray Taylor)

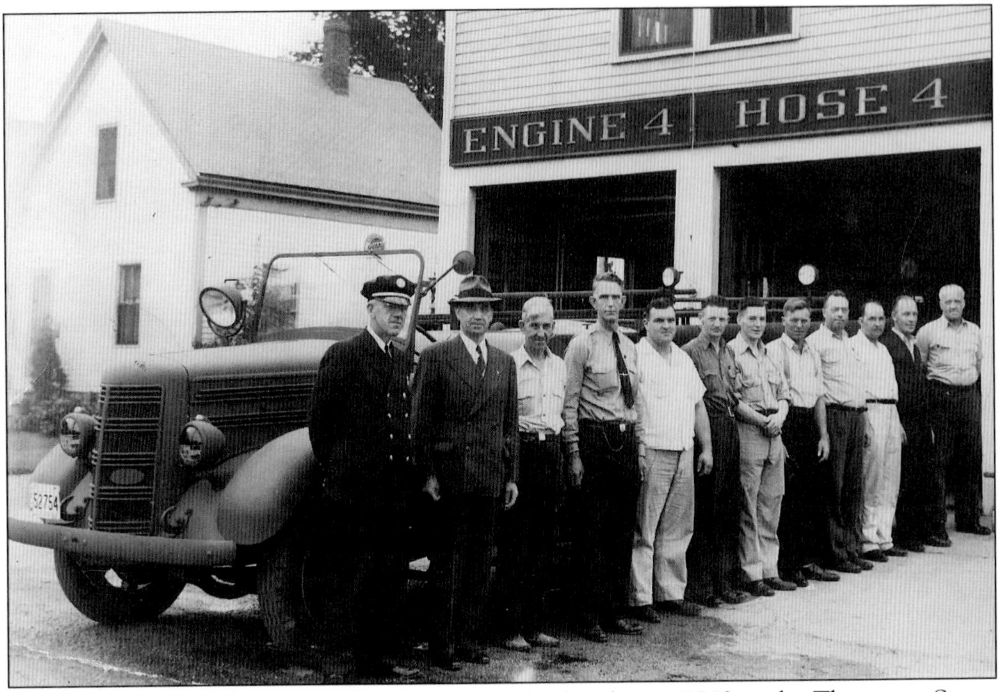

HOSE NO. 4. Firefighters from Engine 4 Hose No. 4 gather in 1943 at the Thompson Street station in South Portland. From left to right are Chief Horace Jose, Harold Webster, Capt. H.A. Nickerson, R.W. Smith, Gleason Hooper, Lawrence McPhearson, Charles D. Heseltine, F.H. Prout, George W. Ridley, Albert W. Nugent, Ralph F. Thompson, and Fred H. Perry (driver). The city's first permanent firefighters were from Hose No. 4. (Tom Heseltine)

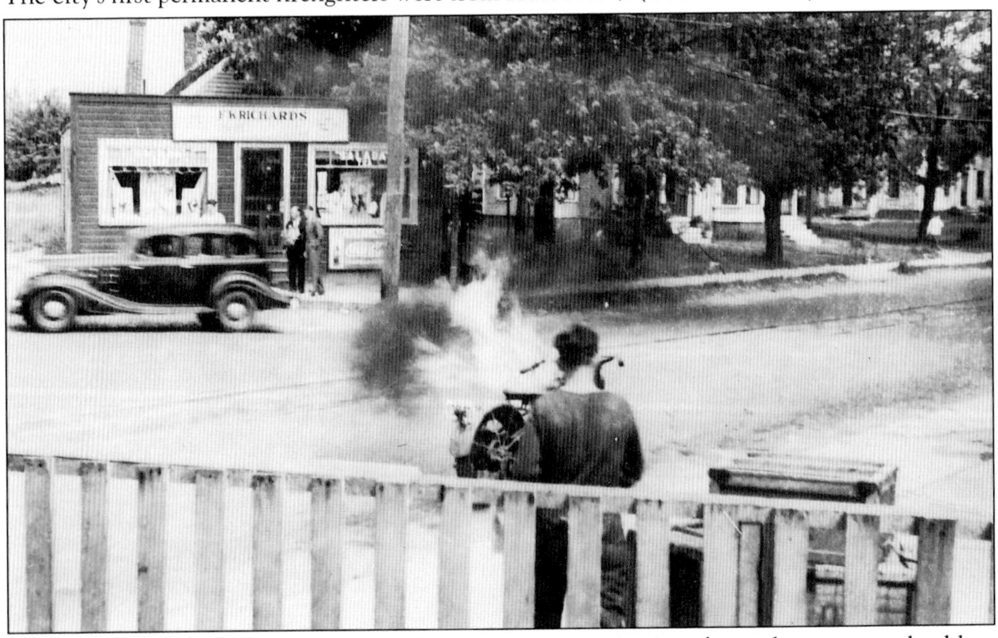

CYCLE FIRE. A call goes out on June 20, 1937, to Hose No. 2 to douse this motorcycle ablaze in Willard Square, South Portland. Coca Cola, Salada tea, and ice cream are advertised at the F.K. Richard's store across the street. (Tom Heseltine)

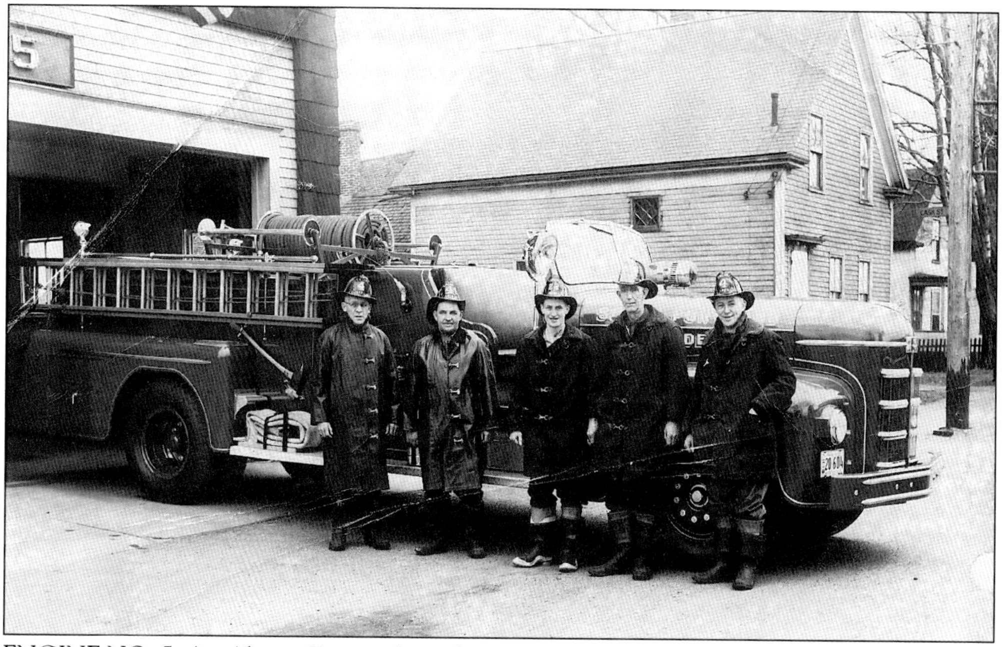

ENGINE NO. 5. An Ahrens Fox truck, with a pumping capability of 1,000 gallons of water per minute, is displayed at the Cash Corner station in South Portland in 1950. From left to right are Ralph F. Thompson (driver), Albert Nugent, Norman Cribby, Captain Raymond W. Smith, and Charles. (Tom Heseltine)

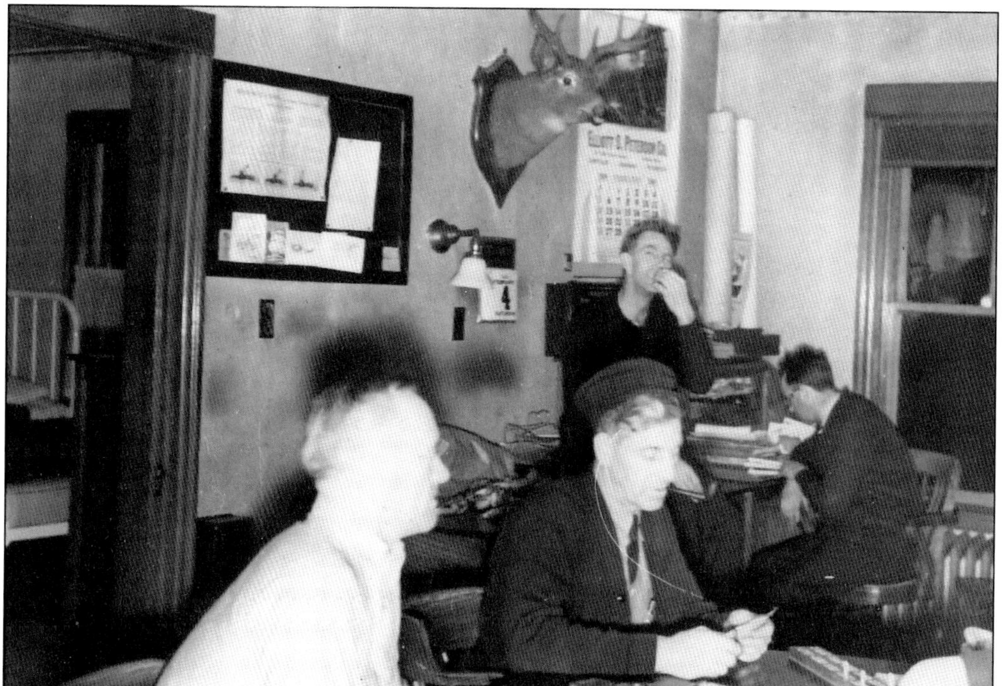

CRIBBAGE GAME. On call at the Thompson Street station are, from left to right, Fred Perry, Nick, Raymond Smith, and George Ridley, *c.* 1940s. (Tom Heseltine)

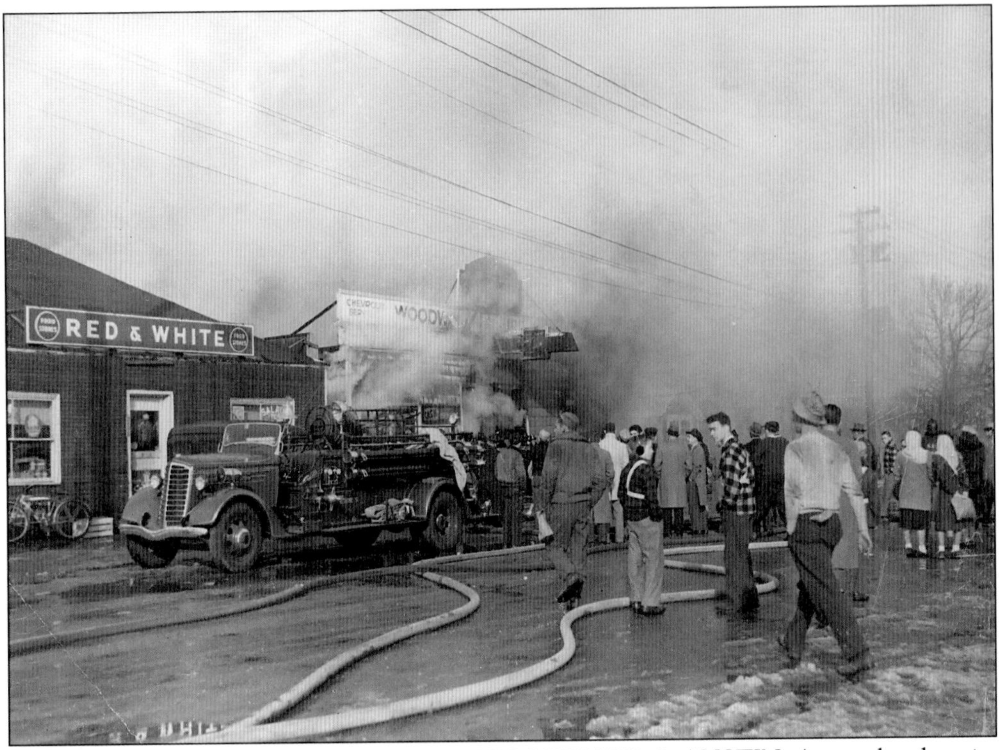

WOODWARD & AUSTIN. A crowd gathers in the 1940s as firefighters scramble to put out a fire at the Woodward & Austin Chevrolet dealership at Cash Corner, South Portland. The dealership opened in Knightville in 1932 and closed in the 1970s. (Tom Heseltine)

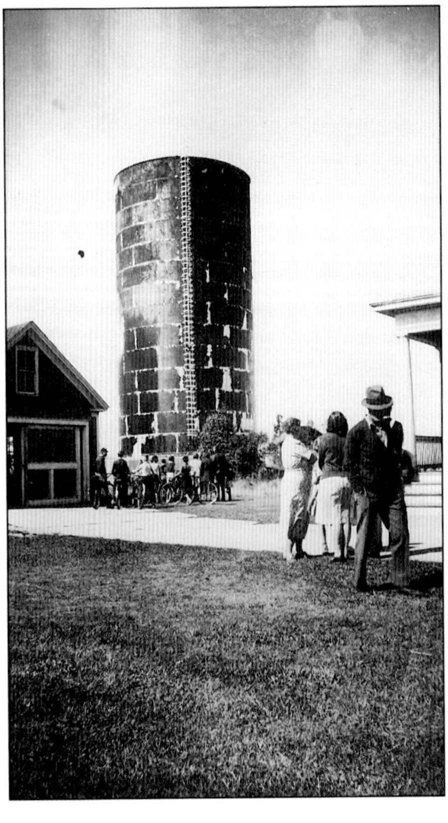

OOOPS! In 1938, workers repairing the water tower on Meeting House Hill, South Portland, accidently caused a fire in the tower that earned them a spot in *Ripley's Believe It or Not*. (Tom Heseltine)

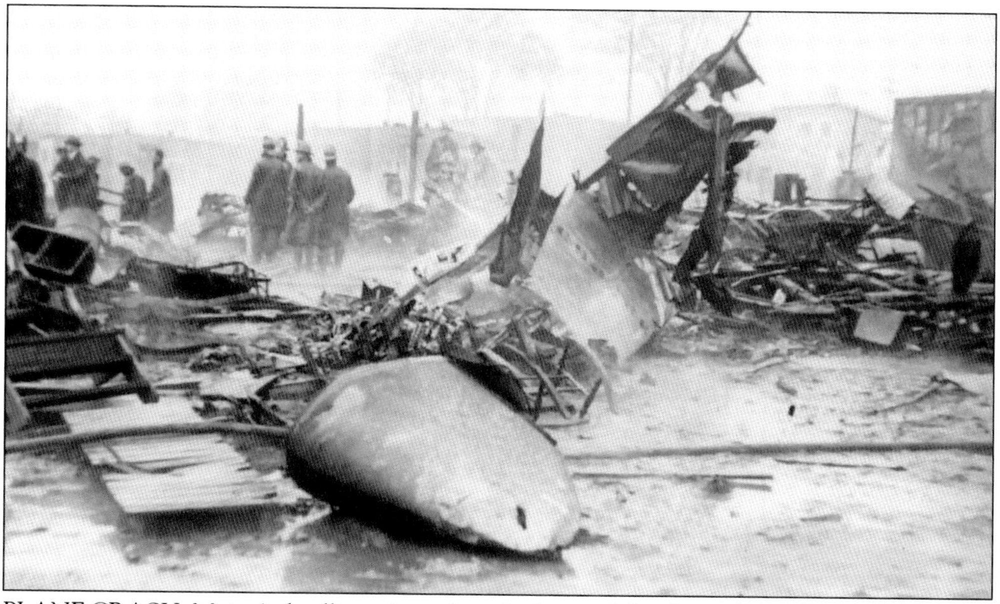

PLANE CRASH. Maine's deadliest air crash took place in July 1944, when a U.S. Army bomber crashed into a trailer park for government workers located in back of Redbank, South Portland. The plane was piloted by 1939 South Portland High School graduate and star athlete Philip I. Russell. A flight instructor, he and eighteen others were killed. (Tom Heseltine)

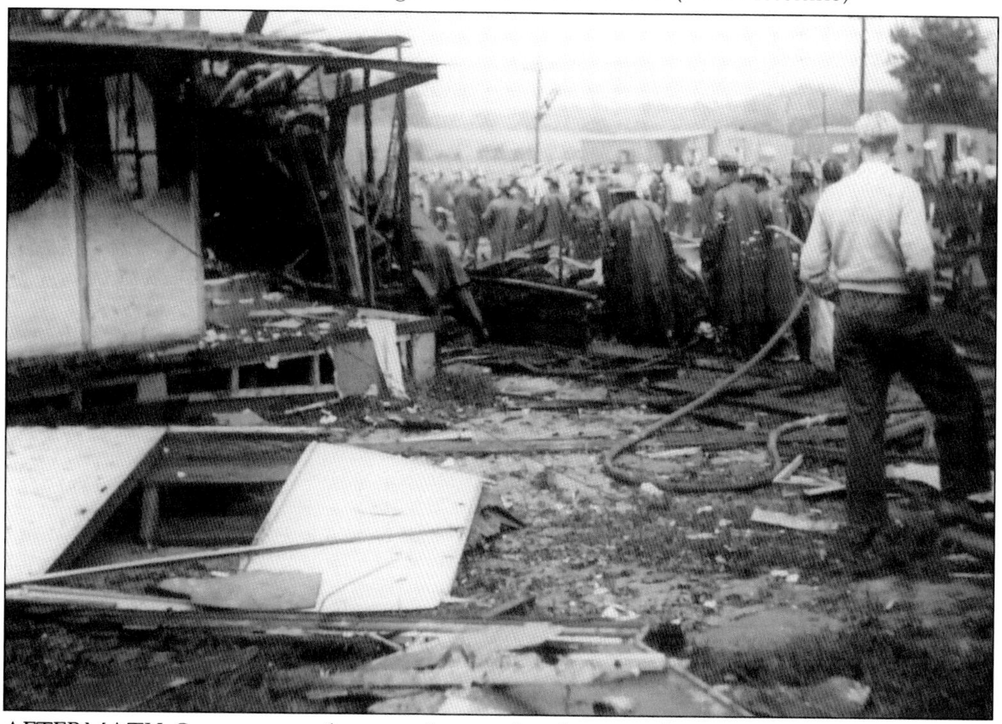

AFTERMATH. Seventeen trailers were destroyed in the 1944 plane crash at the Redbank trailer park in South Portland. Crowds and chaos slowed efforts of rescue workers and ambulances racing to the scene amid dinnertime traffic. The cause of the crash is still unknown, though the airport had been officially closed because of fog. (Tom Heseltine)

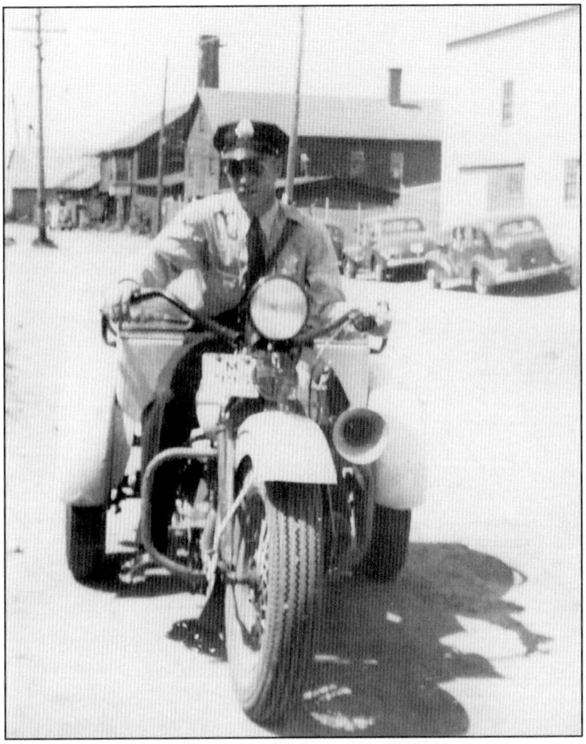

ON DUTY. Sergeant Ernest Darling, a traffic control officer with the South Portland Police Department, patrols Front Street on a three-wheeler that was used into the early 1950s. Sergeant Darling, with only two years on the force in 1944, was the first officer on the scene of the fatal Redbank plane crash. Now age eighty-two, he retired as police chief in 1968 and lives with his wife Merle at Willard Beach, South Portland. (Ernest Darling)

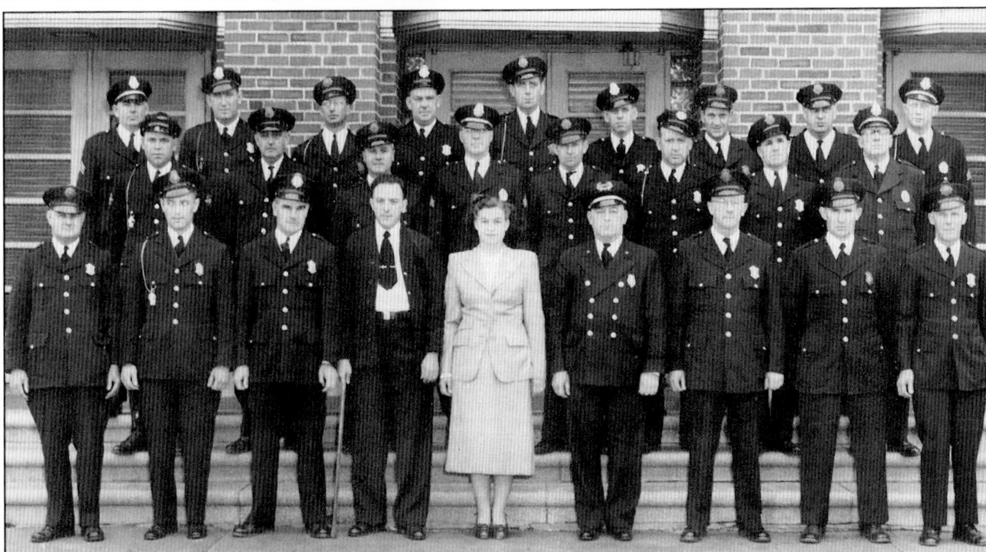

FULL FORCE. Police officers gather at the South Portland Armory in the early 1950s. From left to right are: (front row) Bartley Murphy, Gordon McGrath, William Murphy, clerk George Brownell, matron Doris Angell, Chief Frank Whitten, Donald McDonough, Sterling Kierstead, and Charles Flink; (middle row) George McCubrey, Raymond Dewey, Harold Oliver, Sergeant Ernest Stevenson, Charles Ramsey, William Southard, John Larsen, and Sergeant Carl Murphy; (back row) Sergeant Clifford Welch, Lloyd Oldham, Raymond Fellows, Edward Powers, Karl Sutherland, Nathan Snow, Edward Miller, Frank Bernard, and Sergeant Ernest Darling. (Ernest Darling)

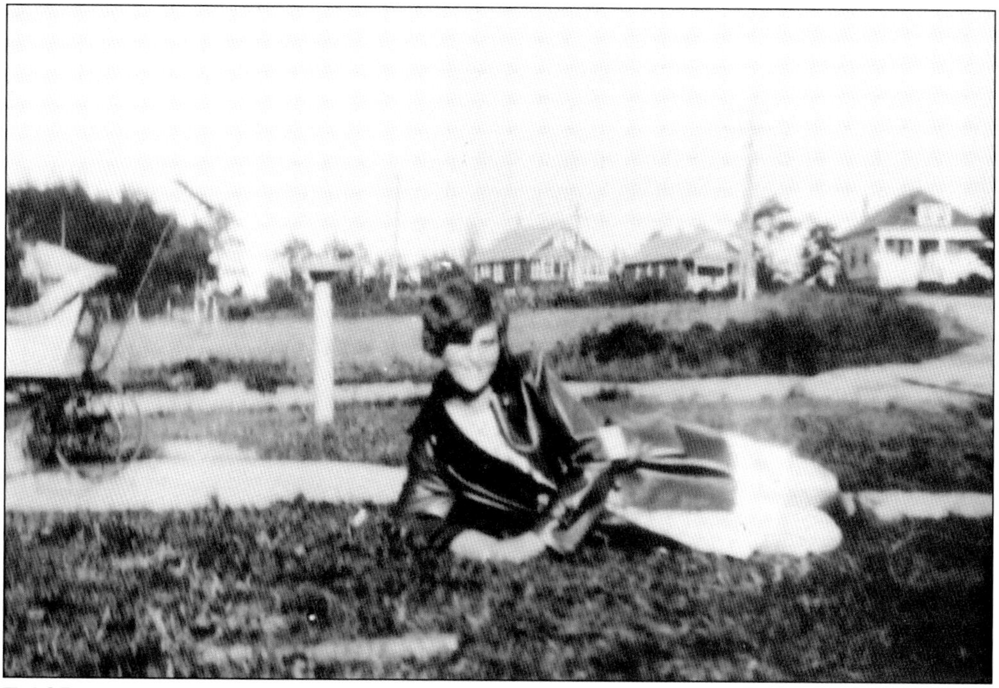

THORNTON HEIGHTS. Thelma Dyke poses near her home, Dyke Farm, off Westbrook Street, *c.* 1920. The house at the far right is still on the corner of Westbrook Street and Keswick Road, South Portland. (Alice Smith)

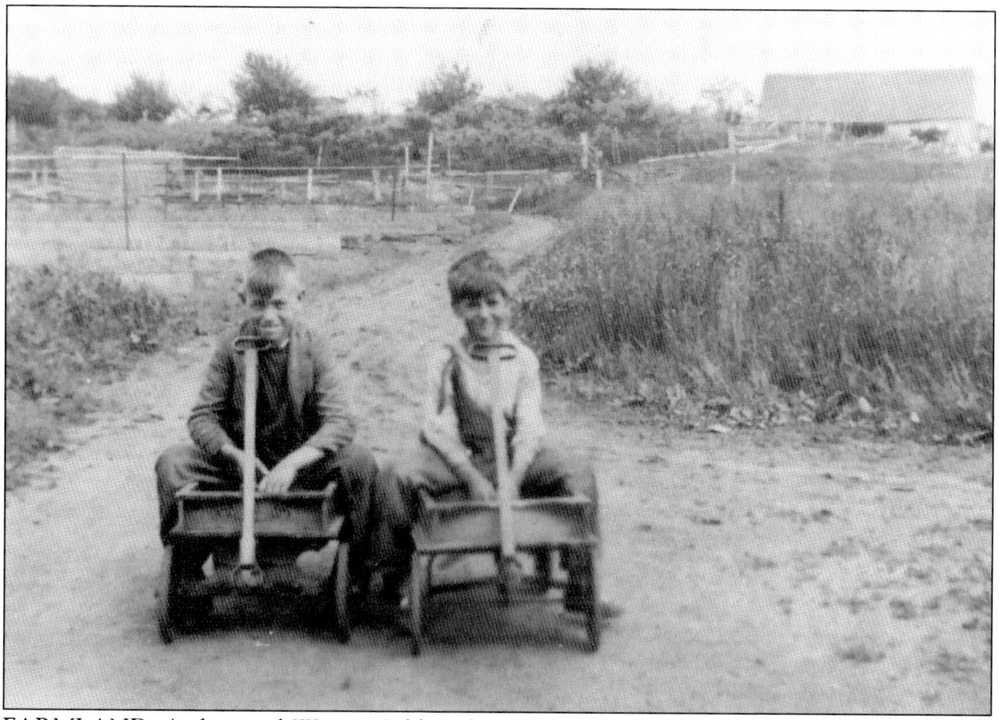

FARMLAND. Arthur and Warren Libby of South Portland ride on Granby Road leading to what now is Country Gardens, *c.* 1930. (Alice Smith)

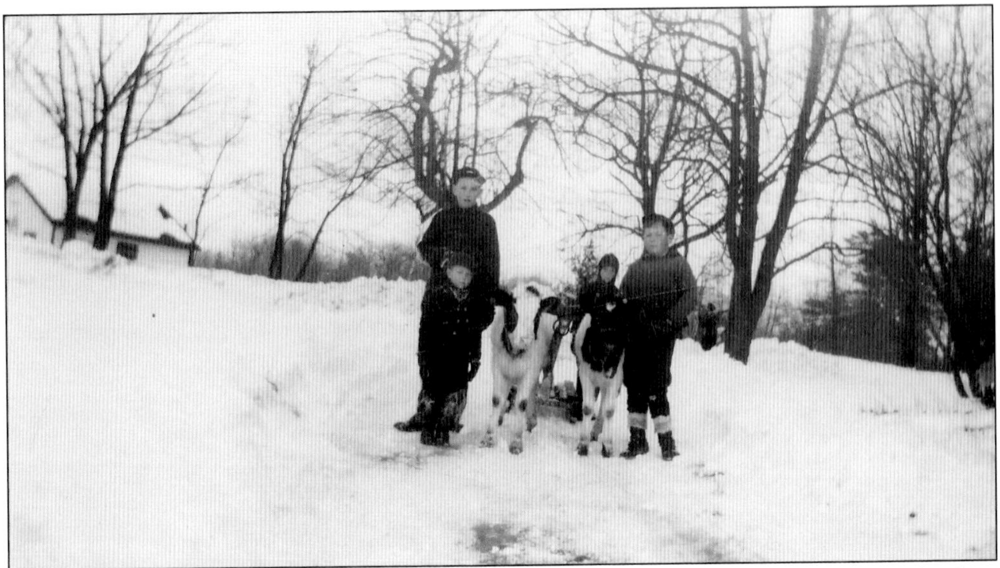

PULL POWER. Al Wilkes and John Dyke, with their two younger sisters, hitch their sleigh to two oxen in the area of the Dyke Farm off Westbrook Street, South Portland. (Dorothy M. Wilkes)

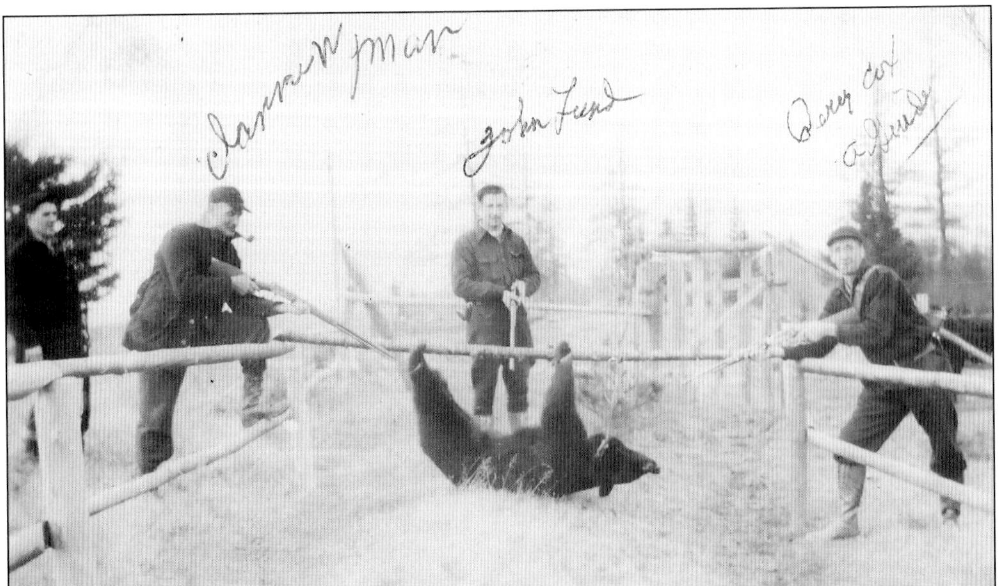

BEAR SEASON. John Lund of South Portland and his buddies brought down a bear during this hunting trip in the 1940s. At that time he operated Lund's Dairy on Thornton Avenue. (Warren & Dorothy Wilkes)

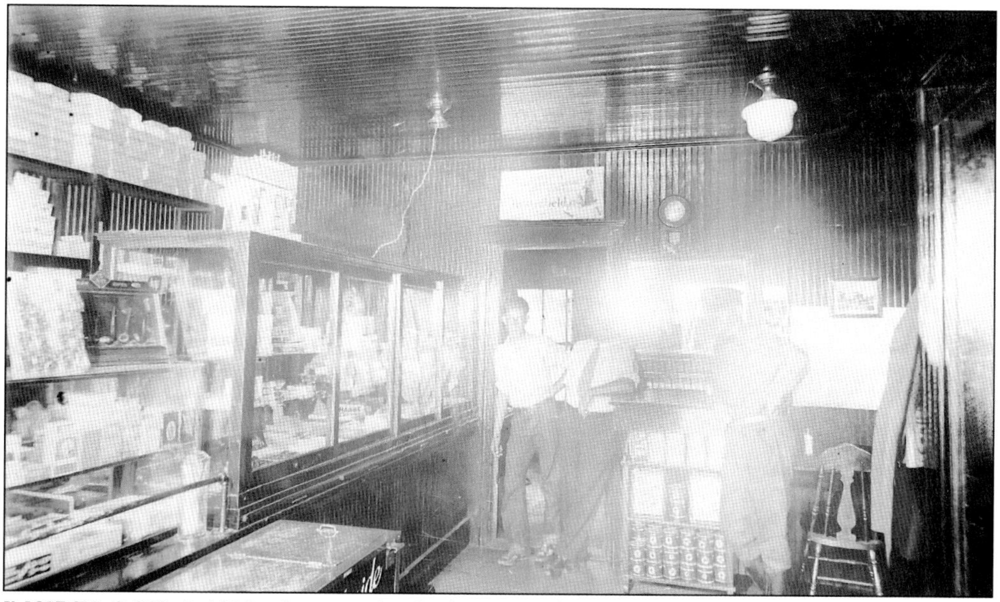

INSIDE LOOK. A 1920s photograph of tobacco products neatly arranged inside glass-enclosed cabinets and Engleside Ginger Ale in an ice-filled chest at A.J. McLean's Texaco station at 620 Main Street, Thornton Heights. The three men are, from left to right, Bill Jackson, Phil Brown, and Ernest Stevenson. (Dorothy M. Wilkes)

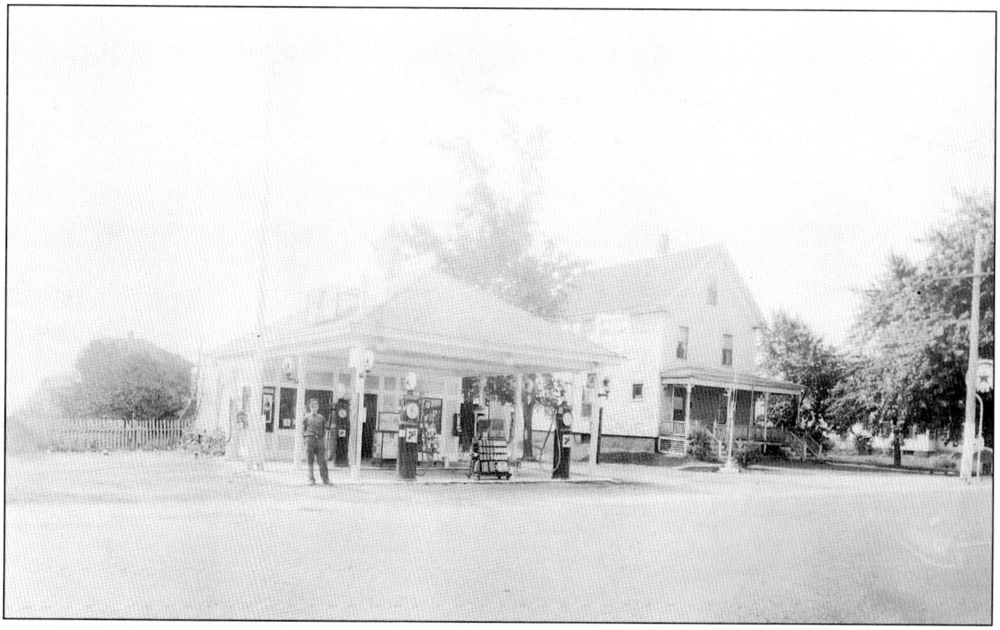

ON THE OUTSIDE. A choice of five kinds of gasoline at 10 gallons for $1 was offered at Albert McLean's Texaco station in the 1950s. The two-family home at right is on the site of the original McLean home, destroyed by fire around 1909 while the family was at church on Brown's Hill. Because no water was available to put out the fire, neighbors pitched in and dismanteled the house. Pieces were used to build the Phinney house on Broadway. Warren Wilkes, standing outside, operated the station for his father-in-law in the 1950s. (Dorothy M. Wilkes)

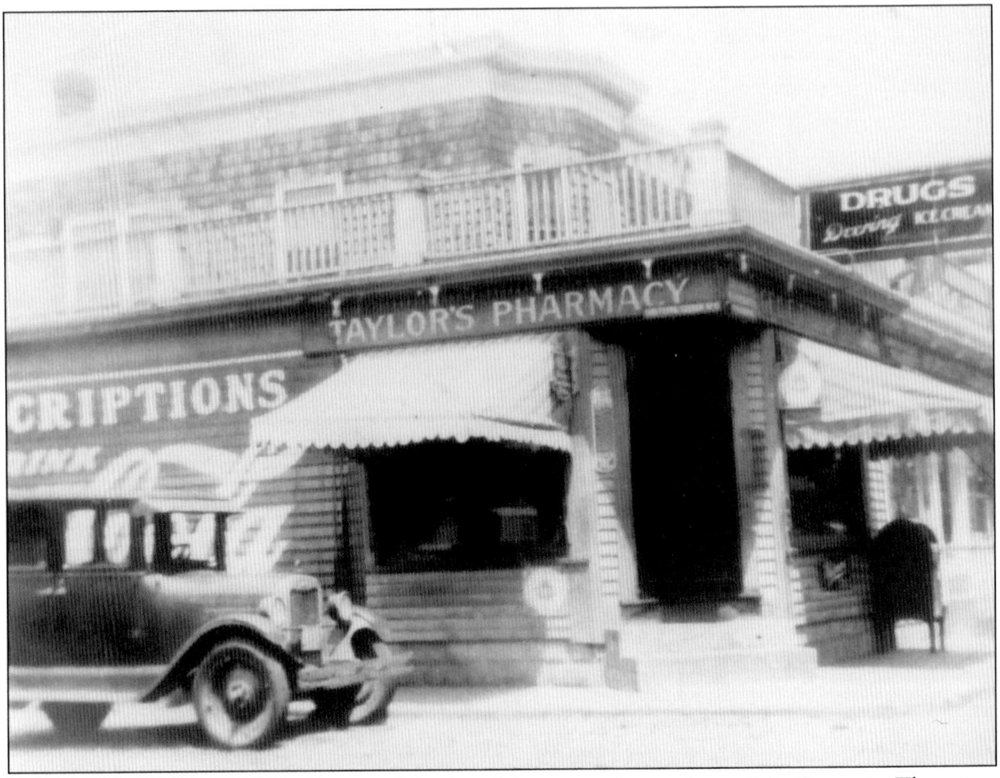

TAYLOR'S PHARMACY. This neighborhood drugstore, located on Main Street in Thornton Heights, was owned by George E. Taylor in 1934. A meat market was next door and its owners lived upstairs. The pharmacy was sold to Ted Gill in the early 1960s. (George Thompson)

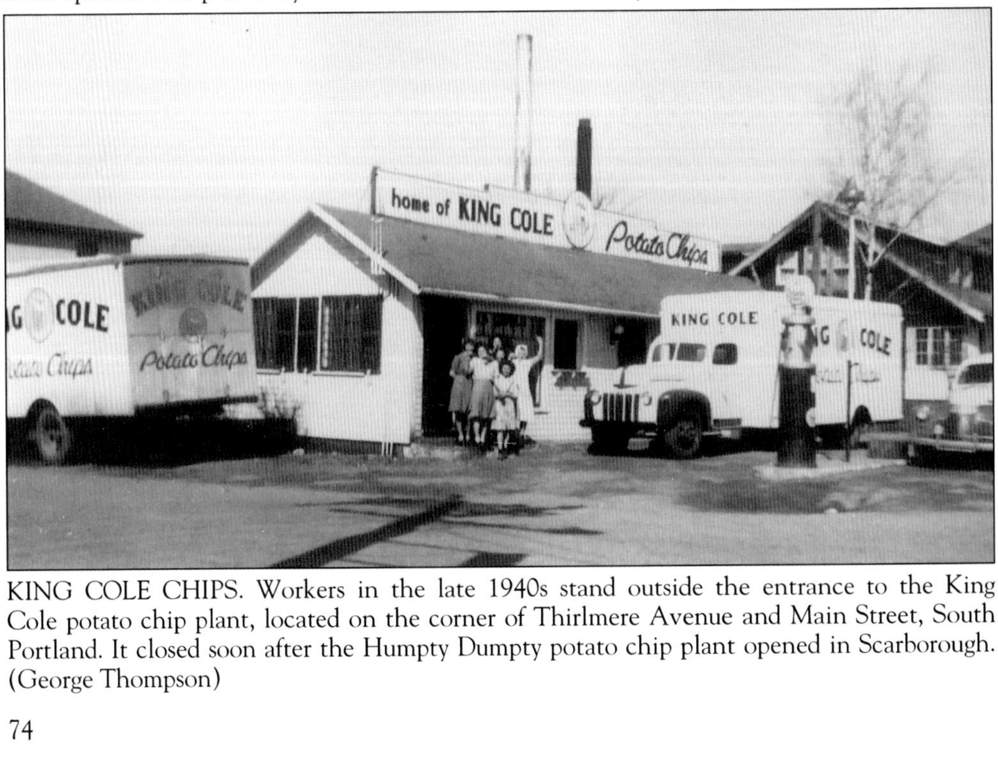

KING COLE CHIPS. Workers in the late 1940s stand outside the entrance to the King Cole potato chip plant, located on the corner of Thirlmere Avenue and Main Street, South Portland. It closed soon after the Humpty Dumpty potato chip plant opened in Scarborough. (George Thompson)

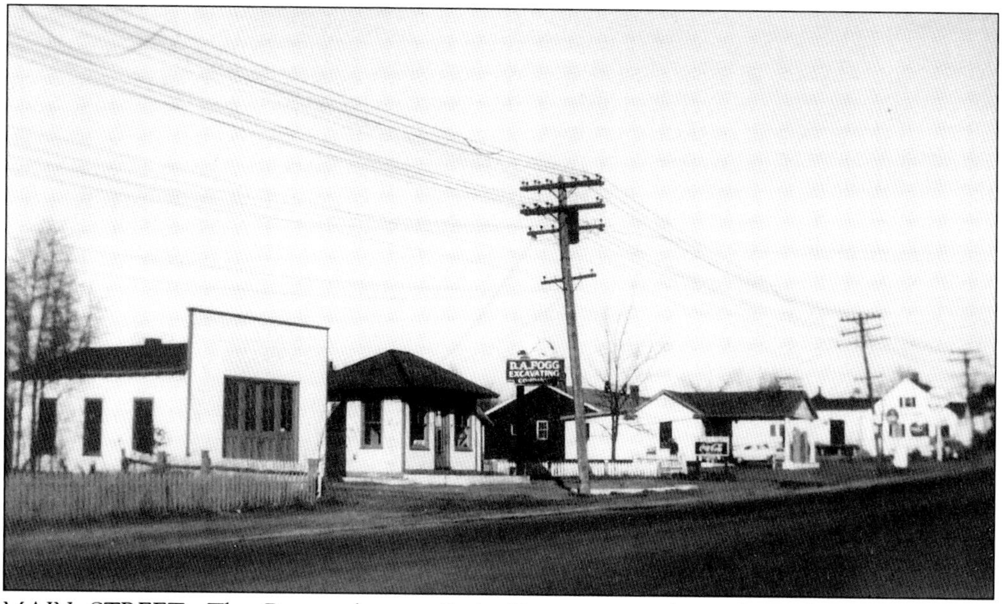

MAIN STREET. The Rosegarden at Cash Corner, once located in the dark building behind the D.A. Fogg Excavating sign, was a hot spot to dine and dance in the 1940s. (George Thompson)

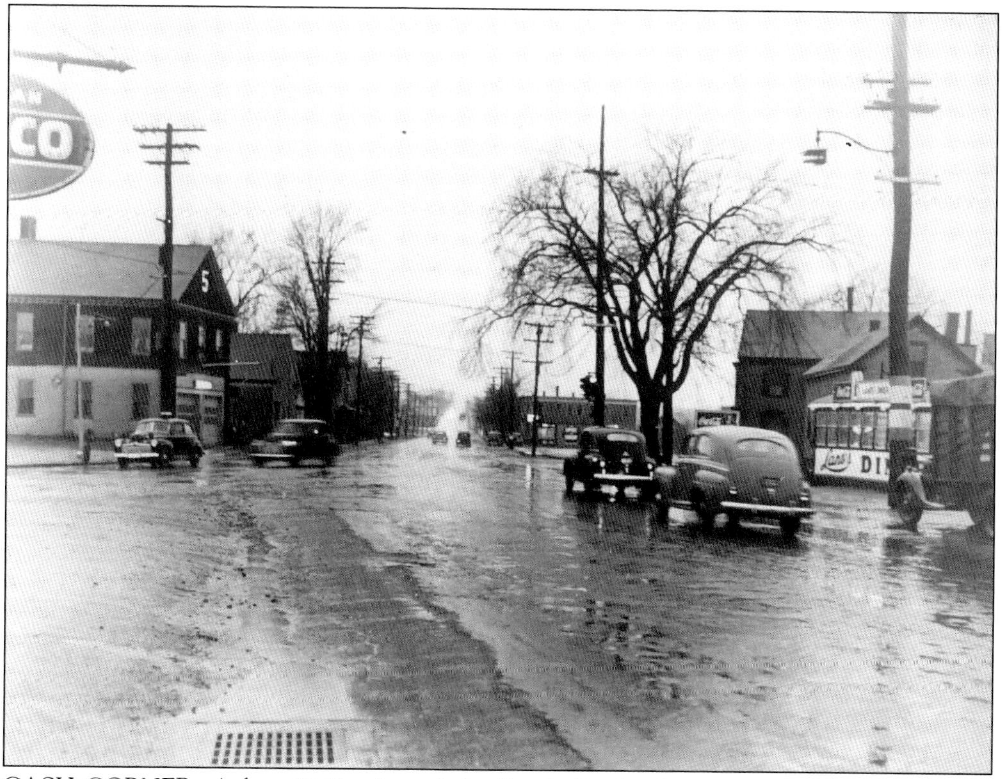

CASH CORNER. A late 1940s view of the South Portland intersection of Broadway and Route 1, heading south, with Lano's Diner on the right and the old firebarn on the left corner. (George Thompson)

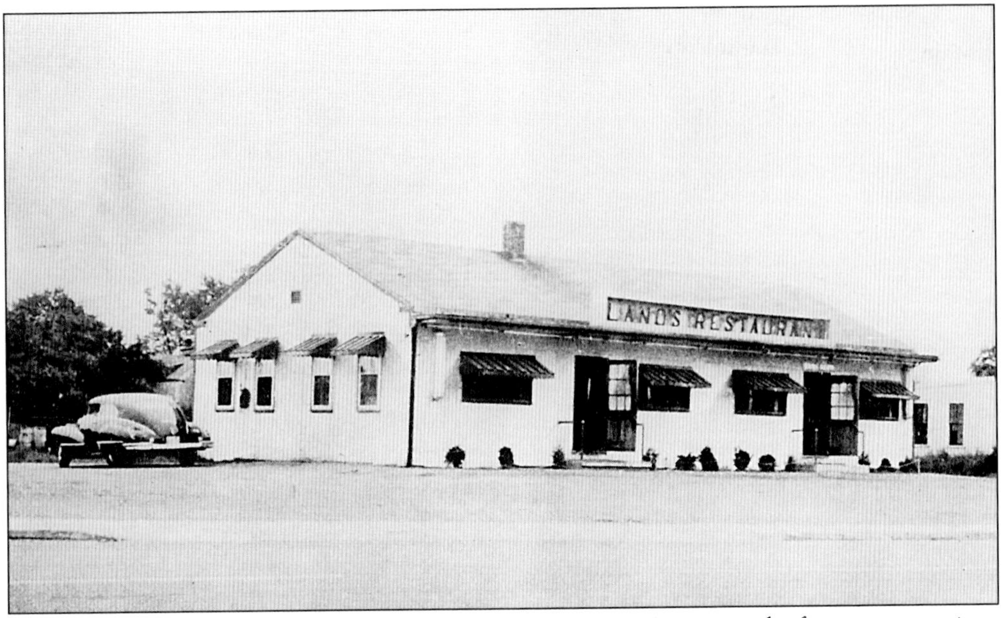

LANDMARK. Considered a landmark in Cash Corner, Lano's remained a favorite eatery into the 1950s in new quarters across the street from the original diner. (George Thompson)

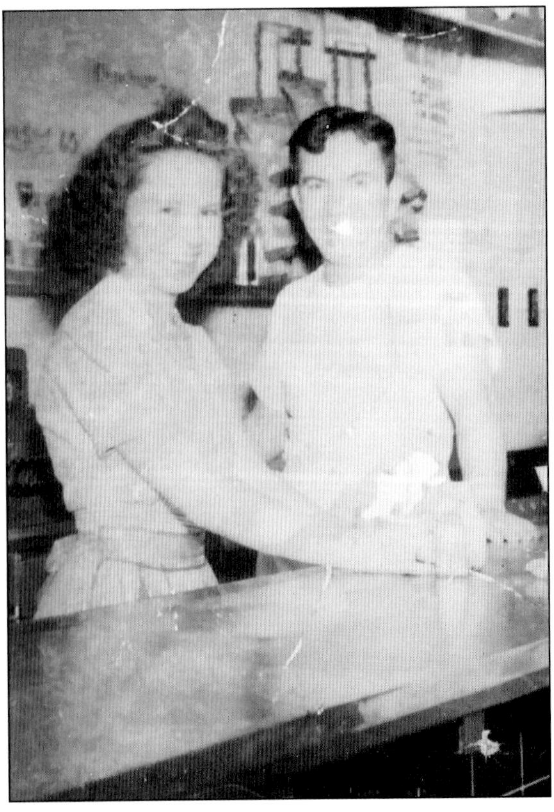

THERE'S JIMMY. Owner Jimmy Lano and waitress Evelyn Kierstead work behind the counter at his South Portland diner, c. 1947. (George Thompson)

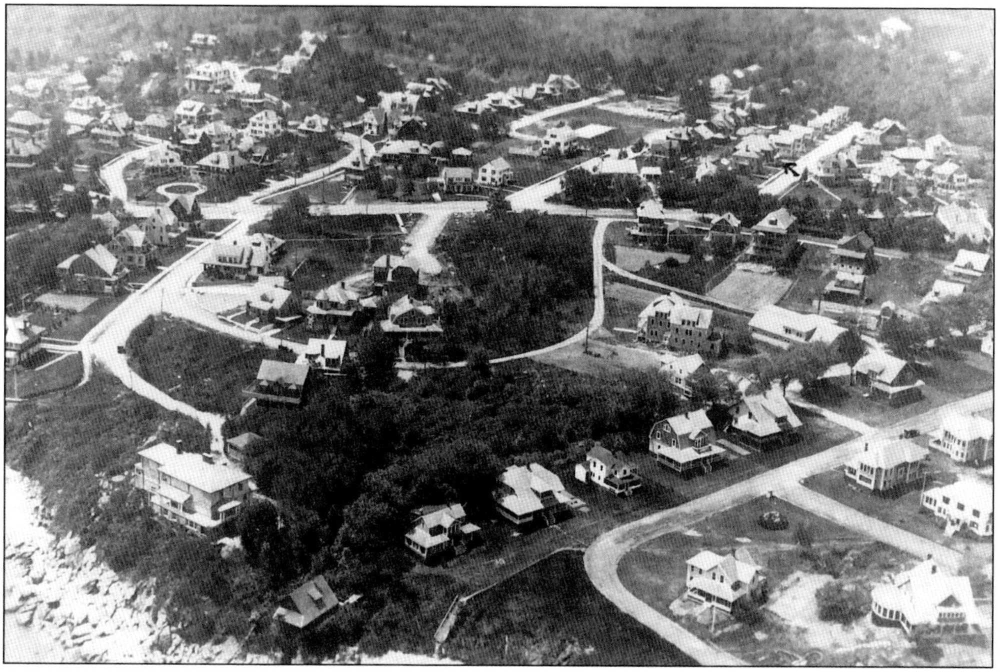

CAPE AERIAL. The Preti residence can be seen in the forefront of this *c.* 1930 view, which includes Mountain View Park (Cape Elizabeth's first housing development) and Cottage Farms. (Sullivan Photo Collection)

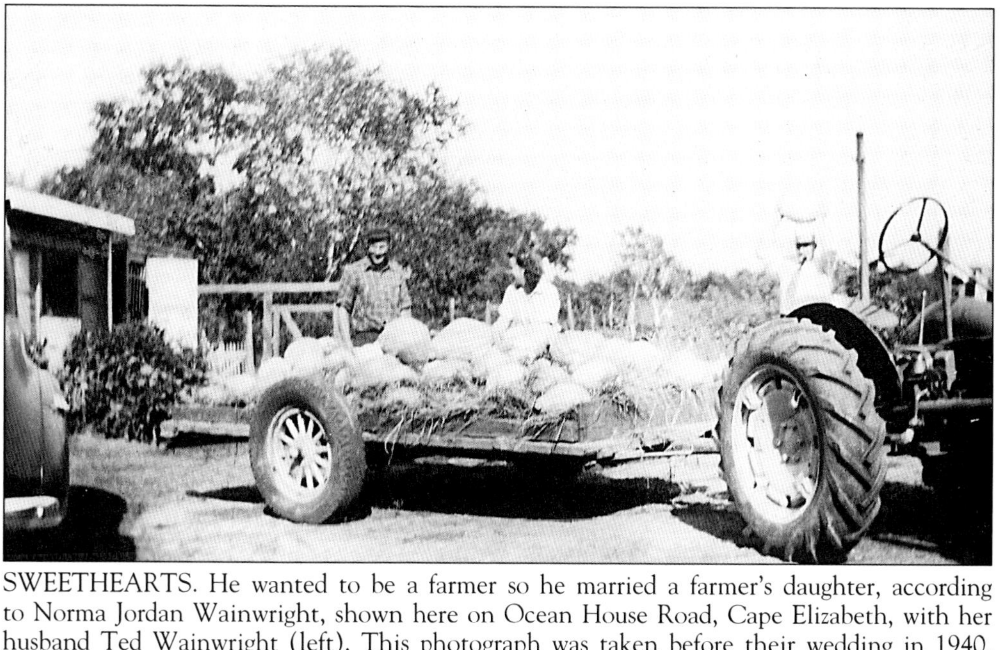

SWEETHEARTS. He wanted to be a farmer so he married a farmer's daughter, according to Norma Jordan Wainwright, shown here on Ocean House Road, Cape Elizabeth, with her husband Ted Wainwright (left). This photograph was taken before their wedding in 1940. Ted's father George is at the right. The Wainwrights have been married fifty-five years. (Ted & Norma Wainwright)

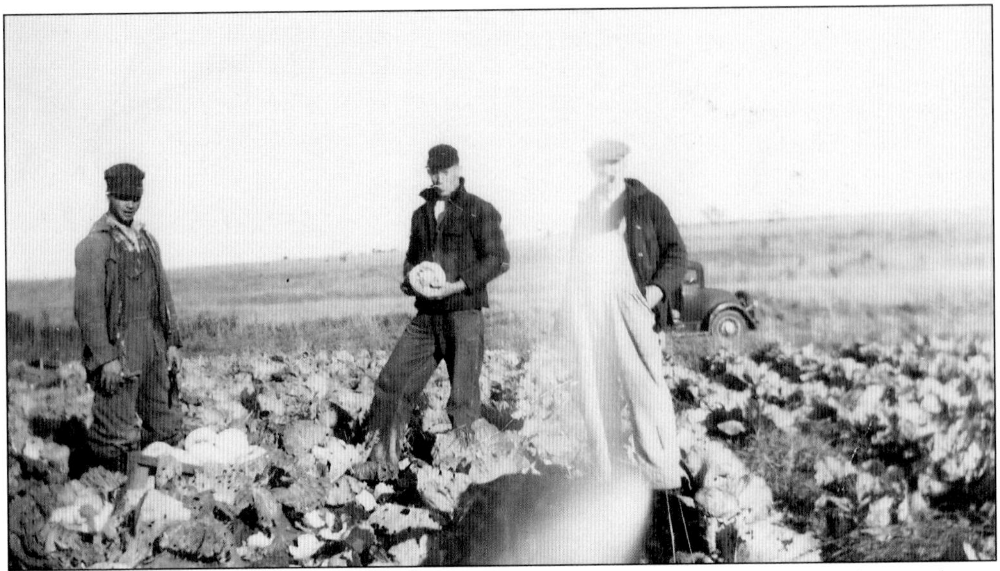

CUTTING CABBAGE. Pete Jordan, Ted Wainwright, and George Wainwright are shown here carrying on the Cape farming tradition of harvesting the cabbage crop, to be sold at local farm stands and the Portland and Boston markets. Spurwink Farm is in the background, c. 1944. (Ted & Norma Wainwright)

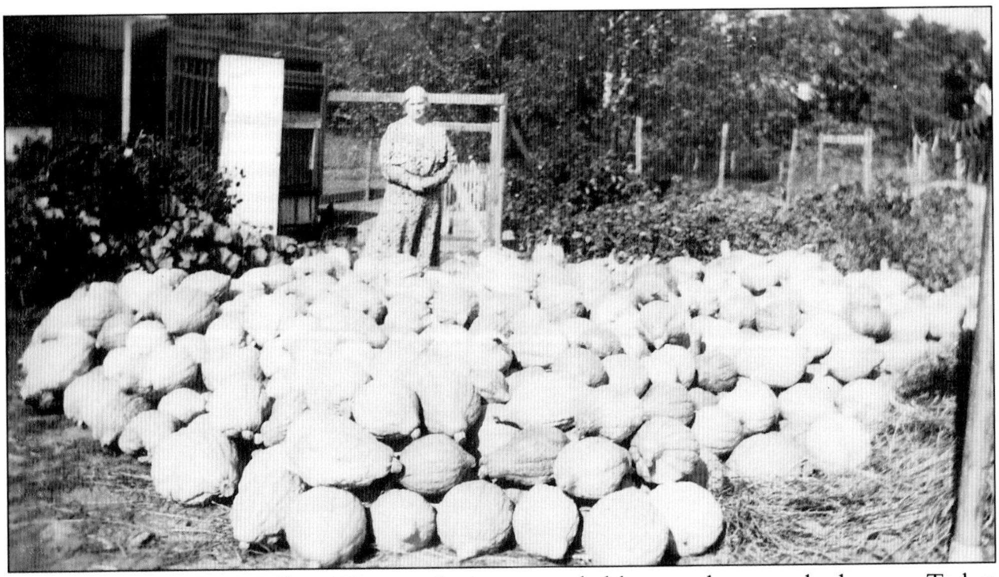

SQUASH APLENTY. Lillian Wainwright is surrounded by squash grown by her son Ted at her home on Ocean House Road, Cape Elizabeth, c. 1943. Lillian hailed from Ireland, and her maiden name was Mskielly. (Ted & Norma Wainwright)

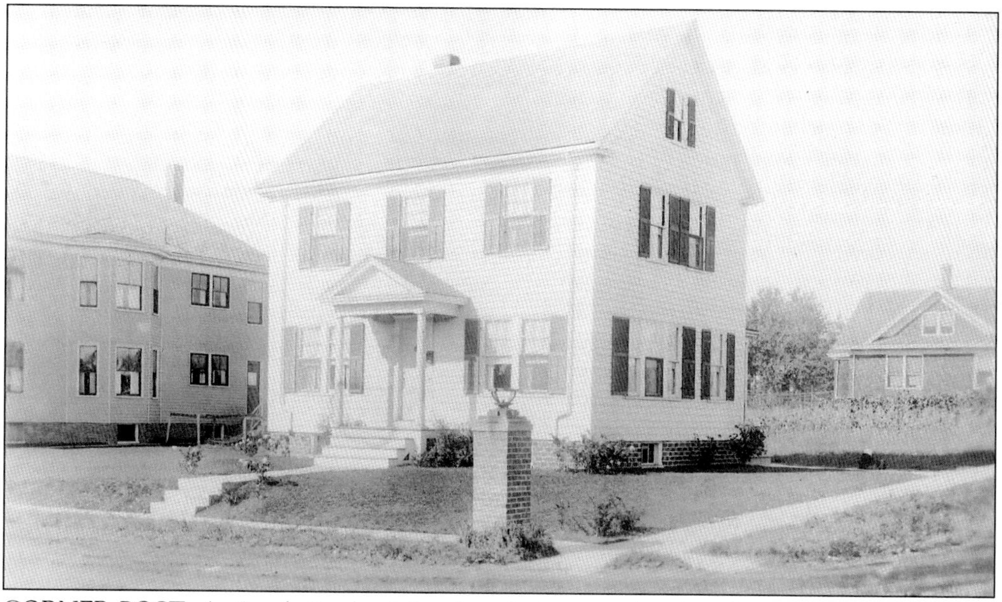

CORNER POST. As South Portland developed, the city placed gas lanterns in brick posts at some street corners, as can be seen in this *c.* 1930 photograph of the Langlois residence on the corner of Fairlawn Avenue and Cedar Street. (Edward Langlois)

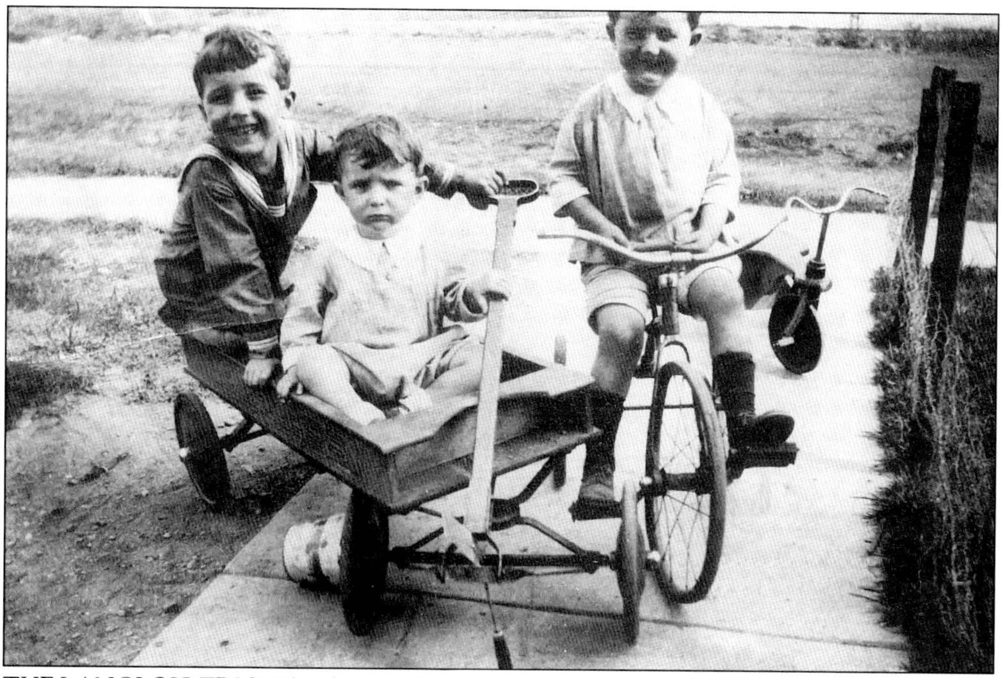

THE LANGLOIS TRIO. The three children of Helen and Alfred Langlois play on the walkway of their home at 43 Fairlawn Avenue in 1925. From left to right are Clement, Jeanette, and Edward. (Edward Langlois)

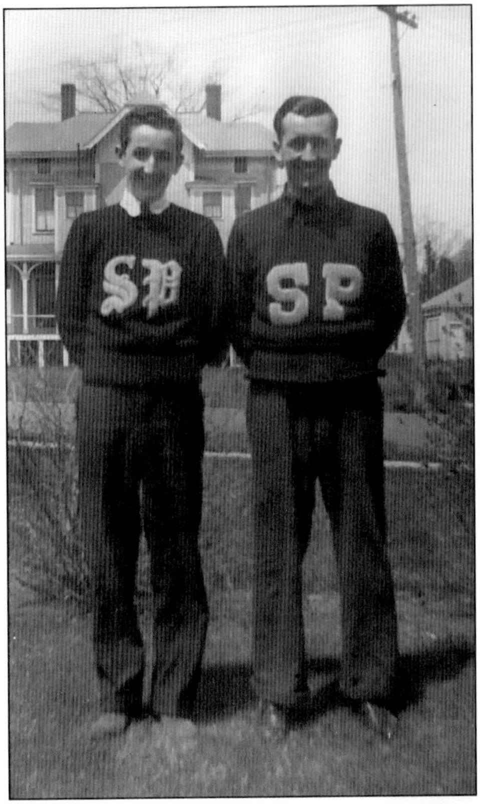

LETTERMEN. Edward Langlois (left), a member of the South Portland High School track team in 1939, and his brother Clement, a member of the school's baseball team, wear the school's letters signifying varsity status. (Edward Langlois)

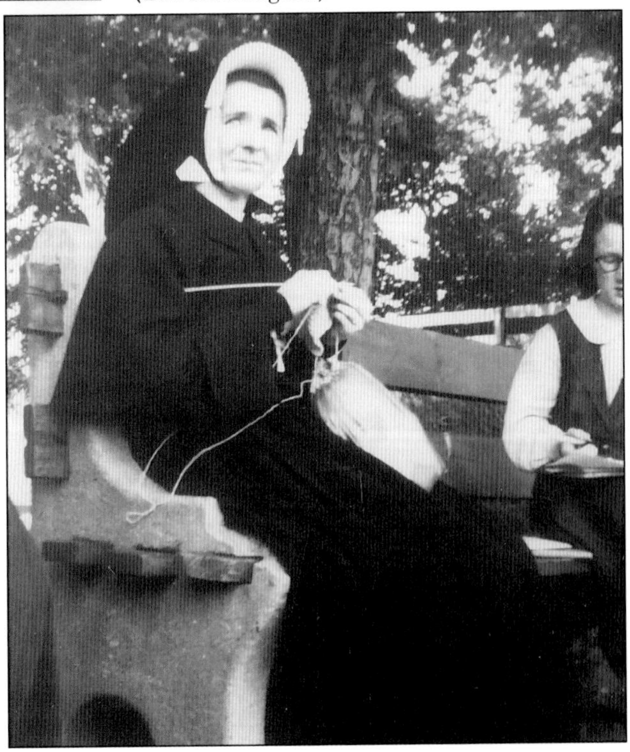

SISTER JEANETTE. Jeannette Langlois became a Roman Catholic nun following her graduation from South Portland High School in 1942. Then known as Mother St. Patrick, she joined the Order of Jesus and Mary in a convent in Quebec, Canada, where she is now Sister Jeanette. (Edward Langlois)

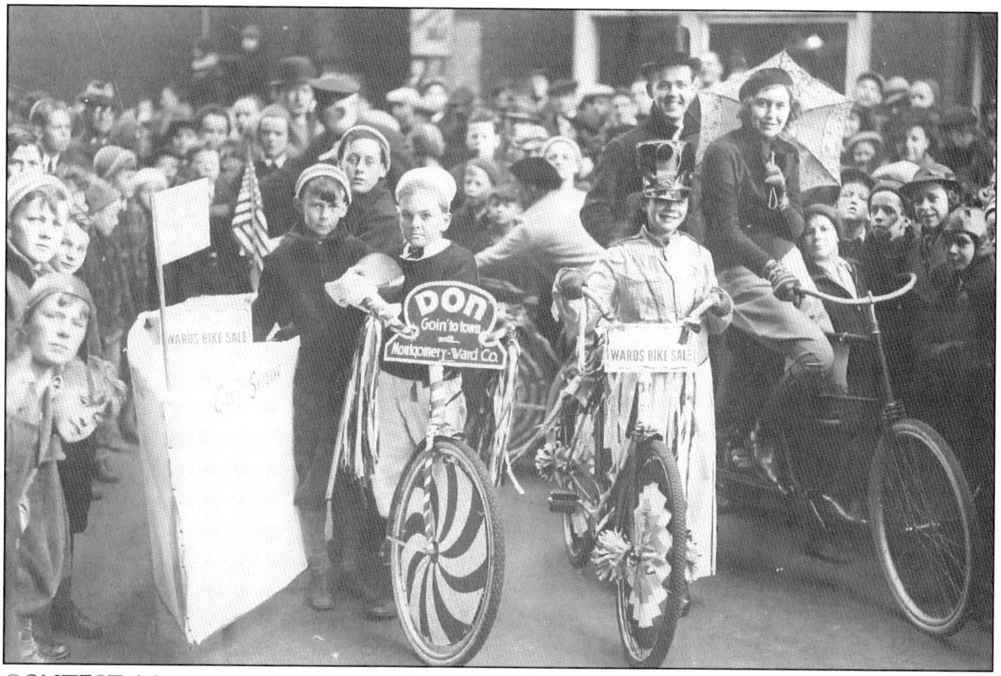

CONTEST. Montgomery Ward, once located on Congress Street in Portland, sponsored a bike parade in 1935 with prizes going to the best-decorated bikes. Twelve-year-old Harris Hinckley (to the left), of South Portland, was a winner with his entry, "Clear Sailing," though it was hard to keep his "boat" on course while parading down Congress Street in the wind. (Harris Hinckley, M.D.)

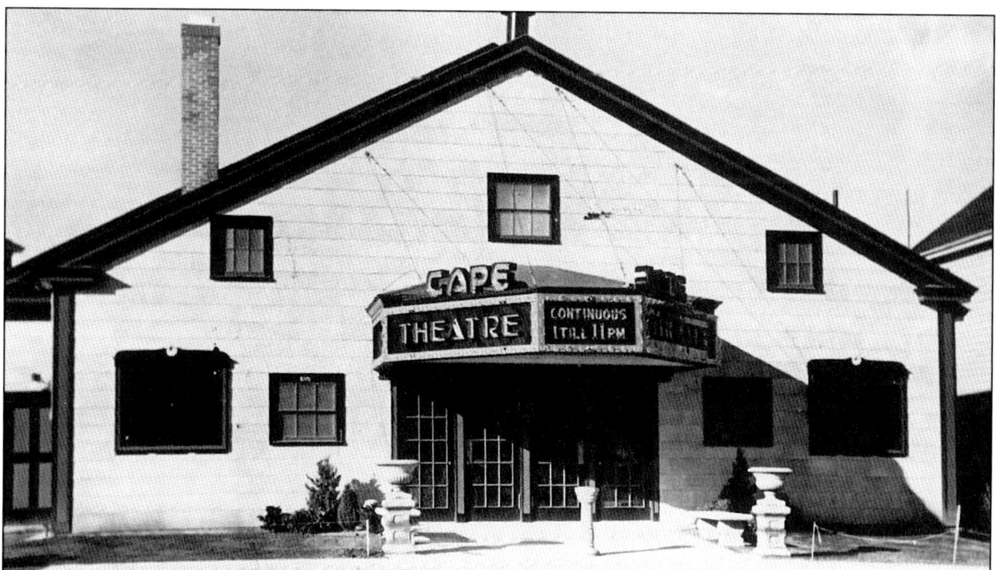

MOVIE THEATRE. *Fire Over England*, starring Flora Robson, Laurence Olivier, Vivian Leigh, and Raymond Massey, was the feature film at opening night in 1937 at the Cape Theatre, Cottage Road, South Portland. At the time, the ticket price was 10¢. The 500-seat theater became home to the Portland Players in 1966 and was renamed the Phyllis Thaxter Theatre. (Edward Langlois)

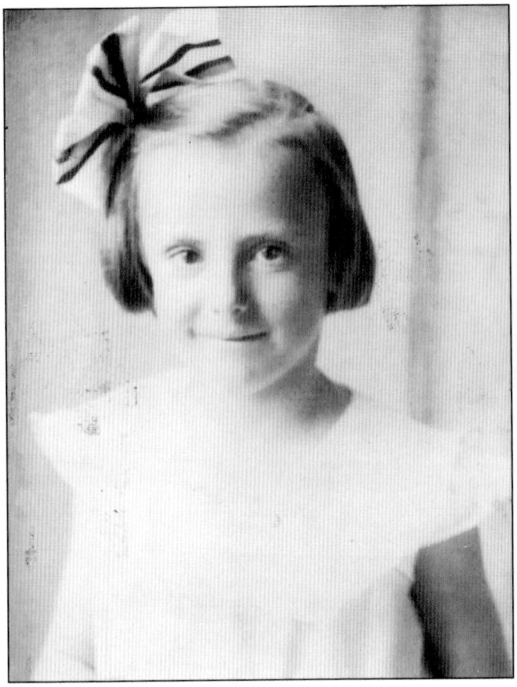

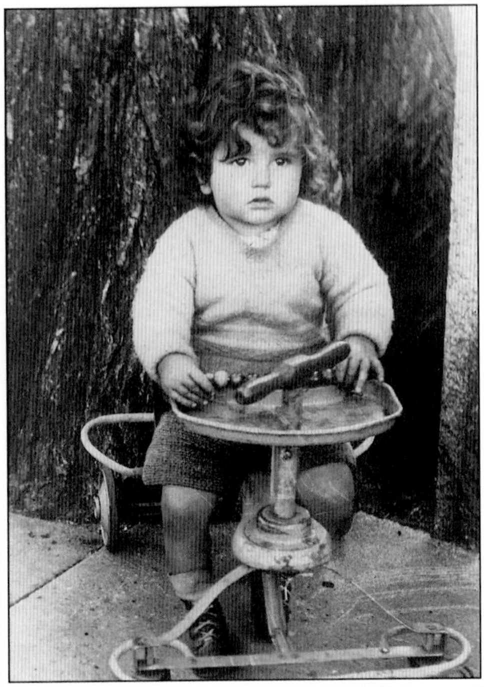

LEFT: NANCY LOVEJOY BEAN. This is a *c.* 1936 photograph of the daughter of Helen and James Lovejoy. Nancy graduated from South Portland High School and lives with her husband Albert Bean on Willard Street. (Helen Goodine)
RIGHT: RICHARD H. LOVEJOY. Two-year-old Richard Herbert Lovejoy, son of James and Helen Lovejoy of Sawyer Street, South Portland, takes a spin in his "kiddie car" in the mid-1930s. He graduated from South Portland High School and lives in Farmington. (Helen Goodine)

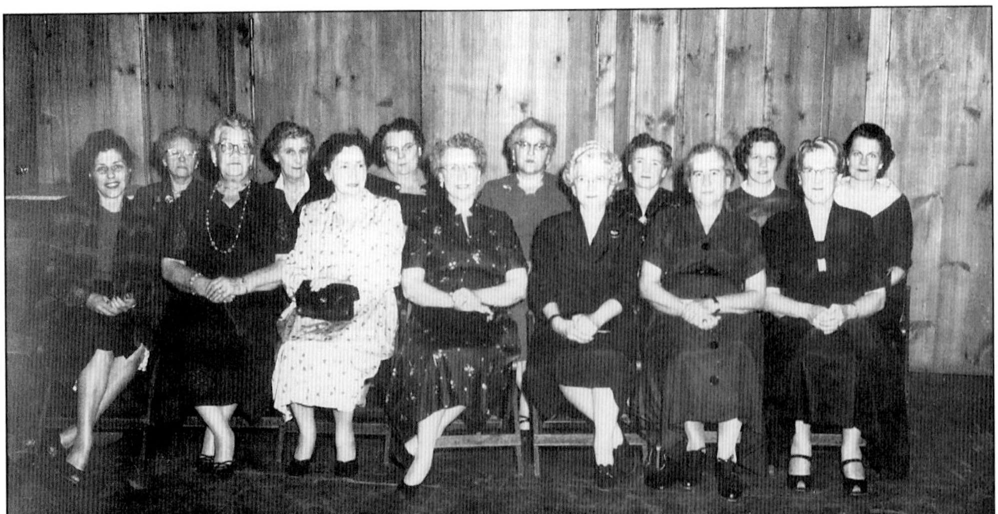

MATRONS. Past presidents of the Matrons group from the First Congregational Church in South Portland get together in 1956. Among them are: (front row) Chris Daner, Etta Strout, Isabelle Spear, Ada Garven, and Esther Leighton; (back row) Pearl Harvey, Hilda Grover, Lena Wetmore, Annie Lawren, Lillian MacPhee, and Pauline Wallace. (Dot Hodgkins)

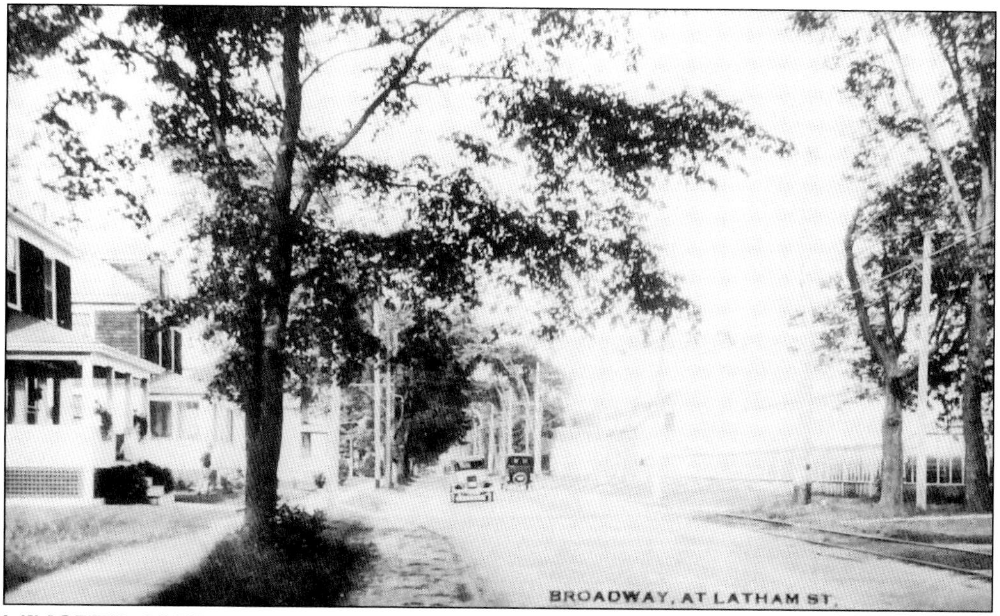

MINOTT'S GREENHOUSE. John Minott and his son George, mayor of South Portland in the 1920s, owned and operated a florist business in these greenhouses located on Broadway, c. 1930. (Ray Taylor)

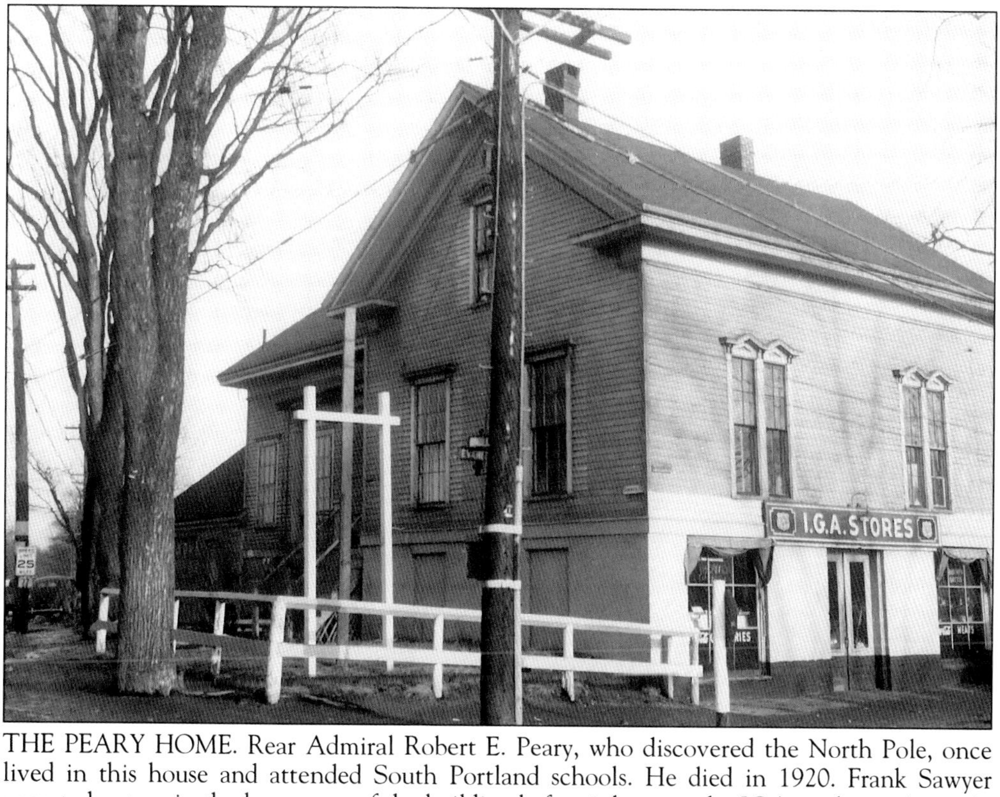

THE PEARY HOME. Rear Admiral Robert E. Peary, who discovered the North Pole, once lived in this house and attended South Portland schools. He died in 1920. Frank Sawyer operated a store in the lower part of the building before it became the IGA, and now Amato's. This photograph was taken c. 1950. (Ruth Morrill)

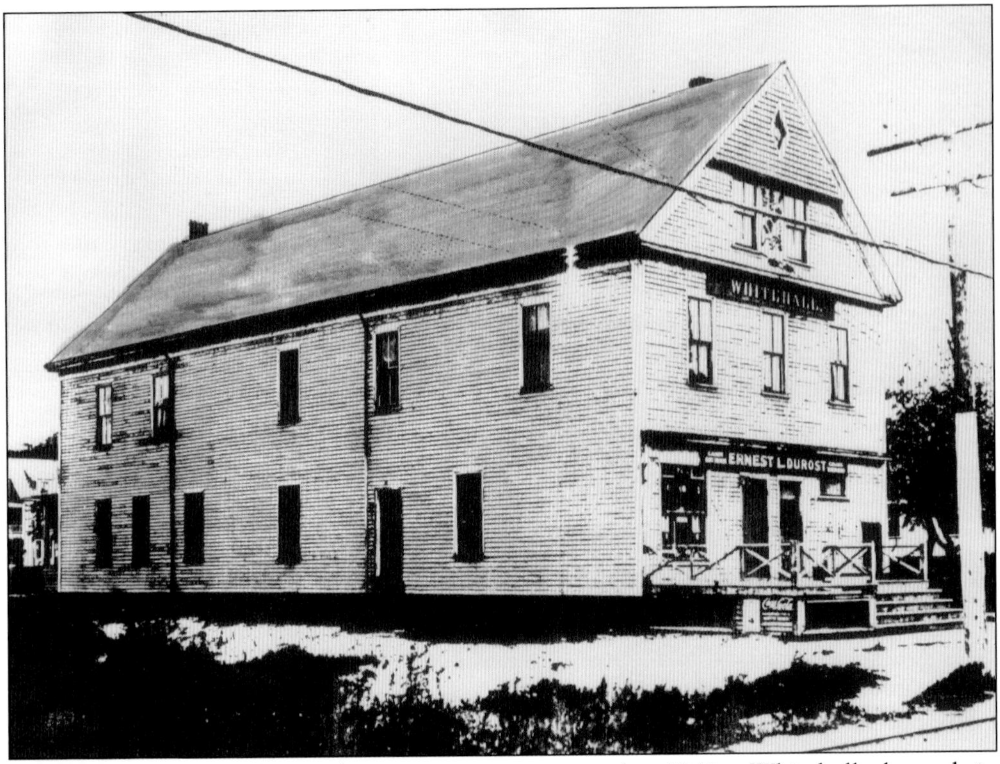

WHITEHALL. An all-around recreation center in the 1940s, Whitehall, located in Pleasantdale, South Portland, included a soda fountain, a pool room with a barber chair, two bowling alleys in the basement, and an upstairs hall for meetings and dances. It burned in the 1950s. (Ray Taylor)

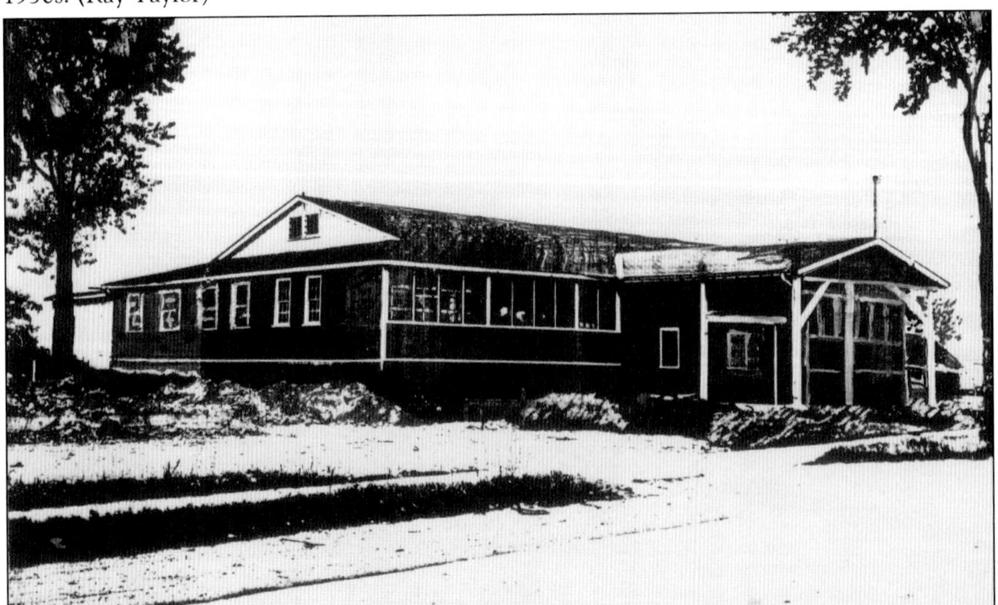

THE JACK-O-LANTERN. A *c.* 1940 photograph of "The Jack," a popular dance hall in the Big Band era, located near the present day Yerxa's on Broadway, South Portland. (Ray Taylor)

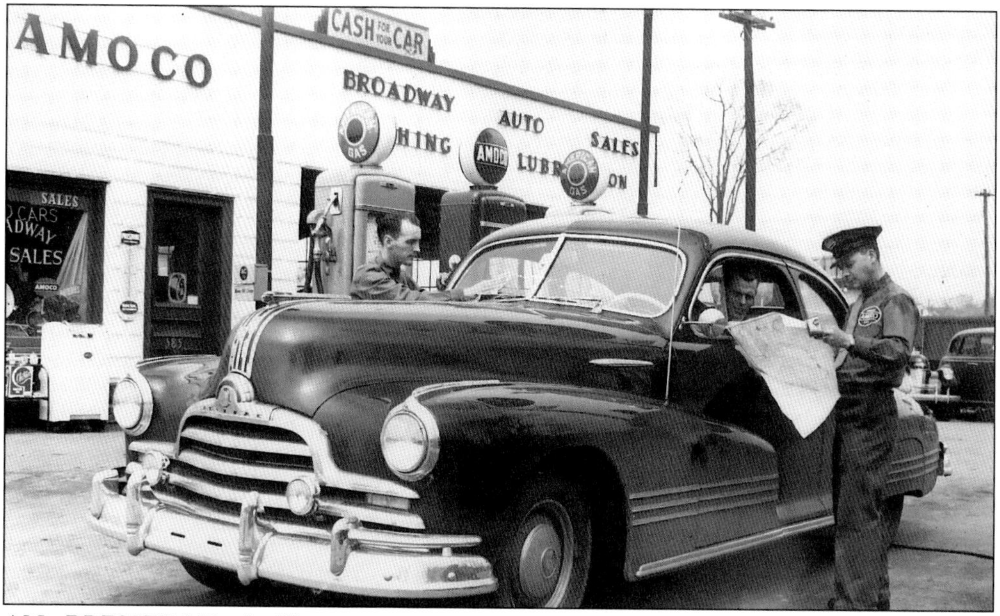

ALL DRESSED-UP. A filling station attendant, attired in the company's uniform, gives directions to a motorist at Broadway Auto Sales in South Portland, while another attendant washes the windows, *c.* 1948. (Sullivan Photo Collection)

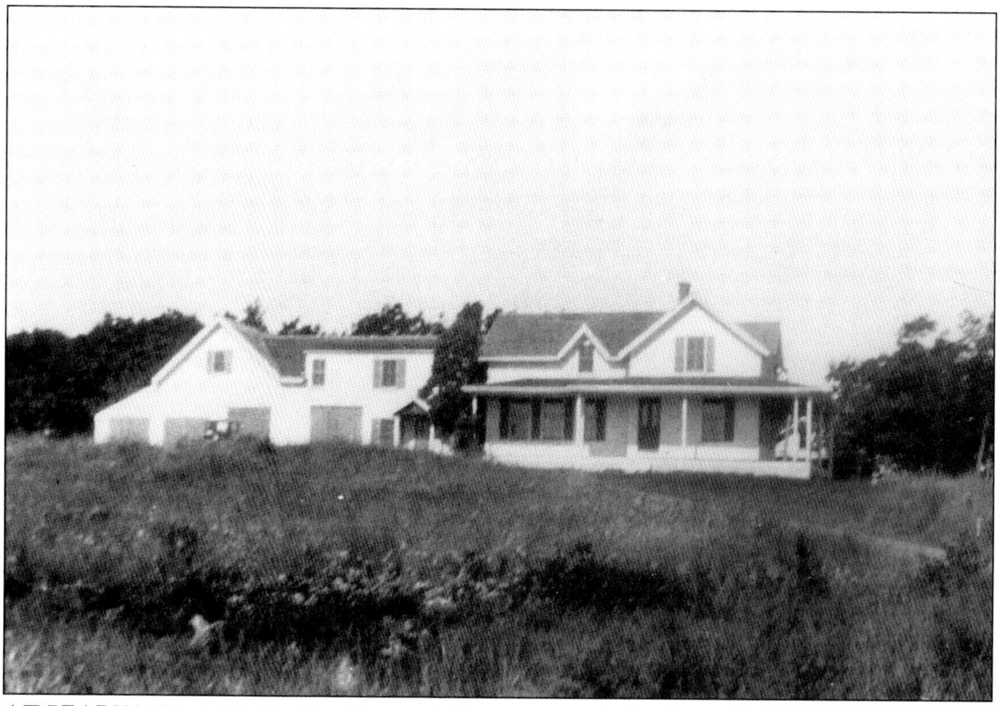

AT PEARY VILLAGE. Marilyn Denbow Thompson, with daughter Sherrie and niece Bonnie, and Alice Pratt Smith, with daughter Nancy, lived at Peary Village in South Portland in the late 1940s. During a blizzard in the early 1950s, the families went without milk and coal delivery for several days before supplies were delivered by toboggan. (Alice Smith)

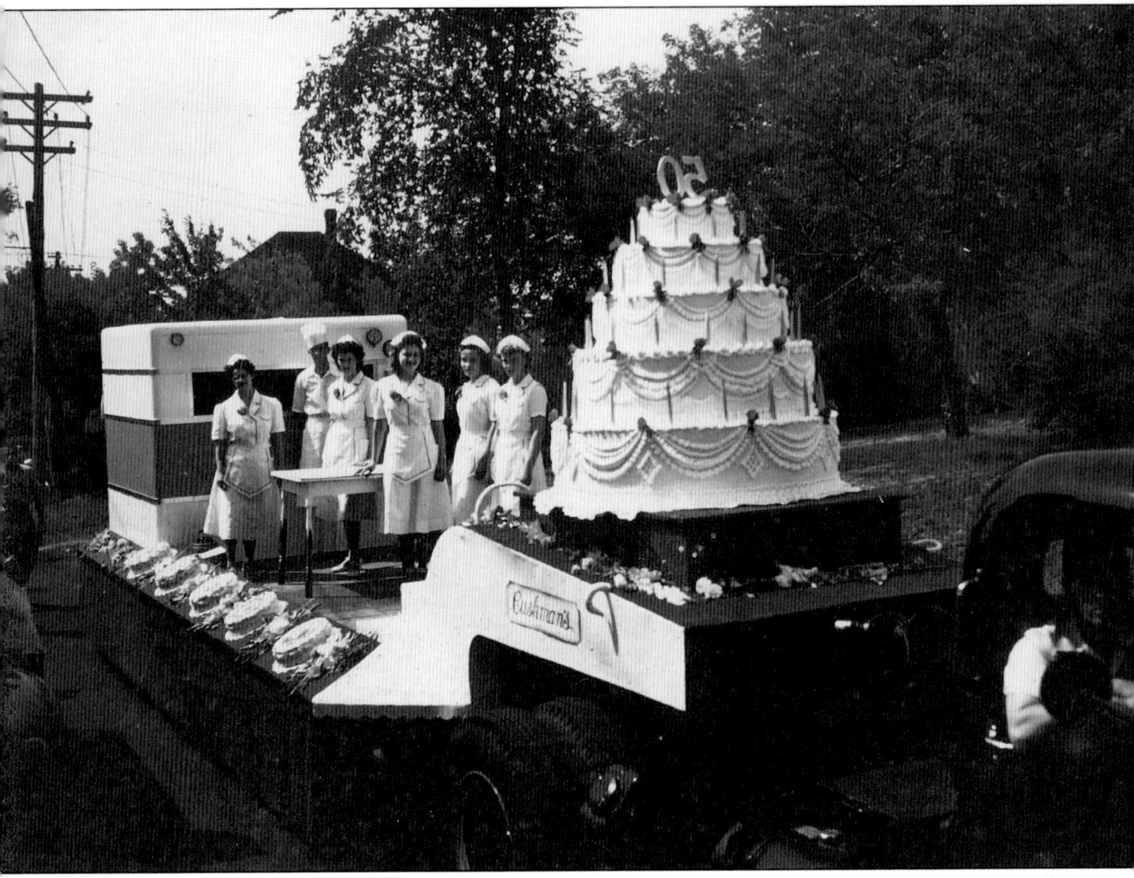

THE CUSHMAN FLOAT. The Cushman Baking Co., which had a store located in Knightville, sponsored this float for the city's 50th anniversary celebration in 1948. South Portland was named an All America City in 1964. (Ray Taylor)

Two

Schools and Activities

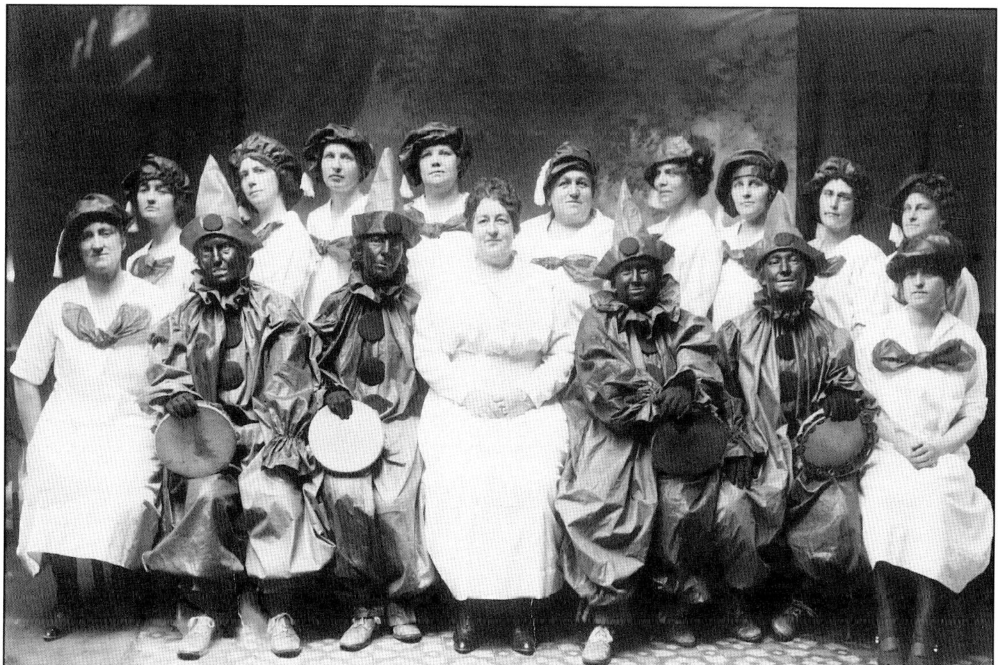

MINSTREL SHOW. Members of the Mothers' Club in South Portland support their school by staging a minstrel show at the Old North Congregational Church on Meeting House Hill. Gertrude Harriman Rodick (back row, fifth from right) sang "Mother," c. 1924. (Nancy Wainwright Woodward)

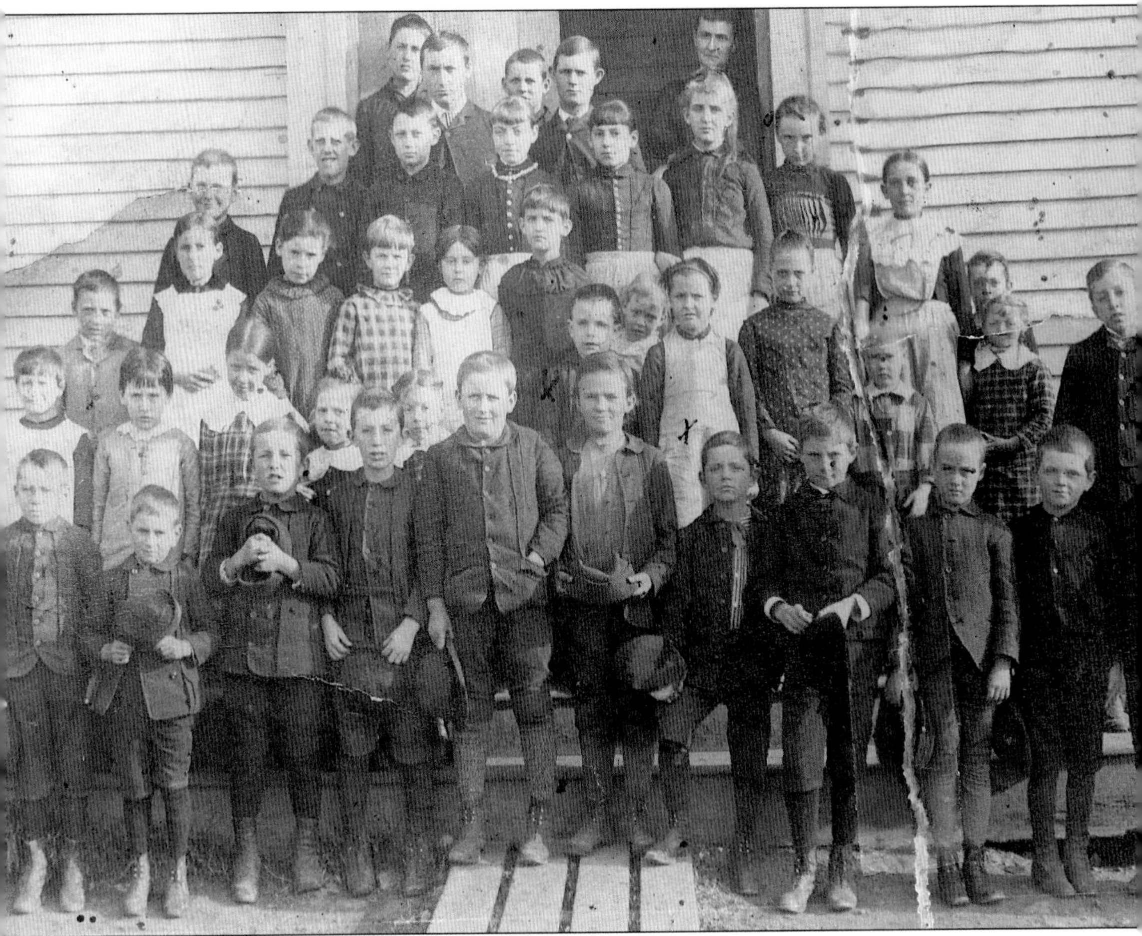

THE EVANS STREET SCHOOL. Alice Taylor, standing in the doorway to the right, taught at this school in South Portland, *c.* 1889. From left to right are: (front row) Lucy Cotton, Fred Sargent, Frank Fickett, John Burgess, Charles Taylor, Charles Graffam, Lester Whitney, Howard Latham, Frank Walker, Charles Green, Howard Worth, and Harry Latham; (second row) Ella Cotton, May Skillings, Susie Tarbox, Ethel Fullerton, Minnie Whitten, Albert Green, Fred Dyer, Harry Skillings, Sam Libby, Cora Richardson, and Alice Green; (third row) Charles Richardson, Bess Burgess, Georgia Libby, ? Nutter, Edith Smith, and Mary Nutter; (back row) ? Small, Mildred Cotton, E. Mountfort, Bertha Sargent, Nellie Skillings, Bess Nutter, Nellie Richardson, and Lottie Whitney (the remaining names were unavailable). (Ray Taylor)

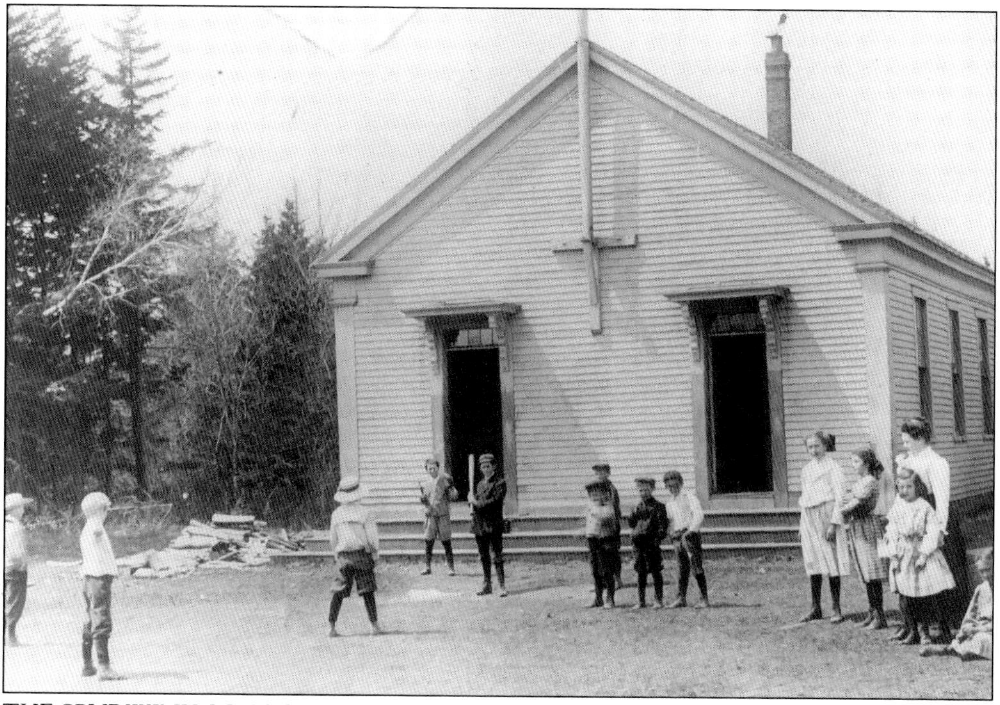

THE SPURWINK SCHOOL. A *c*. 1900 photograph of children playing ball on the grounds of Spurwink School, one of the first schools in Cape Elizabeth before the turn of the century. Other early schools included Bowry Beach, Pond Cove, and Ridgeway. The Spurwink School was later moved to Pond Cove and is now part of the Thomas Memorial Library. (Norman Jordan)

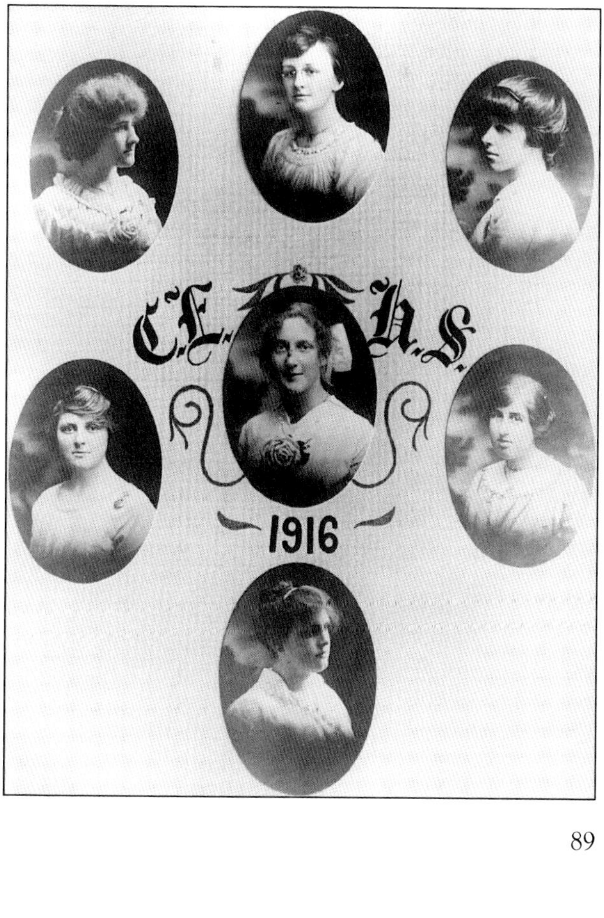

CEHS 1916. Valedictorian Vesta E. Brown earned the center spot in the Cape Elizabeth High School 1916 senior photograph. Clockwise from the top are unknown, Esther Foss, Alice May Sanborn, Ethel Olsen, unknown, and Bessie May Foster. Other graduates were Isabel Carrie Libby, Leora Elizabeth Weld, and Edith Louise Jordan. Commencement was held in June at the town hall. (Norman Jordan)

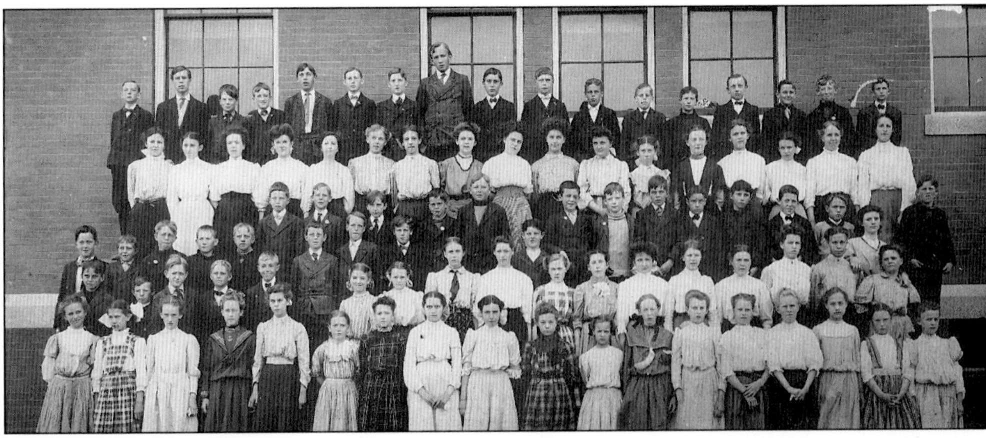

THE SUMMER STREET SCHOOL. In 1909 these youngsters attended the new Summer Street School in South Portland. From left to right are: (front row) Ethel Sawyer, Lucille Libby, Helen Marden, Marguerite King, Elsie McLaughlin, Mary Sturk, Emma Gardiner, Isabel Banks, May Skillin, Louise Johnson, Ruth Curtis?, Anna Bowers, Bessie Worth, Grimmer, ? Green, Gertrude Burke, and Julia Whitten; (second row) P. Gilman, W. Hughes, Chester Carles, Frank Gilman, Raymond Dyer, Ruth Herbert, Lila Willett, Kitty Tanner, Alice Flynn, Lizzie White, Ida Skillins, Bessie Manning, Helen Silvia Akeley, Annie Bell, and Beulah Gilman; (third row) Reginald Lombard, C. Kittelson, L. Cash, H. Cook, Carl Ward, Brick Campbell, C. Grimmer, Frank Murphy, and Warren Cash; (fourth row) Howard Chick, Ralph Curtis, Cliff Richardson, William Manning, E. Ryall, unknown, Ralph Bell, Roland Dyer, unknown, J. Norton, E. Kierstead, and Asa Morse; (fifth row) Annie Smith, Lillian Thompson, Mildred Chick, Ella Moody, Ella Brophy, Hazel Webster, Winnie Curtis, Alice Arnold, Bea Benson, Gladys Miles, Annie Rundlett, Mollie Thomas, Helen Coyne, unknown, Margaret Watson, Lilly Goff, and Nell Goff; (back row) Robert Strout, Clayton Kennedy, George Minott, L. Hunnewell, C. Libby, Eddie Flynn, Howard Skillin, Dan Rodick, Percy Carter, F. Ryder, George Gavett, C. Kemp, D. Hackett, C. Skillin, E. Christianson, Jimmie Duffy, and Dave Blanchard. The school later became the Edward C. Reynolds School. (Ruth Morrill)

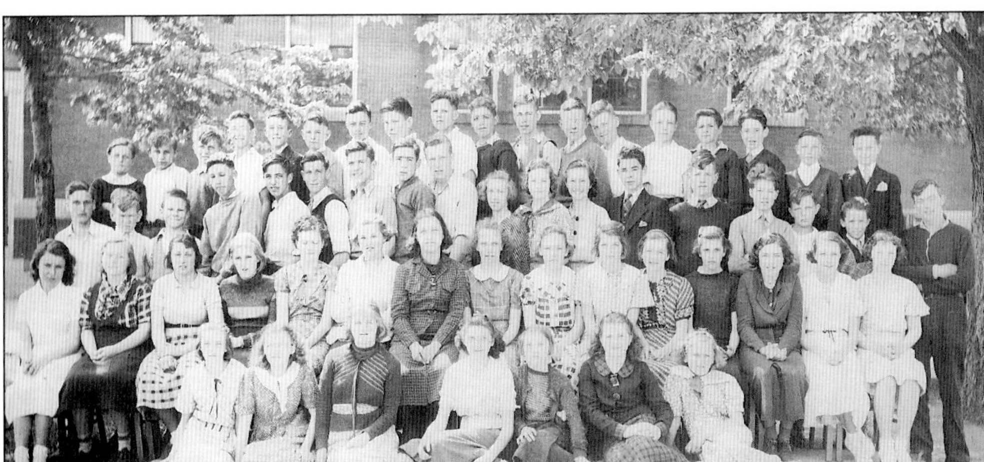

SECOND GENERATION. This is a 1935 photograph of the last class to graduate from the Edward C. Reynolds School, Broadway, South Portland. (Ruth Morrill)

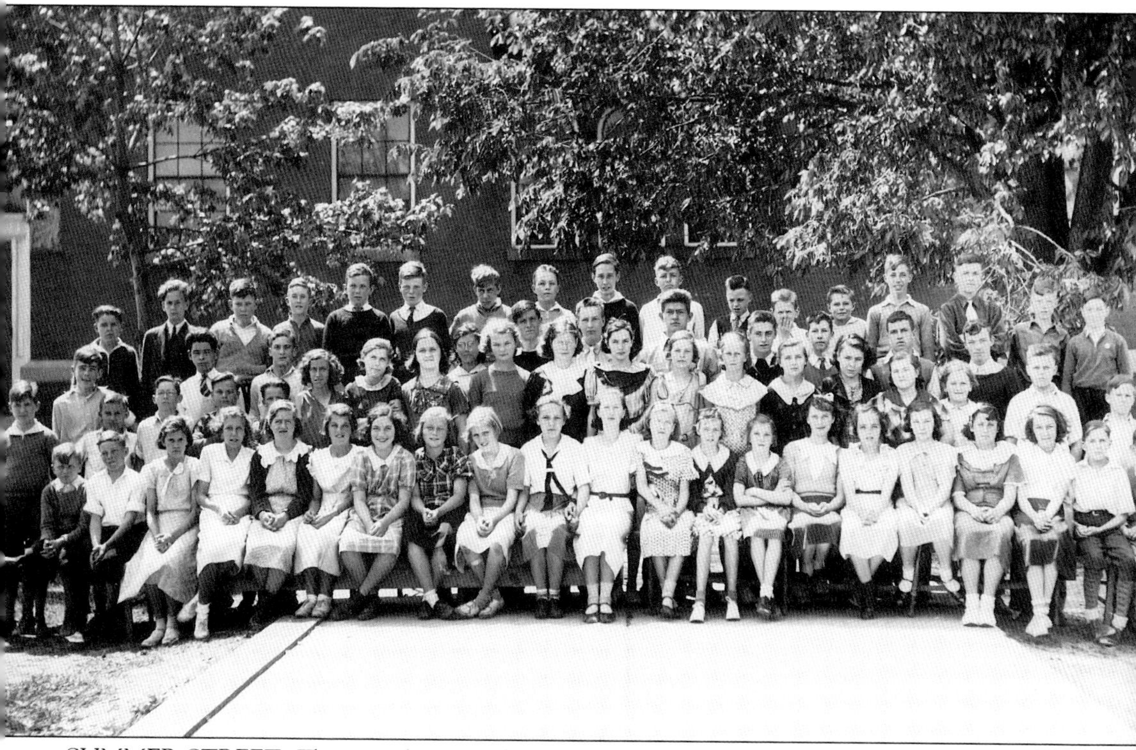

SUMMER STREET. These students in the seventh and eighth grades at the Summer Street School changed classes for different subjects in the mid-1930s. (Mary Olssen)

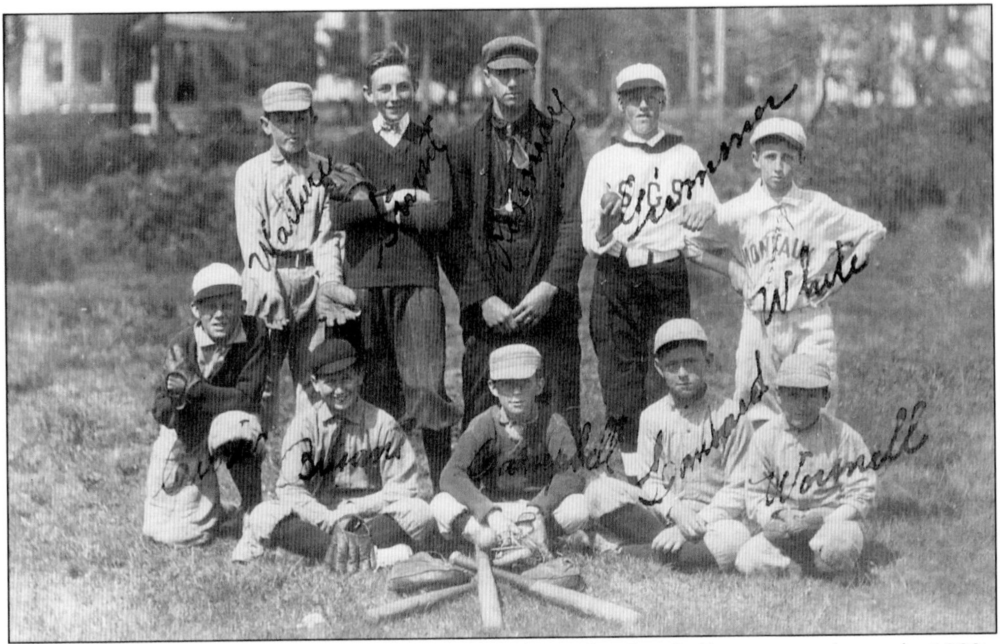

PLEASANTDALE KIDS. Neighborhood boys formed a baseball team in the early 1900s. From left to right are: (front row) Ralph Curtis, unknown, Brick Campbell, Reg Lombard, and Wormell; (back row) Wallace, Robert Strout, Clayton Kennedy, Grimmer, and White. (Ruth Morrill)

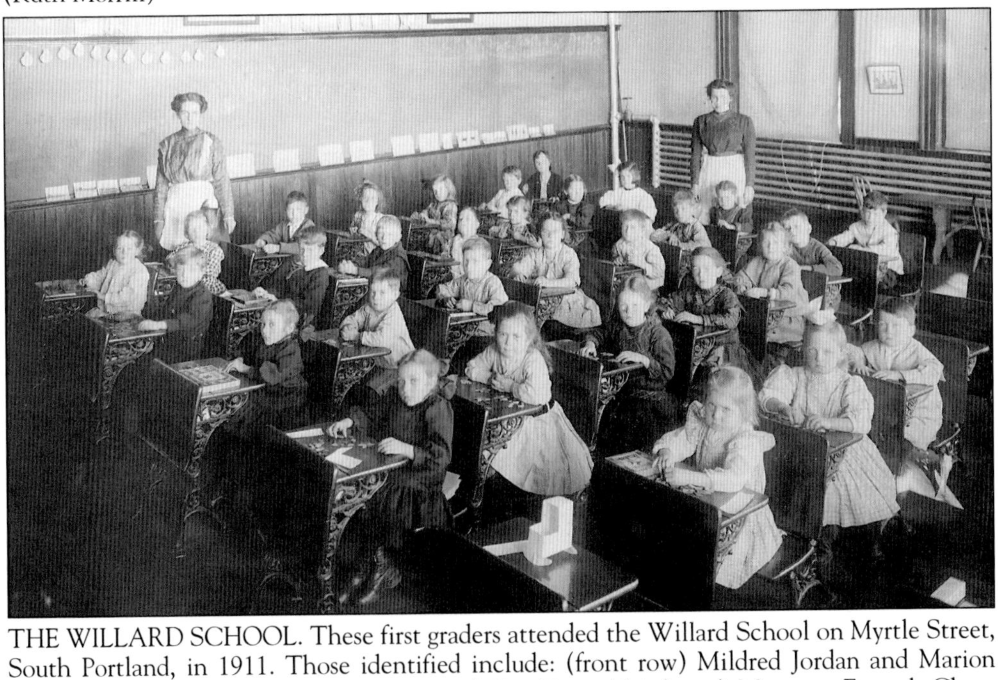

THE WILLARD SCHOOL. These first graders attended the Willard School on Myrtle Street, South Portland, in 1911. Those identified include: (front row) Mildred Jordan and Marion Willard; (second row) Ruth Thompson and Ora King; (third row) Margaret Fuessel, Chase Thompson, Sybil Eaton, and Mabelle Smart; (fourth row) Mildred Feussel, Ide? Brown, and Florence Stephenson; (back row) Arminth Lewis?, Elizabeth Huntress, and Lowell Smith. The teachers were Alice Chase and Corinne Genn. (Rosella Loveitt)

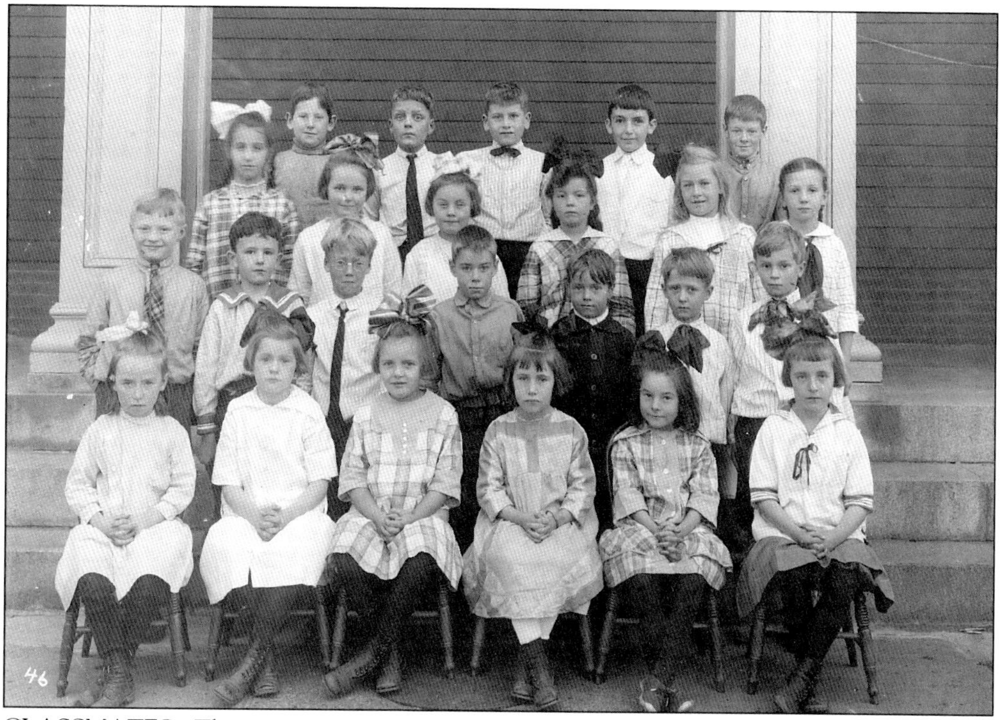

CLASSMATES. These youngsters in high-buttoned shoes attended the Willard School, c. 1915. (Nancy Wainwright Woodward)

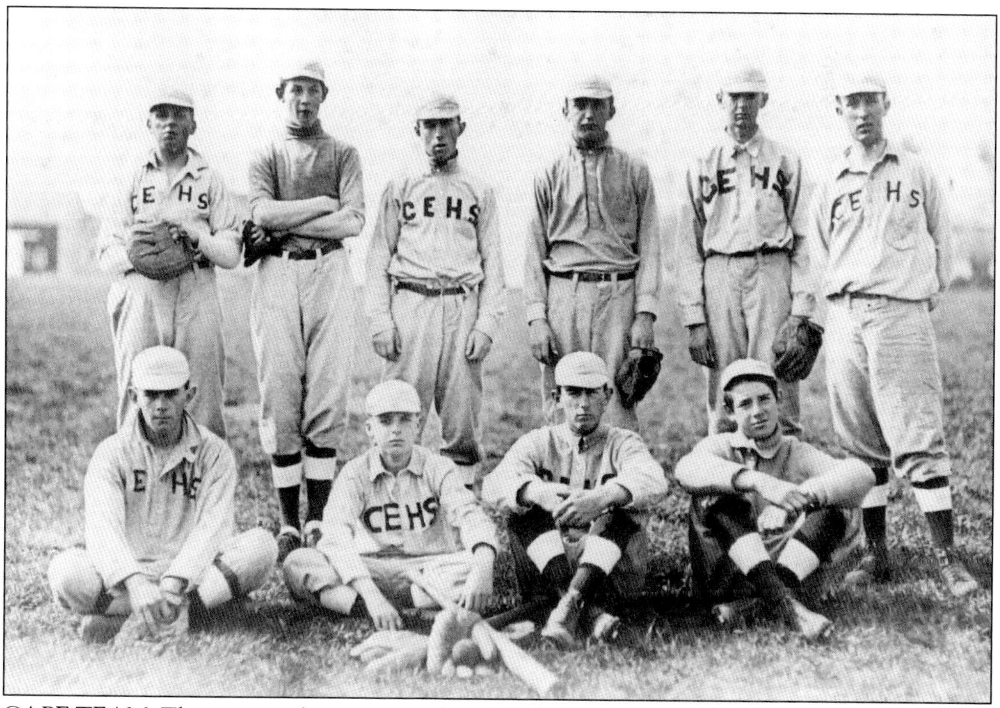

CAPE TEAM. There was only one extra player on this ten-man baseball team at Cape Elizabeth High School in 1916. (Norman Jordan)

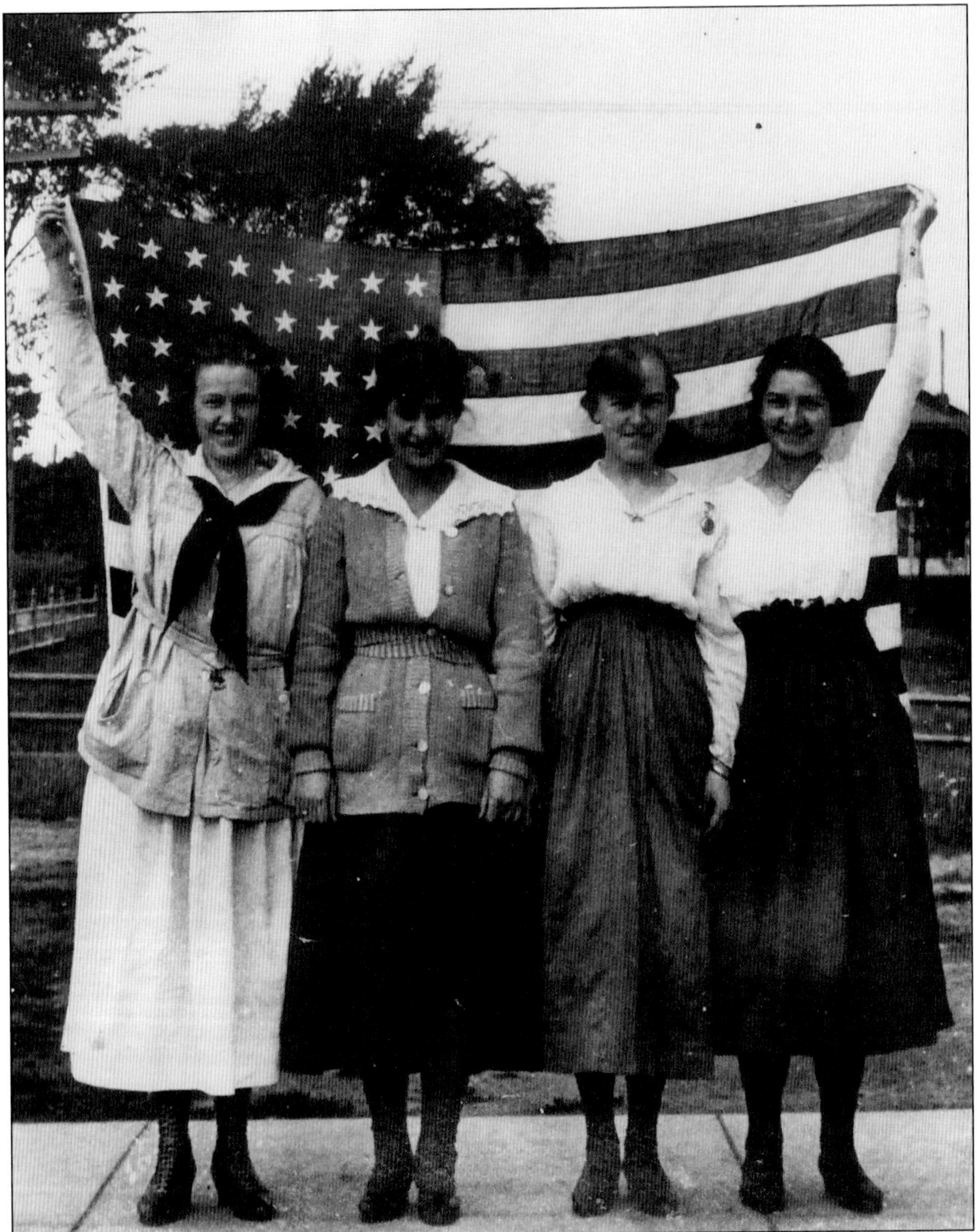

CLASS OF 1918. Patriotism was in vogue when these girls graduated from Cape Elizabeth High School. From left to right are Gladys Jordan, Adra Clark, Irene Sanborn, and Viola King. (Norman Jordan)

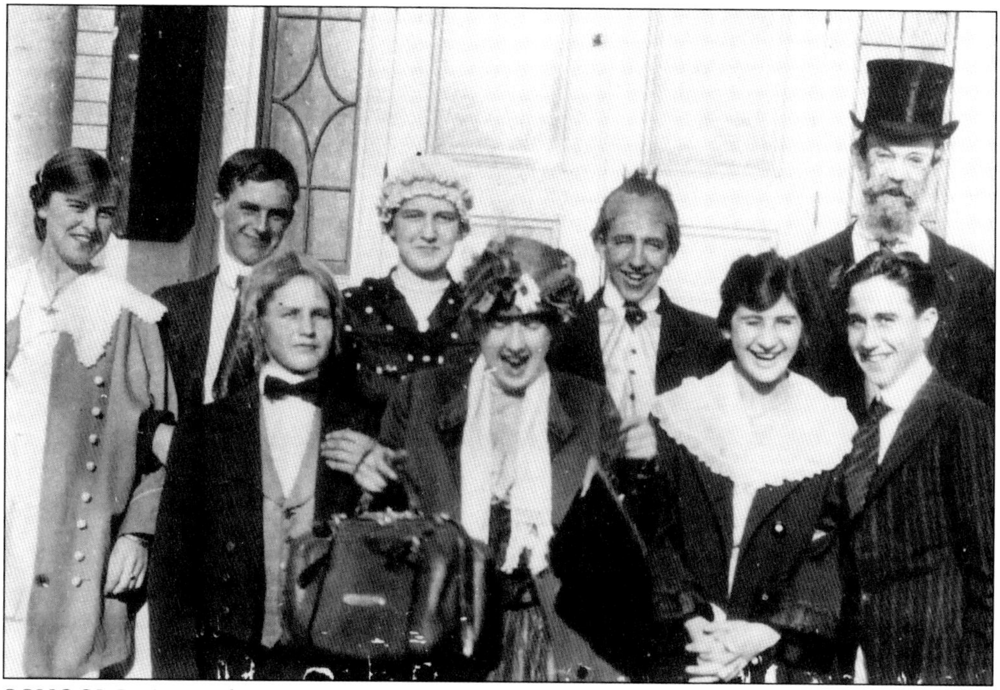

SCHOOL PLAY. *Higbee of Harvard* was the Cape Elizabeth High School play in 1918. The cast members were, from left to right: (front row) Ralph Dresser, Helen Newcomb, Edra Clark, and C. Ela; (back row) Irene Sanborn, Rossell Ela, Gladys Jordan, Chester Hannaford, and Charles Maxwell. (Norman Jordan)

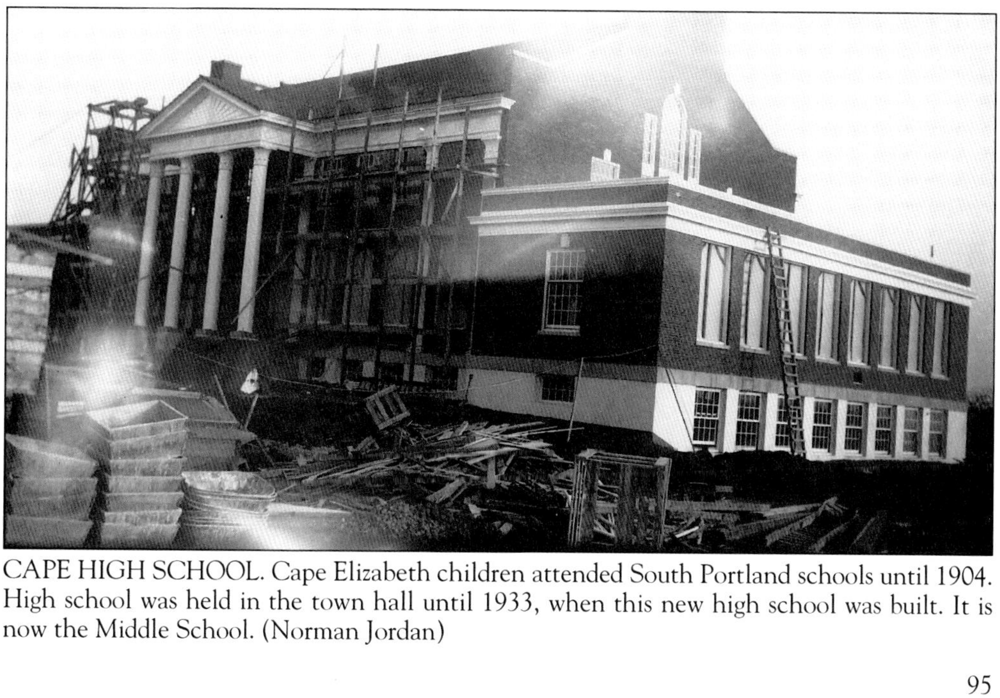

CAPE HIGH SCHOOL. Cape Elizabeth children attended South Portland schools until 1904. High school was held in the town hall until 1933, when this new high school was built. It is now the Middle School. (Norman Jordan)

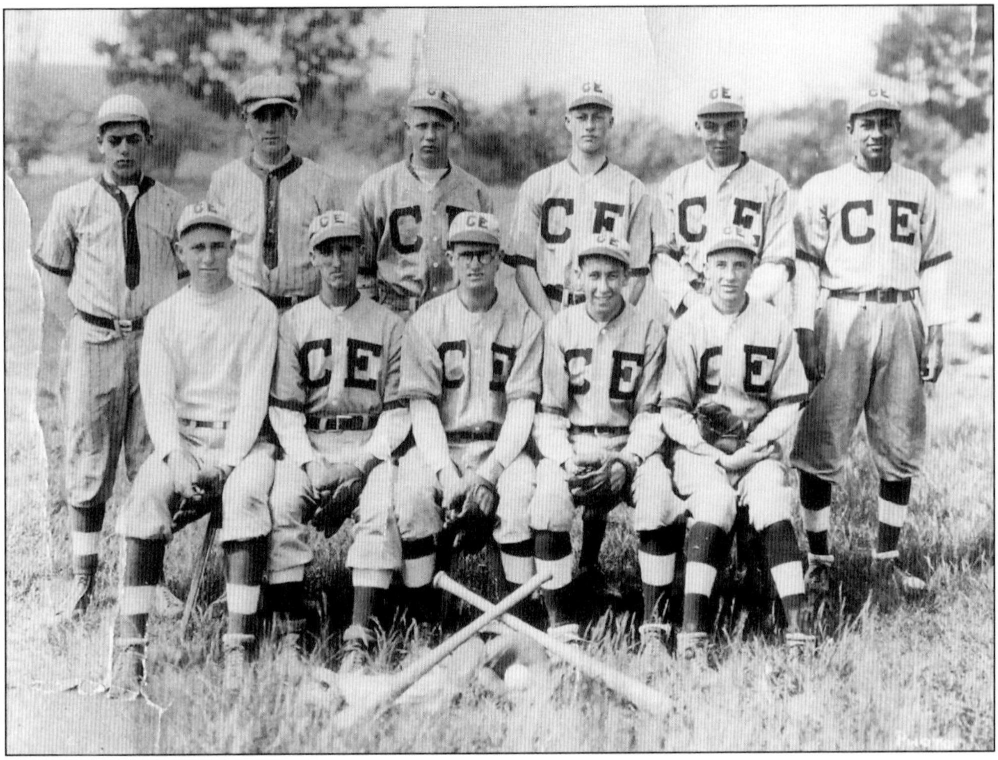

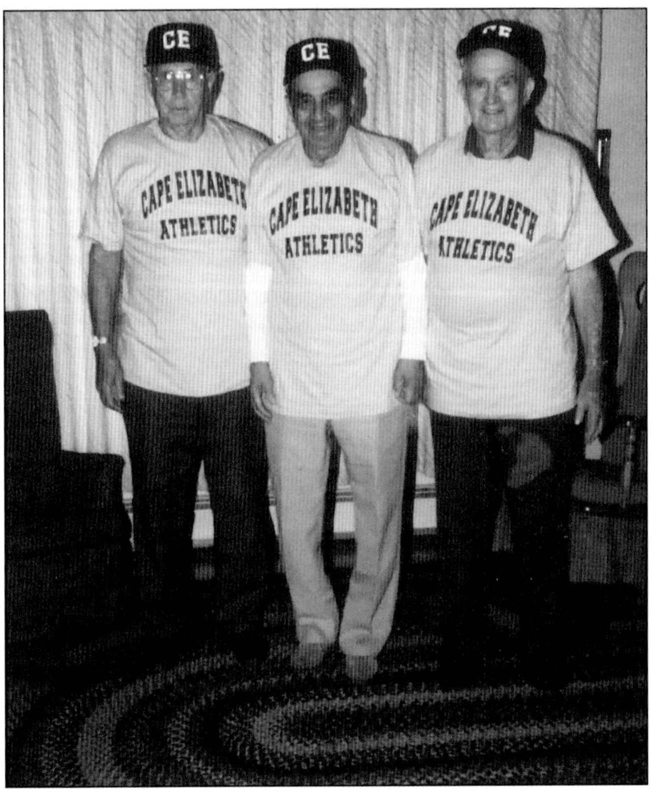

THEN. The members of the Cape Elizabeth High School baseball team in 1929 were, from left to right: (front row) C. Richard Jordan, Charles Crozier, Stan Prout, Philip Bagley, and Carroll Hannaford; (back row) Willliam Murray, Harry Prout, Ernest Darling, G. Jordan, Dwight Leighton, and Richard Gomes. (Ernest Darling)

AND NOW. Getting together in 1992 are these former Cape Elizabeth High School team members. From left to right are: Ernest Darling, pitcher, of South Portland; Richard Gomes, catcher, of Westbrook; and Stanley Prout, pitcher, of Florida, since deceased. (Ernest Darling)

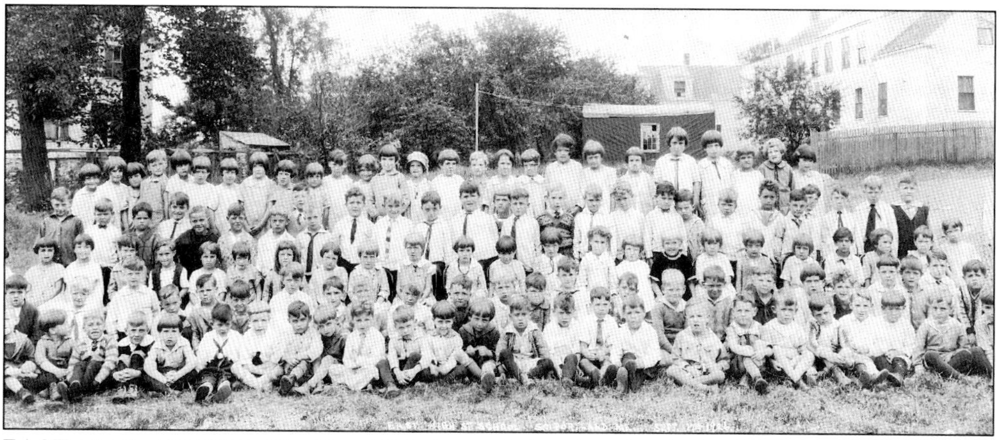

EAST HIGH STREET. The East High Street School in South Portland housed this banner class in 1926. (Tom Heseltine)

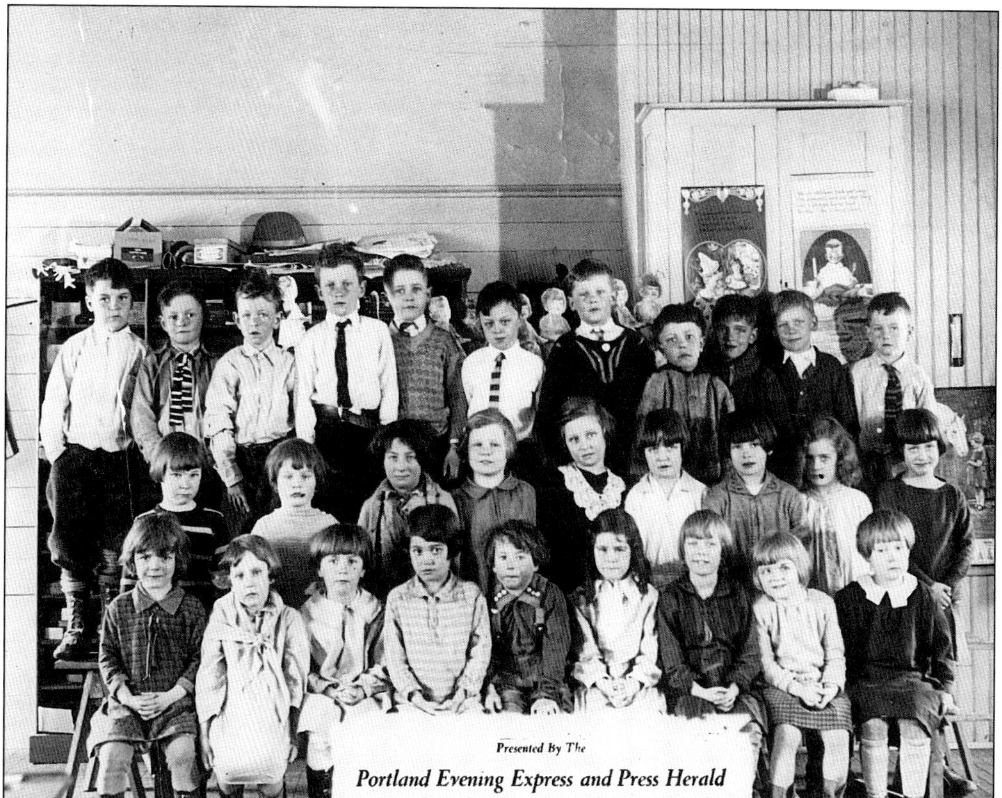

THE EVANS STREET SCHOOL. This first grade class in 1928 includes, from left to right: (front row) unknown, Jean Morgan, unknown, Frances Spaltro, L. Sio, Minnie Parker, Adelaine Willette, Margaret McCormack, and unknown; (middle row) Mary Olssen, Betty Jean Minott, Julia Sio, Richard Bean, unknown, Eleanor Brice, Rachael Larochelle, Evelyn Rosoborough, and Charlotte Minott; (back row) Wellington Dyer, Donald Messer, unknown, Paul Davis, Gerald Shorey, Louis Anderson, Roger Shorey, Patsy Spaltro, Louis Larochelle, unknown, and A. Messer. (Mary Olssen)

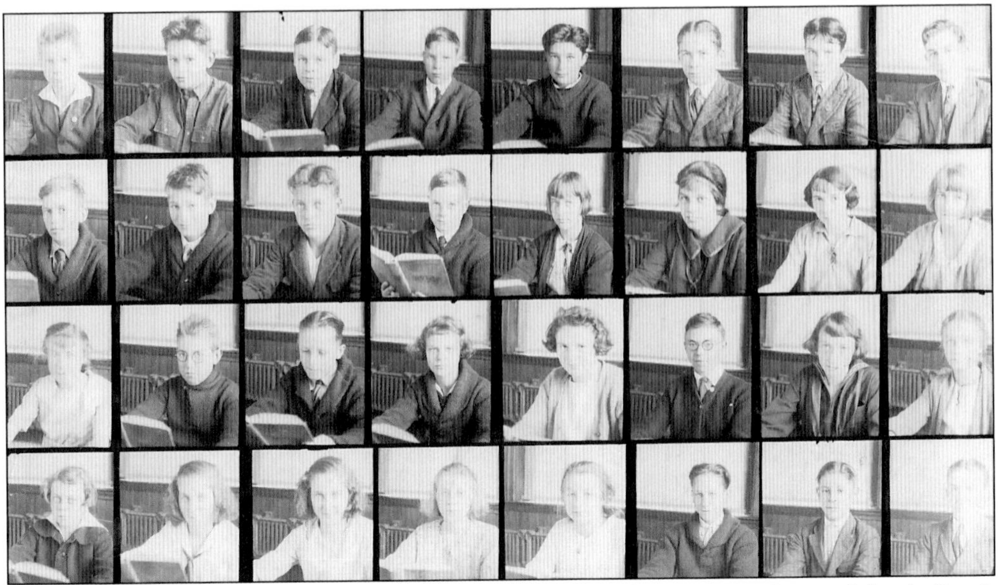

EIGHTH GRADERS. In 1923, these students attended the Summer Street School, South Portland. From left to right are: (front row) E. Palmer, Annie Davis, Beatrice Davis, Annie Kilman, Ernestine Dyer, Arthur Jones, Alfred Crockett, and Norman Fozzard; (second row) Helen James, Harry Bartch, Donald Cheney, Edith Anderson, Dorothy McLean, K. Noyes, Carolyn White, and Verna Cromwell; (third row) Robert Foshay, Edwin Morrill, Freman Brown, Merle Brigham, Beatrice Plummer, Bernice Cotton, Alice Taylor, and B. Gordon; (back row) Edward Smith, Lawrence Fickett, Donald Bean, George Chesley, Merle Cook, Keith Denison, Kenneth Hogston, and Reginald Conner. (Dorothy M. Wilkes)

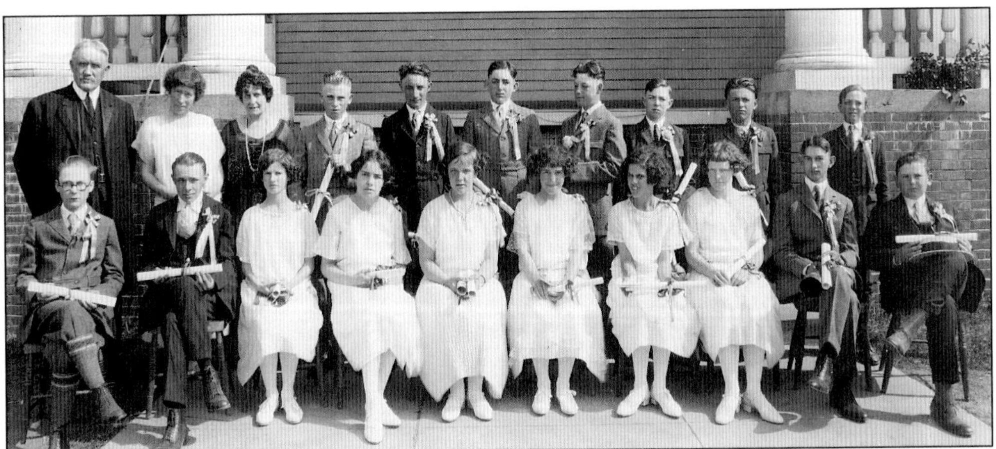

JUNE GRADS. Diplomas in hand, these 1924 Cape Elizabeth eighth graders sit for a class photograph in front of the present Thomas Memorial Library. From left to right are: (front row) unknown, ? Pennell, Dorothy Wing, ? Darling, Anna Anderson, ? Adams, Elizabeth Murray, Helen Bothel, Arthur Willard, and Russ Peables; (back row) Di ? Hamlin, Edith Murray, the music teacher (name unknown), Joe Key, Stan Doughty, unknown, Russell Hannaford, Henry Wainwright, ? Darling, and unknown. (Nancy Wainwright Woodward)

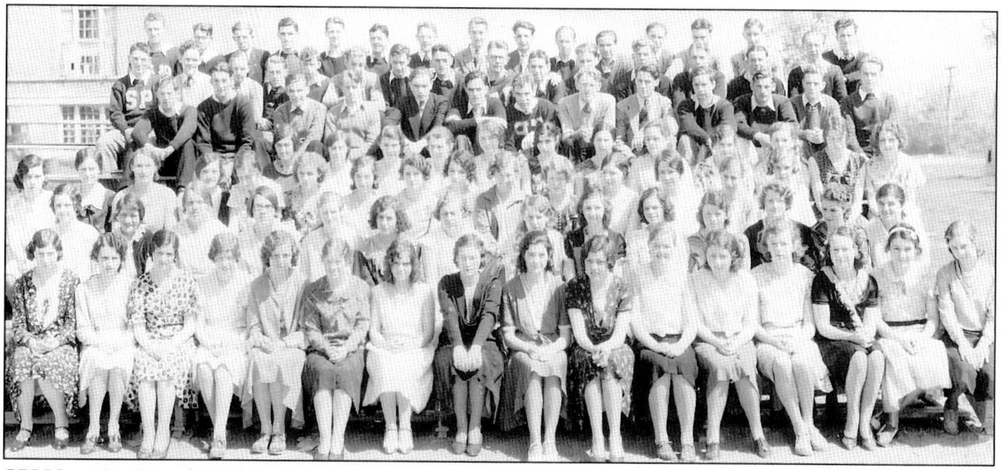

SPHS 1931. Josiah Cobb was mayor of South Portland when this class graduated from the high school. (Dot Hodgkins)

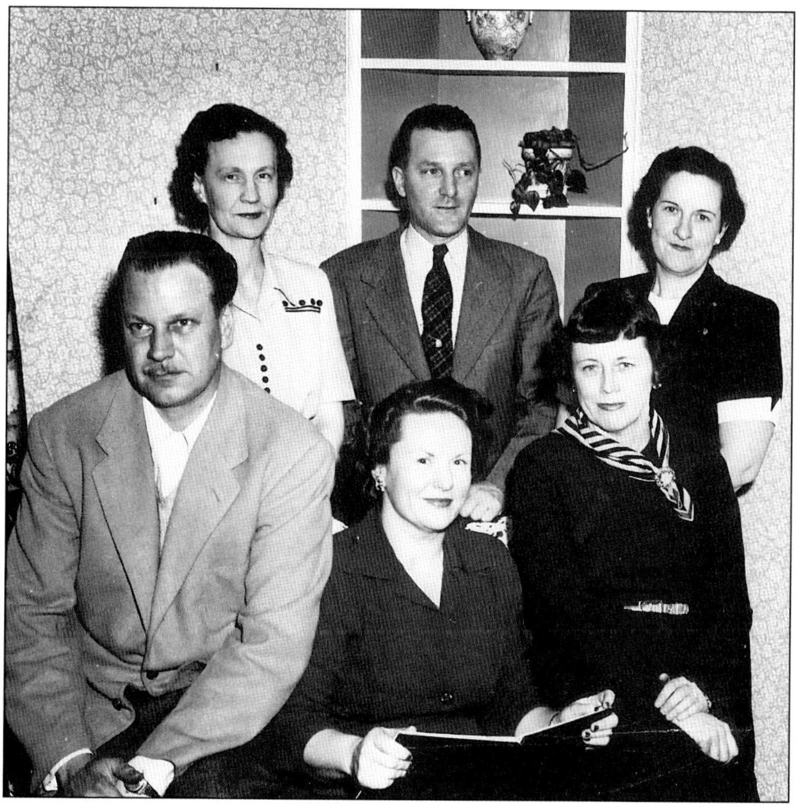

REUNION 1931. Planning the 20th reunion of the South Portland High School Class of 1931 are, from left to right: (front row) Ernie Curtain, Anne O'Connor, and Alice Ryder; (back row) Eleanor Butler, "Pete" Roach, and Dot Hodgkins. (Dot Hodgkins)

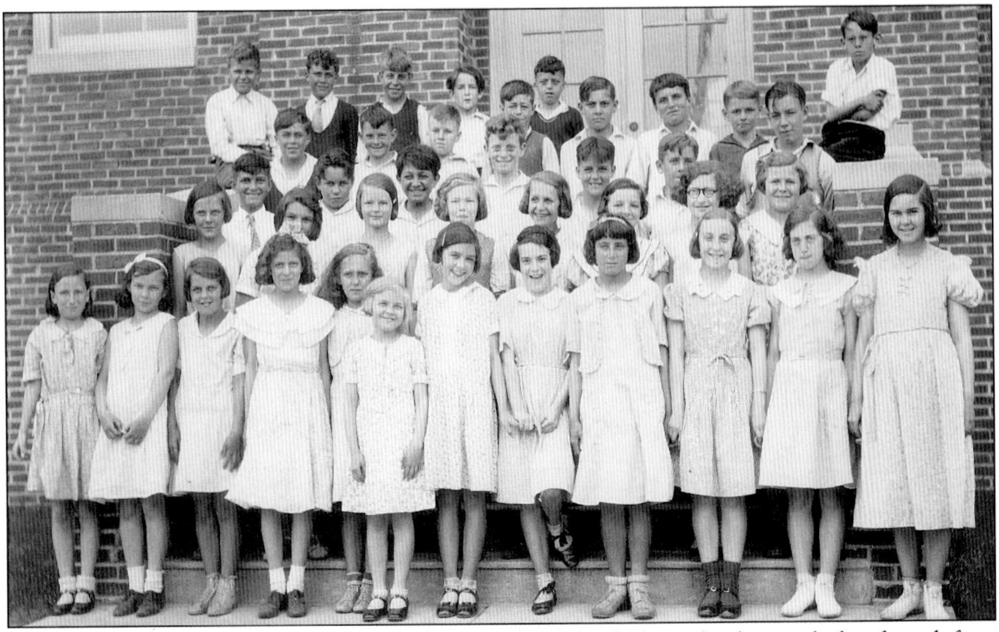

THE KALER SCHOOL. This *c.* 1929 photograph of the fifth grade class includes, from left to right: (front row) Frances Pettingill, Mary Olssen, Helen Snow, Charlotte M., Jean Morgan, Mary ?, Adelaide Sweeney, unknown, Julia Sio, Shirley Michaud, and ? Bryant; (second row) Eleanor Henderson, unknown, unknown, Mary Lydon, Phyllis Legere, ? Heath, and Rachel Bean; (third row) unknown, unknown, Dominic Spaltro, Paul Davis, Wellington D., Gerald Shorey, and unknown; (fourth row) unknown, Edmond Dyer, unknown, Arnold Parker, unknown, ? Leberge, and Donald Messer; (back row) unknown, unknown, Forest Littlefield, unknown, Louis Anderson, and ? Ingraham. (Mary Olssen)

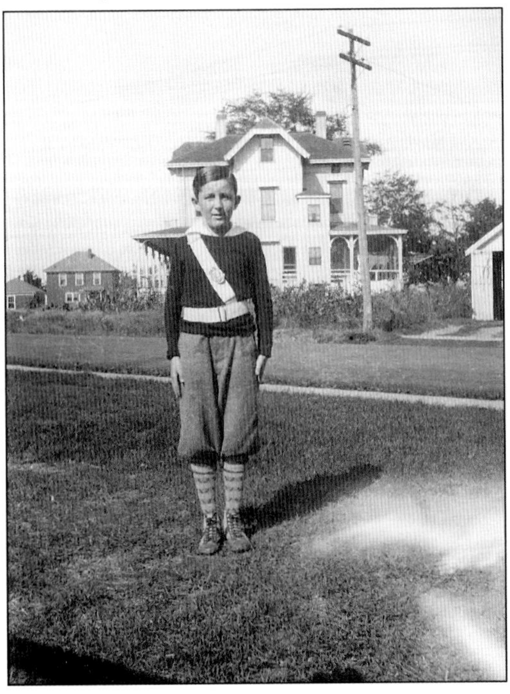

CROSSING GUARD. Edward Langlois, a pupil at the Roosevelt School in South Portland, wears the familiar belt of a crossing guard, *c.* 1932. He was one of many such boys chosen to help classmates cross streets safely to and from school. (Ed Langlois)

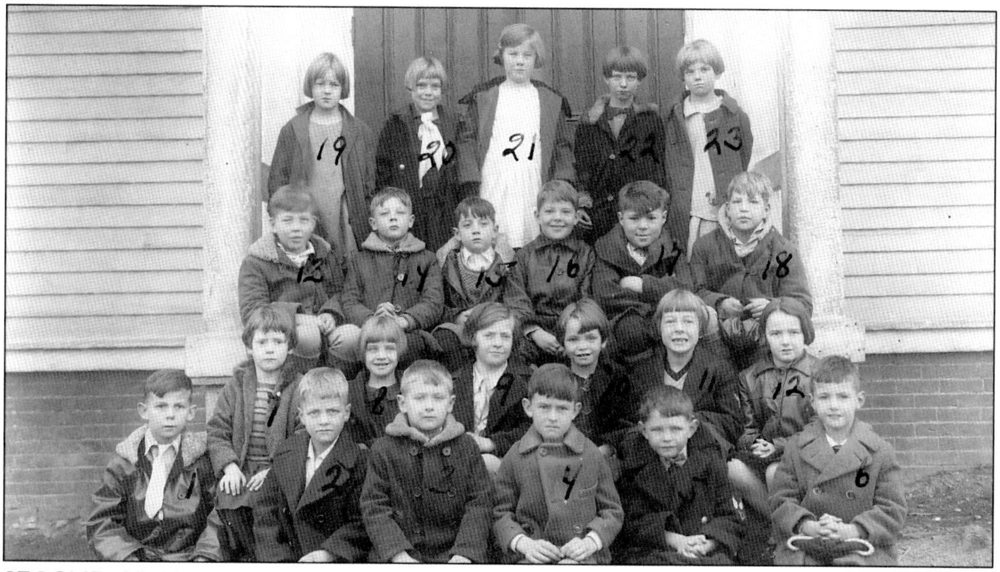

SECOND GRADE. An early 1930s photograph of the second grade of the South Portland Heights School (now Hamlin). From left to right are: (front row) Harris Hinckley, Gerald Merriman, Clayton Ellis, Robert Millett, Billy Jewell, and Robert Preti; (second row) Caroline Prout, Virginia Worthen, Dorothy Collins, Pearl Lang, Alice Knotts, and Jane Strachan; (third row) Donald Wiggins, Jack Watson, Frank Timberlake, John Gault, Raymond Shalaand, and George Wiggins; (back row) Audrey Dinsmore, Esther Lunn, Grace Hazlett, Phyllis Chesley, and Viola Brown. (Harris Hinckley, M.D.)

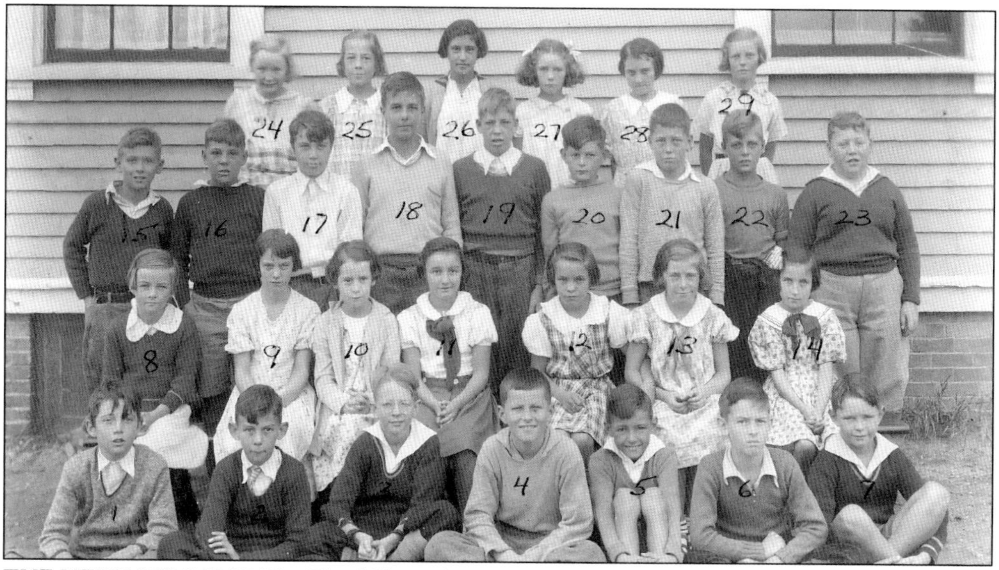

THE HEIGHTS SCHOOL. The fifth graders at this school in 1933 include, from left to right: (front row) Frank Timberlake, Harris Hinckley, Lloyd Chesley, Charles Flaherty, Robert Preti, Robert Millet, and Billy Jewell; (second row) Margaret Griffin, Phyllis Chesley, Caroline Prout, Jane Strachan, Pearle Lang, Dorothy Collins, and Diana Lervey; (third row) Clayton Ellis, John Gault, Paul Timberlake, Edwin Burt, George Wiggins, Paul Donahue, Donald Wiggins, Thomas Merriman, and Fred Rolfe; (back row) Charlotte Ross, Alice Knotts, Jean Hannaford, Patsy Jewell, Mary Griffin, and Ruth Brown. (Harris Hinckley, M.D.)

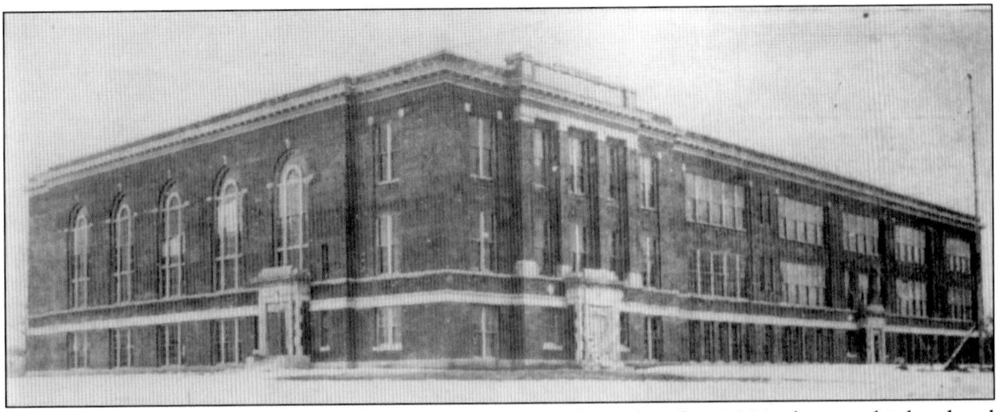

THE NEW SOUTH PORTLAND HIGH SCHOOL. Completed in 1924, the new high school on Ocean Avenue was touted as having ". . . an auditorium accommodating 1200 people, stereopticon and motion picture apparatus and one of the largest and best equipped gymnasiums in any high school in the country . . . and, what possibly no other high school may possess, a one-quarter mile track . . ." (Ruth Morrill)

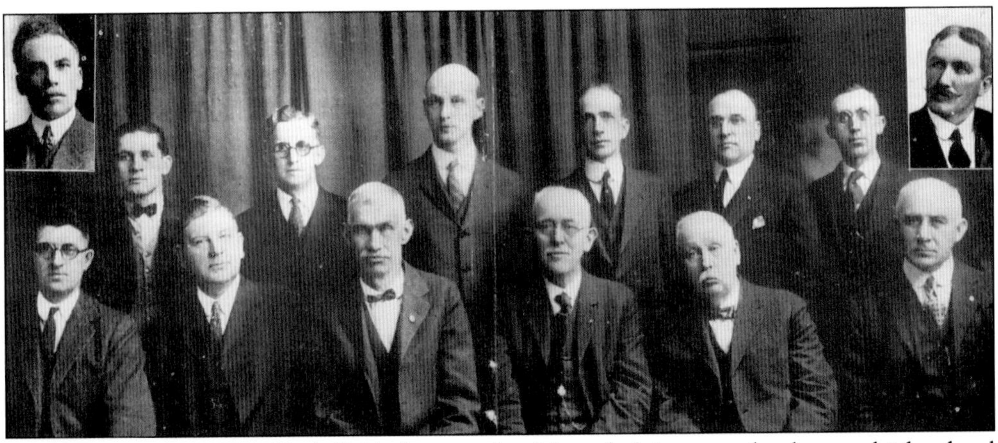

BUILDING COMMITTEE. A 1924 photograph of those helping to make the new high school a reality. From left to right are: (front row) Henry B. Walton, Lewis E. Rich, James A. O'Neil, Everett C. Dyer, Fred W. Bryant, and Leslie E. Norwood; (back row) Allen H. Cobb, William L. Walker, Dr. Frank I. Brown (the oldest member of the school board), Harold B. Haggett, Howard P. Knight, and Charles D. Sawyer; (left insert) William R. MacDonald, mayor and board chairman; (right insert) Simon M. Hamlin, superintendant of schools. Absent were George G. Boynton, John W. Thomas, Albert E. Sylvester, Charles H. Brimecombe, Edgar O. Hawkes, Alfred N. Plummer, and Charles H. Perkins. (Ruth Morrill)

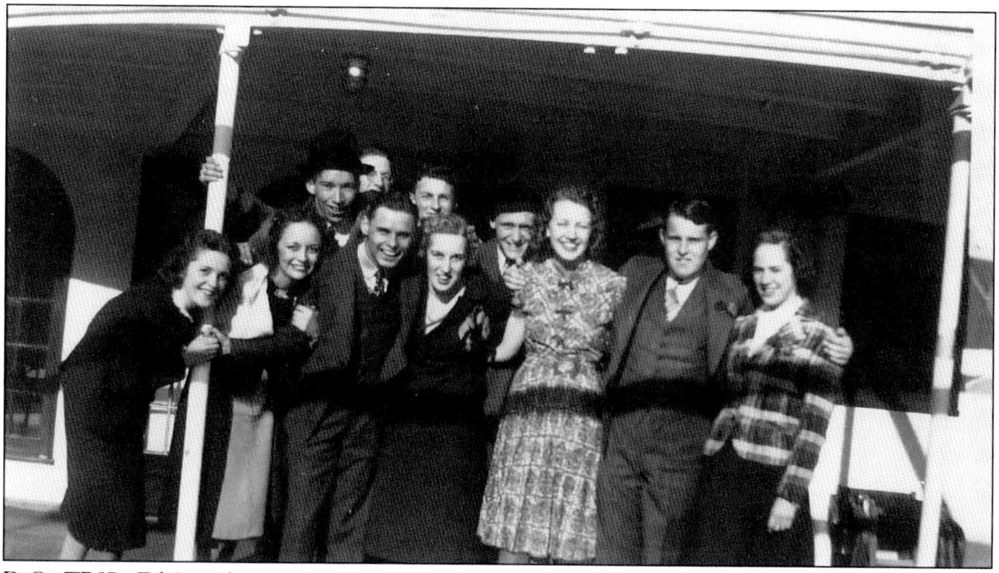

D.C. TRIP. Ed Langlois took this 1939 photograph of those aboard ship during the South Portland High School senior class trip to Washington, D.C. From left to right are Charles Appleton, Jackson Long, Betty Griffin, Kenneth Robinson, Ruth Lunt, Lennie Singer, Margaret Prout, Tom Winston, Ben Graves, and John O'Donovan. (Edward Langlois)

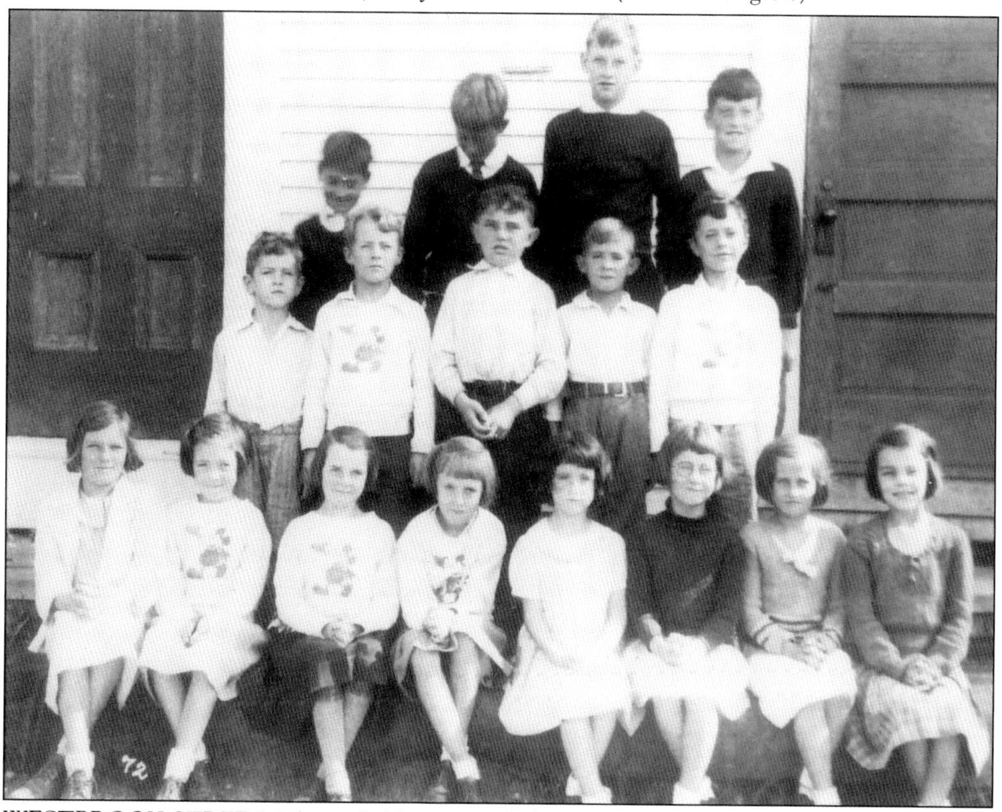

WESTBROOK STREET. These children attended a one-room school on Westbrook Street in South Portland, in the mid-1930s. (George Thompson)

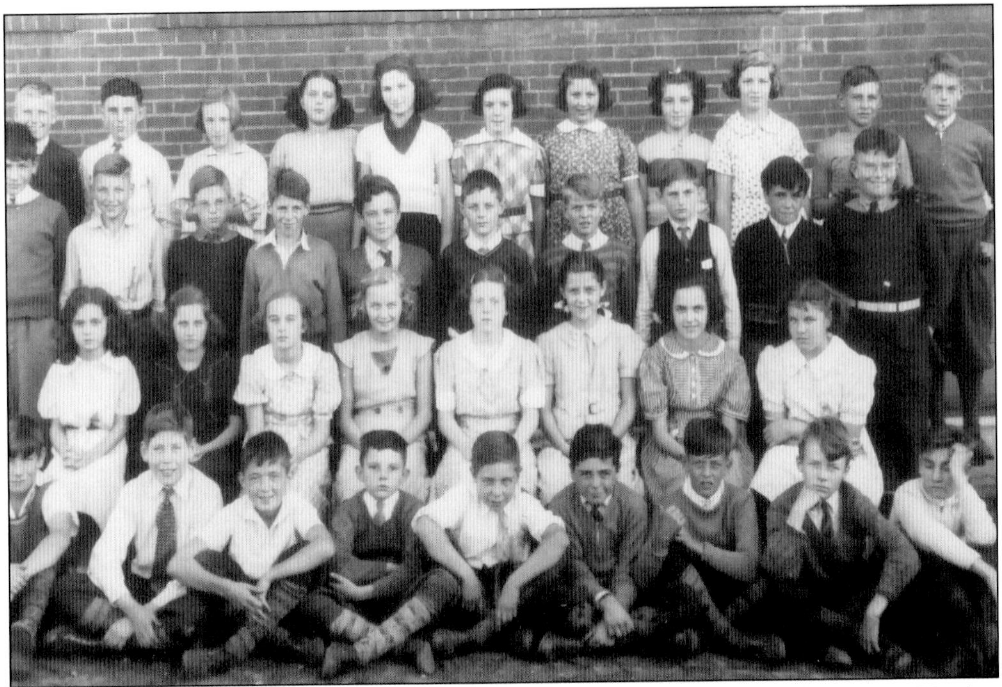

THORNTON HEIGHTS. A 1939 photograph of the students of the Thornton Heights School on Westbrook Street, South Portland. From left to right are: (front row) Peter Everest, Ira Stoddard, unknown, George Thompson, E. Garnum, Dick Boucher, Bob Pratt, Leonard Greenlaw, and John Curry; (second row) Barbara Bogus, Mary Currie, Mildred Colby, Janice Worthing, Ruth Paine, Anna Lee, unknown, and Eleanor Ladd; (third row) John Kendall, T. Pennel, Lloyd Mills, Ted Beety, Ernest Greenlaw, Arthur Washburn, unknown, Purington, Paul Trueland, Paul Boucher, and George Goodwin; (back row) Charles Brice, Estha Tapley, unknown, unknown, Gloria Garren, Jackie Cole, Catheryn Smith, Lorane? Mayo, ? Nelson, and Charles Reef. (George Thompson)

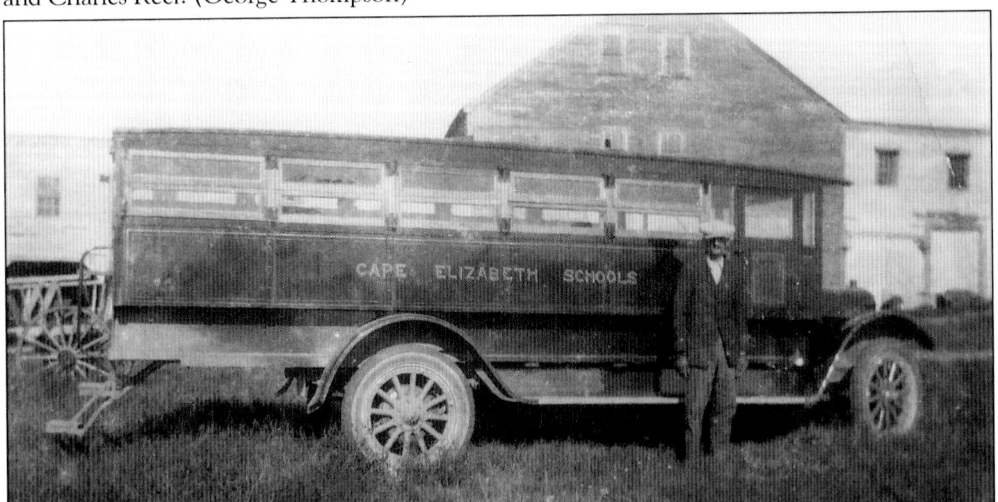

BUS DRIVER. Clarence Phinney was the Cape Elizabeth school bus driver in the 1930s. He also was a caretaker at the town's Poor Farm (on the right), which was built in 1874 by William Murray and destroyed by fire in 1974. (Emma Phinney)

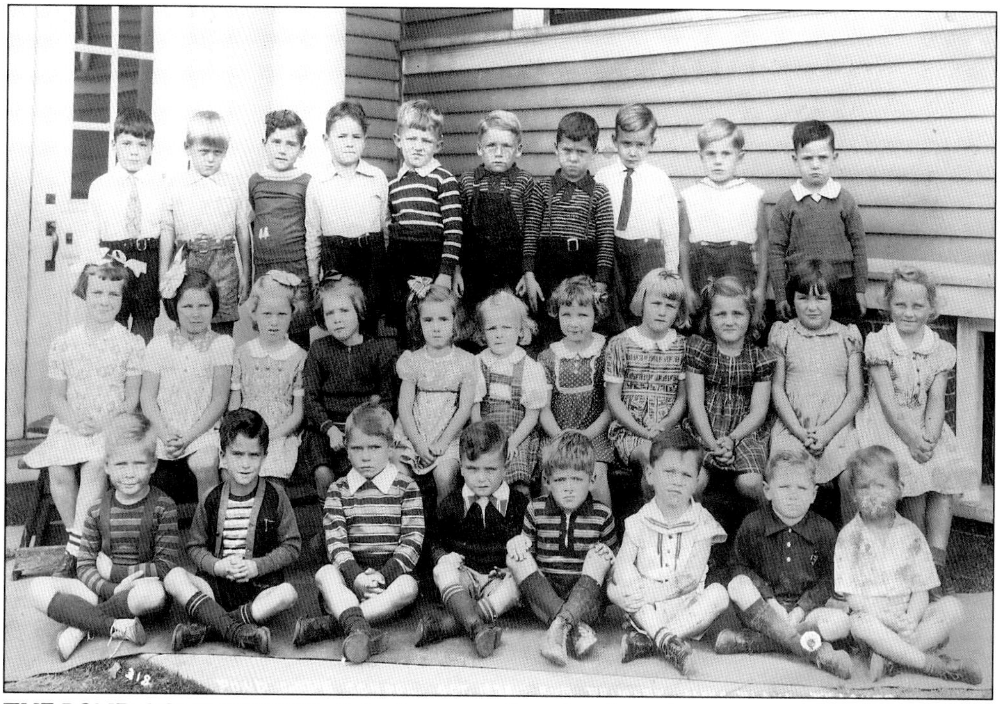

THE POND COVE SCHOOL. Subprimary pupils gather for a class picture in 1939 at the Pond Cove School, built in 1912 in Cape Elizabeth. From left to right are: (front row) W. Holman, Clayton Knight, John Coker, unknown, Gordon Murray, Wendell Tucker, William Will, and ? Trafton; (middle row) unknown, Lucille Beal, Violet Sweetser, Jane Hanscom, unknown, Florence Foss, Doris Anderson, Janet Mercer, unknown, Mary Emery, and Sonja Olsen; (back row) Laurence Peabbles, Charles Mercer, Ronald Schwartz, Wayne Brooking, Norman Jordan, unknown, Kenneth Barrett, Roland Melcher, Robert Berry, and unknown. (Norman Jordan)

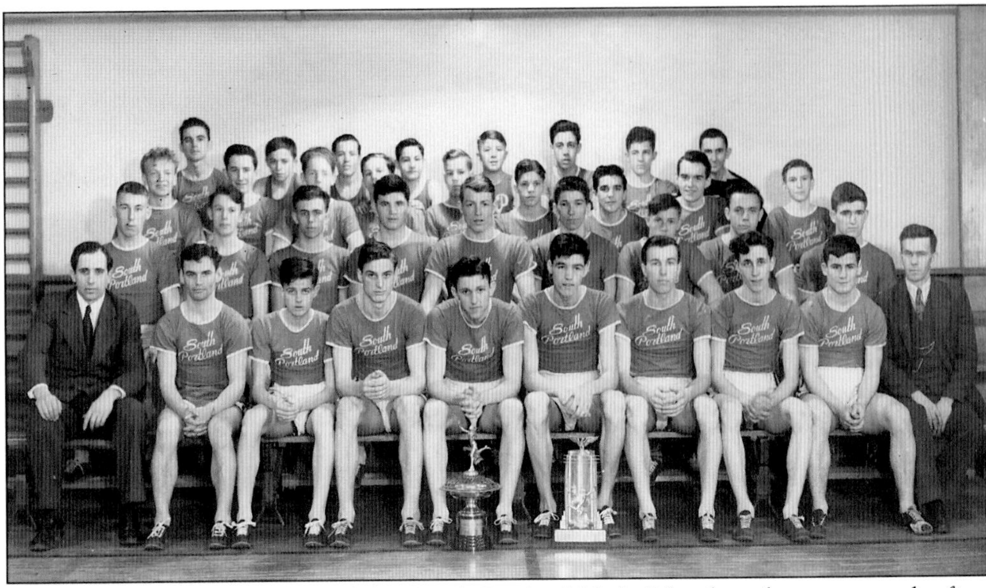

FIRST PLACE. The members of this South Portland High School track team were the first-place winners at the meet held in 1939 at Portland's Exposition Building. From left to right are: (front row) Coach Kahill, Hannaford, Hale, Foster, Captain Strchan, Coyne, Redmond, Lydon, DeCosta, and Coach Nason; (second row) Wood, Kelley, Greenlaw, McDonald, W. O'Donell, Winston, Wender, Morrill, and Maloney; (third row) Craig, Langlois, Collins, Bragdon, Kenney, Millett, Legere, Burke, and Cannon; (back row) LaBerge, Kenniston, Cribby, DeCosta, Payne, Quinn, E. O'Donell, and Rines. Coyne set two records that day, in the high hurdles (6 feet) and the high jump (5 feet 10 1/8 inches). (Edward Langlois)

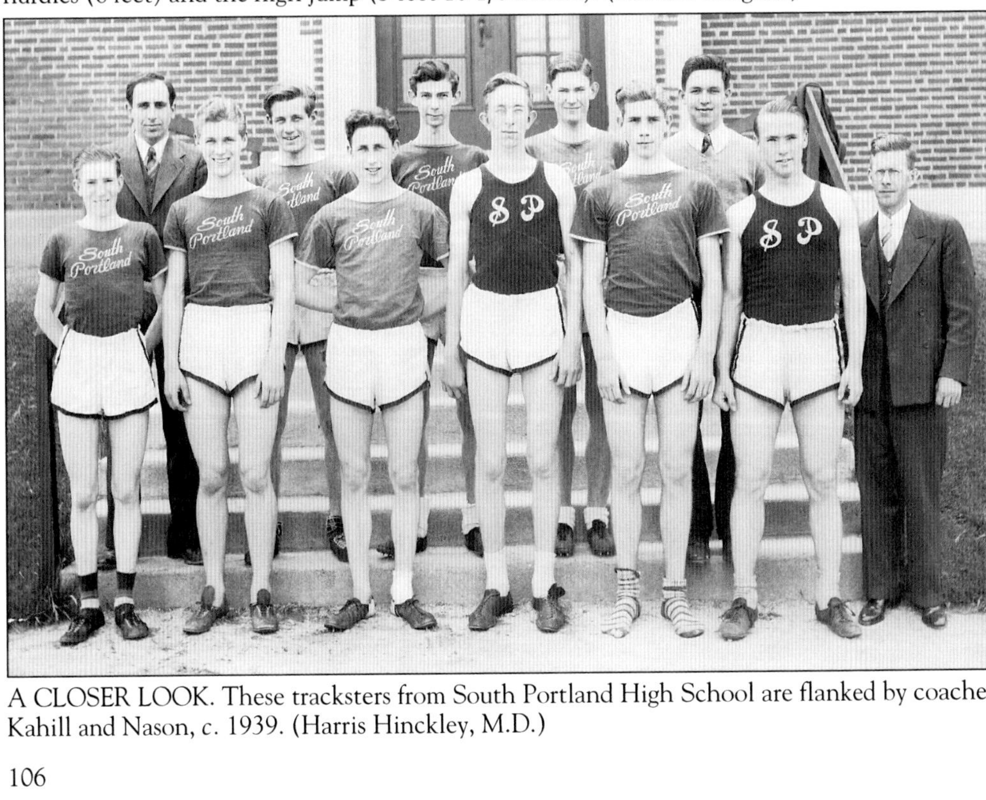

A CLOSER LOOK. These tracksters from South Portland High School are flanked by coaches Kahill and Nason, c. 1939. (Harris Hinckley, M.D.)

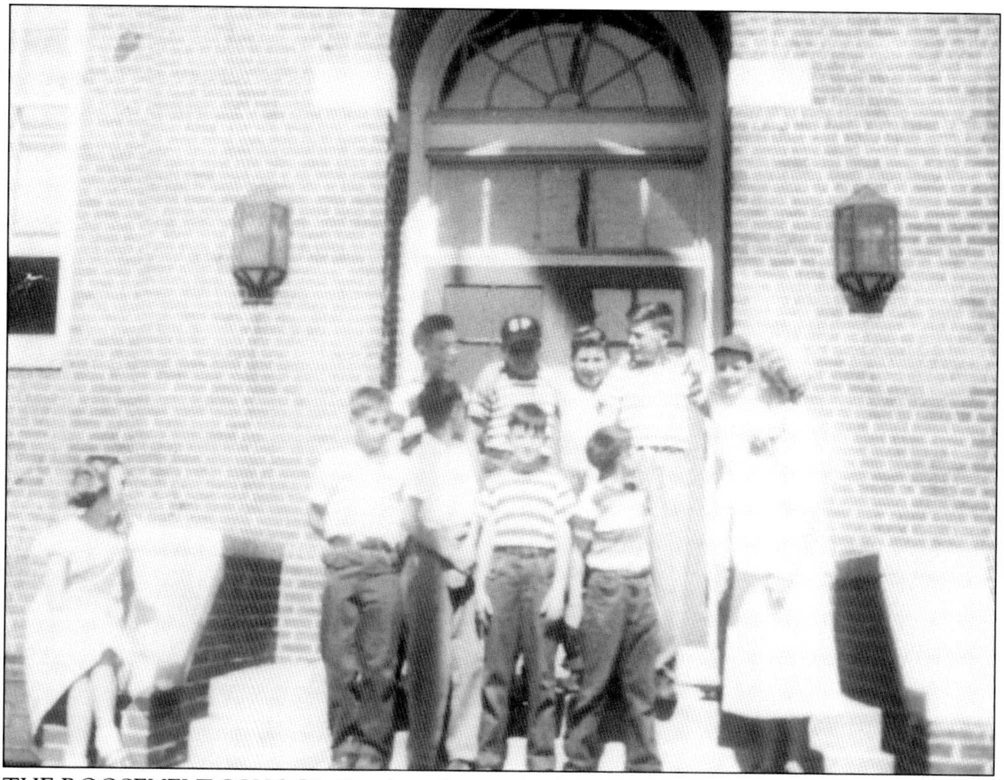

THE ROOSEVELT SCHOOL. Pupils gather in the doorway of the Roosevelt School, c. 1948, with teacher Dora L. Small, for whom the Dora Small School on Thompson Street was named. From left to right are: (front row) Janice Spear, Ronald Tripp, Carleton Hackett, Ronald Dyer, Dana Willard, and Dora Small; (back row) Paul Frost, Robert Call, William Barry, Richard Tuttle, and ? Crozier. The building now houses the Spurwink School. (Pat Pender Fucciani)

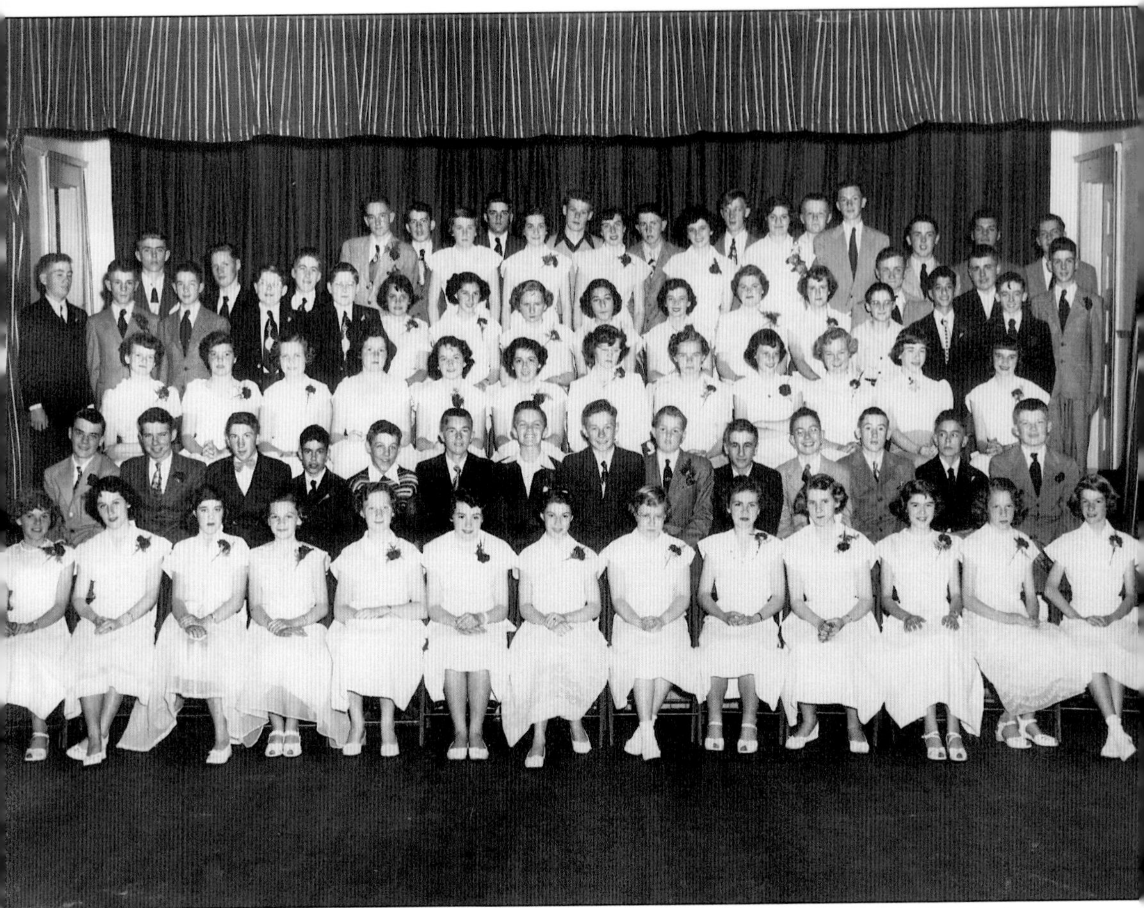

THE HENLEY SCHOOL. This is a 1951 photograph of the eighth graders of the last graduating class at the George F. Henley School, located on Broadway in South Portland. From left to right are: (front row) Rita M. Ledger, Corinne Oliver, Betsy Jordan, Aldana Odlin, Carol Chambers, Muriel Taylor, Anne Patenaude, Carol Gustafson, Isabelle Emerton, Louise Mansfield, Nancy Hogan, Louise Worthing, and Judy Gay; (second row) Henry Brosseau III, Raymond MacLean, J.N. Grant Quirk, Richard Roberge, Robert Pray, Robert Grindle, Chandler DeMelle Jr., Bill James, George Hazel, Ronald Tripp, Paul Frost, Tom Cheney, James Yalouris, and Leon Burns; (third row) Karen Seabury, Sandra Wood, Connie Austad, Gloria Cunningham, Patricia Atwood, Margaret Darling, Georgina Mansfield, Letitia Walsh, Muriel Hagerthy, Mary Anne Kemp, Janice Spear, and Louise Doane; (fourth row) Charles Kennedy, Robert Upton, Peter Tanguay, Ronald Dyer, James Mulvey, Bailey, William Barry, Bailey (twins), Carolyn Day, Mary Jordan, Roberta Kendall, Joanne Lowell, Loretta Dobson, Elizabeth Butler, Patricia Staples, Dana Willard, Clyde Simmons, Rocco Frallicciardi, W. Francis Strout, Gordon Burnham, and Carleton Hackett; (back row) Donald Clark, Lawrence McDonald, Elizabeth Hay, Wayne Gray, Eleanor Willey, Robert Call, Patricia Pender, Leman French, Marlene Dobson, Steve Osgood, Donna Scott, Eric Vaule, John Tolman, Richard Tuttle, John Swierzynski, and Donald Anderson. The school is now the Henley condominiums. (Loretta Dobson Coughlin)

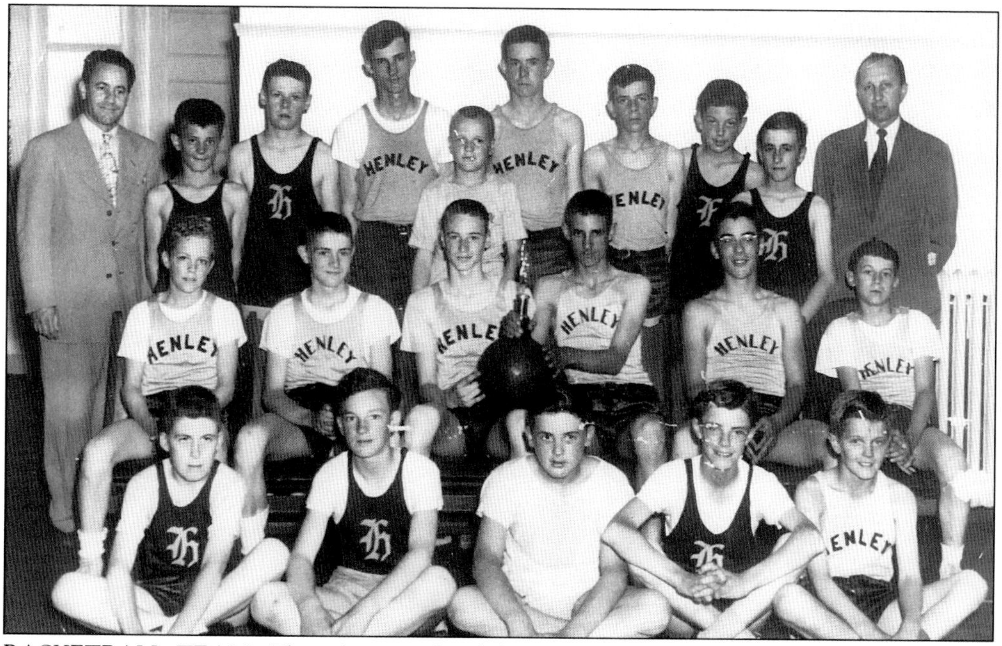

BASKETBALL TEAM. This photograph of the members of the 1950 basketball team was taken at the George E. Henley School, South Portland. From left to right are: (front row) William Barry, John Tolman, Richard Tuttle, Bill Harris, and Chandler DeMelle Jr.; (middle row) Richard Sweat, Clifton Burrows, Gerald Doane, Bruce Pineo, William Parker, and Charles Sawyer; (back row) Coach Ray Boman, Robert Upton, Robert Call, Ronnie Fournier, George Hazel, Arthur Lailer, Neil Bruns, Kenny Ames, Ronald Tripp, and Principal Gilbert Miller. (Loretta Dobson Coughlin)

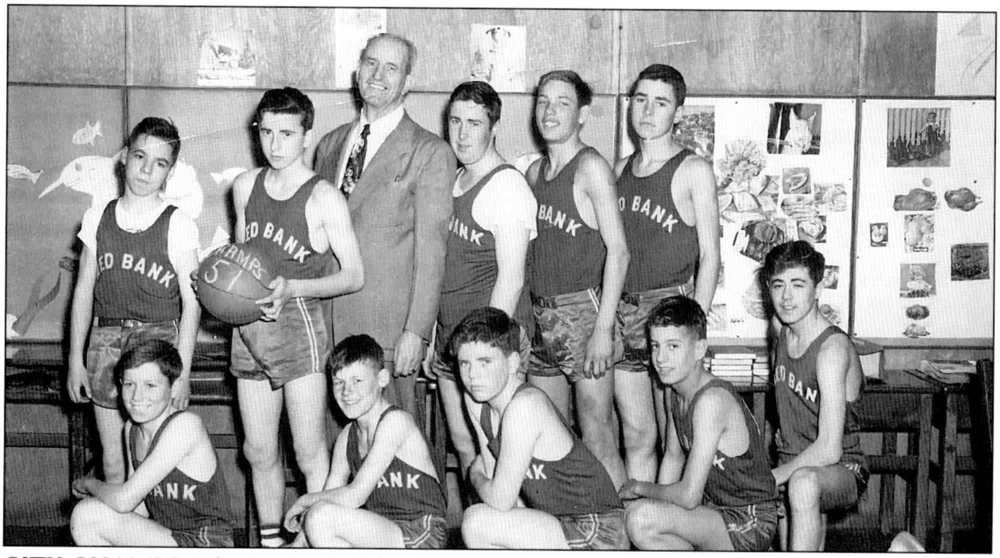

CITY CHAMPS. The Redbank School boys basketball team beat Thornton Heights to take the championship in 1951. From left to right are: (front row) John Whalen, Maurice Hinks, David Sturgeon, Carl Miller, and Donald Parker; (back row) David McHugh, Richard Totman, Coach Stanhope (also the principal), Robert Thompson, George Watts, and Raymond Totman. (Connie Porter Scott)

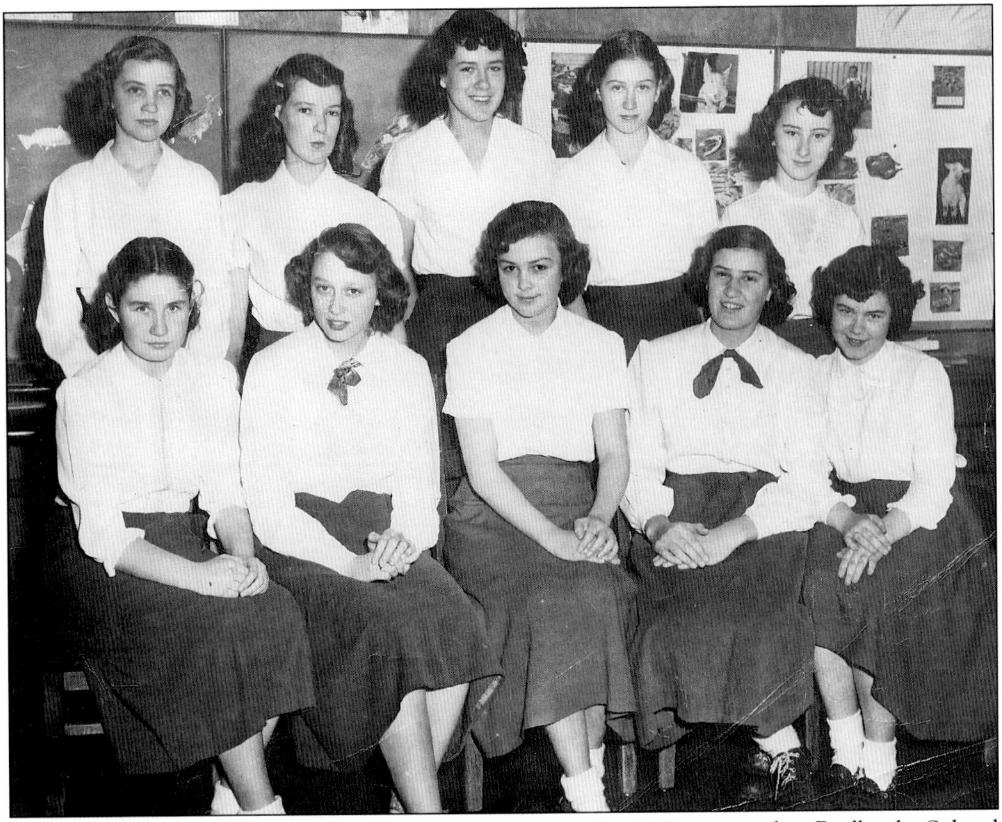

CHEERLEADERS. Rooting for the winning team in 1951 were the Redbank School cheerleaders. From left to right are: (front row) Ellen Furguson, Connie Porter, Roberta Kinney, Charlotte LeBlanc, and Joan Hodgkins; (back row) Carol Ronan, Pauline Whalen, Helen Sawaska, Margaret McMennamin, and Fern Forty. (Connie Porter Scott)

Three

The Shipyard Years

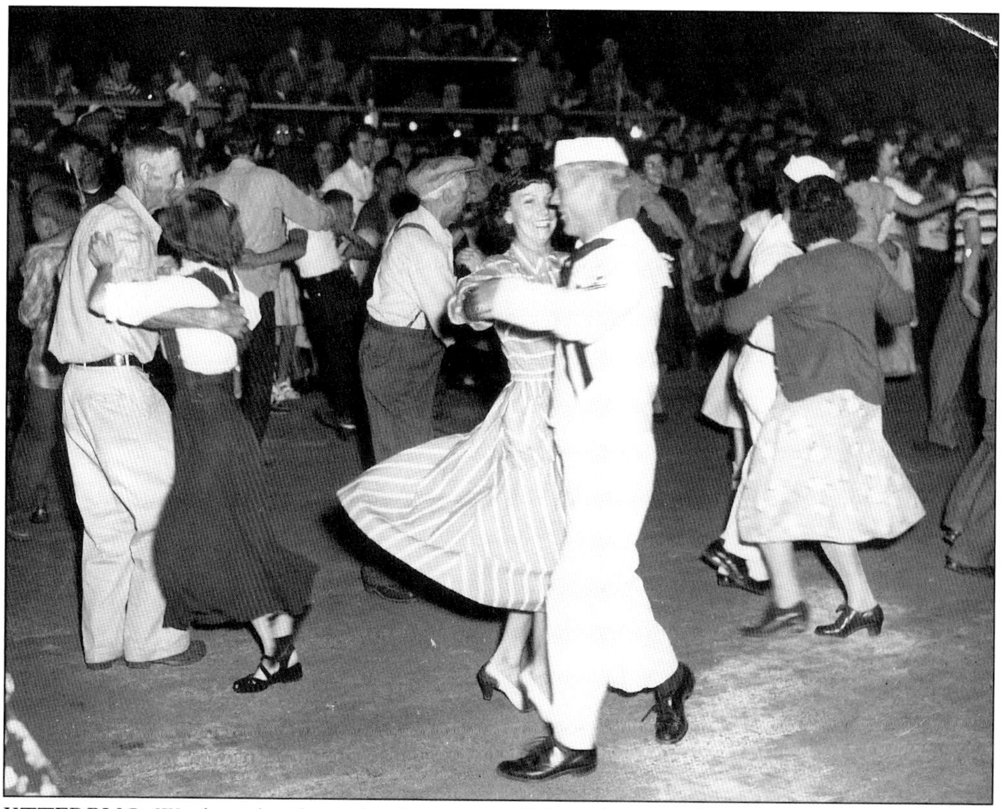

JITTERBUG. Workers, locals, and sailors show off their dance skills during the Big Band era of the 1940s. With hundreds of ships and Navy personnel in and around Casco Bay, the economy surged and nervous parents warned daughters to beware of sailors who, reportedly, had "a girl in every port." (Edward Langlois)

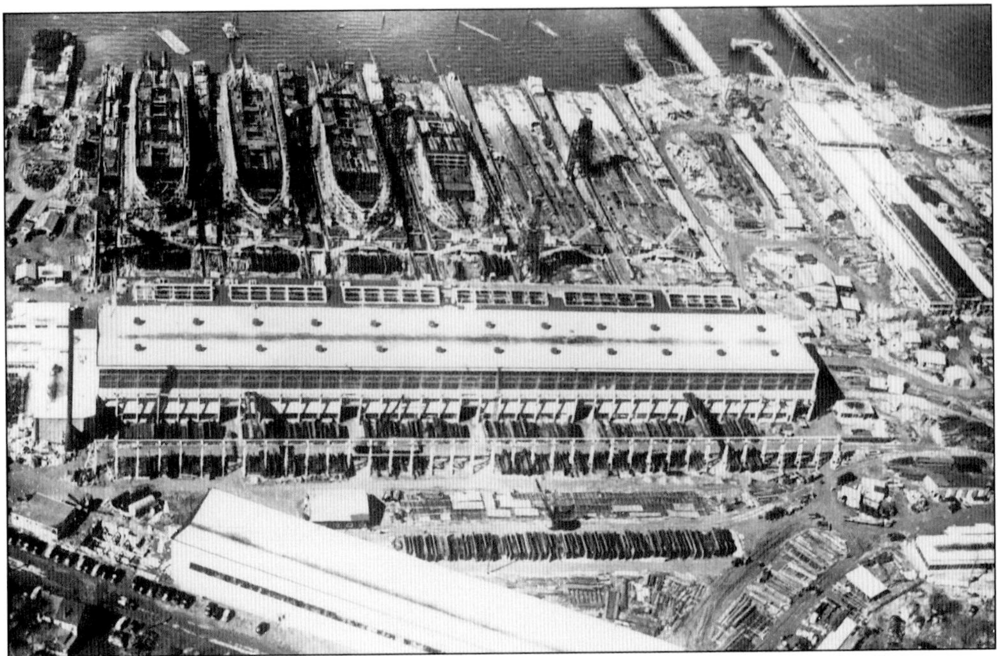

THE WEST YARD. This was the second of the two shipyards on the South Portland waterfront during World War II. It turned out its first vessel in 1942, while the last of the thirty British "Ocean" ships were being completed at the East Yard. The two yards eventually combined as The New England Shipbuilding Corp. and were among eighteen U.S. yards turning out Liberty Ships. (George Thompson)

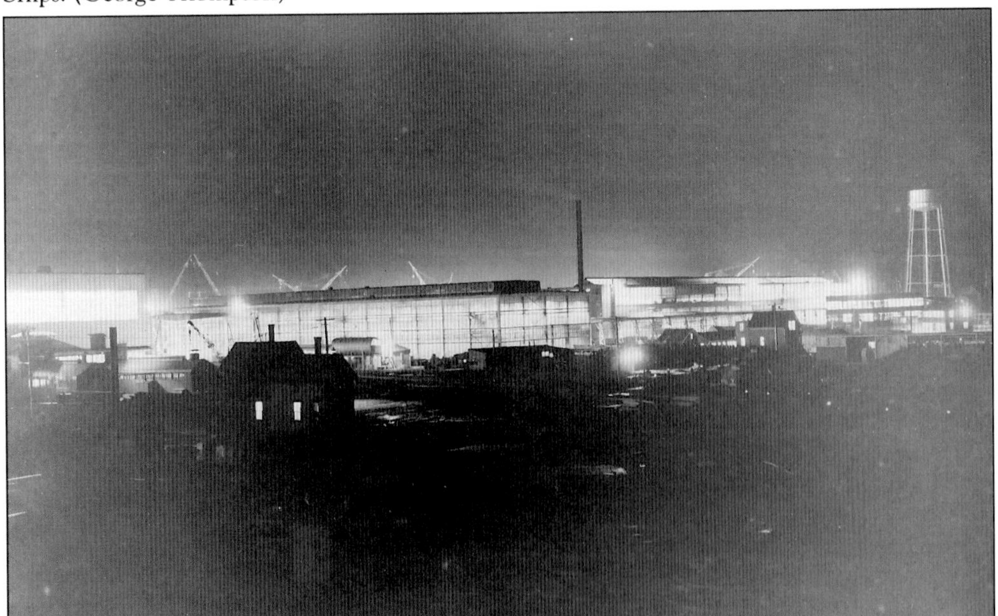

NIGHTSCAPE. Lights from South Portland's East Yard illuminate the skyline as night crews continue the twenty-four-hour-a-day production of Liberty Ships that transported supplies and troops to the Allies during World War II. Of the 236 Liberty Ships built at South Portland, 21 were lost during the war. (Edward Langlois)

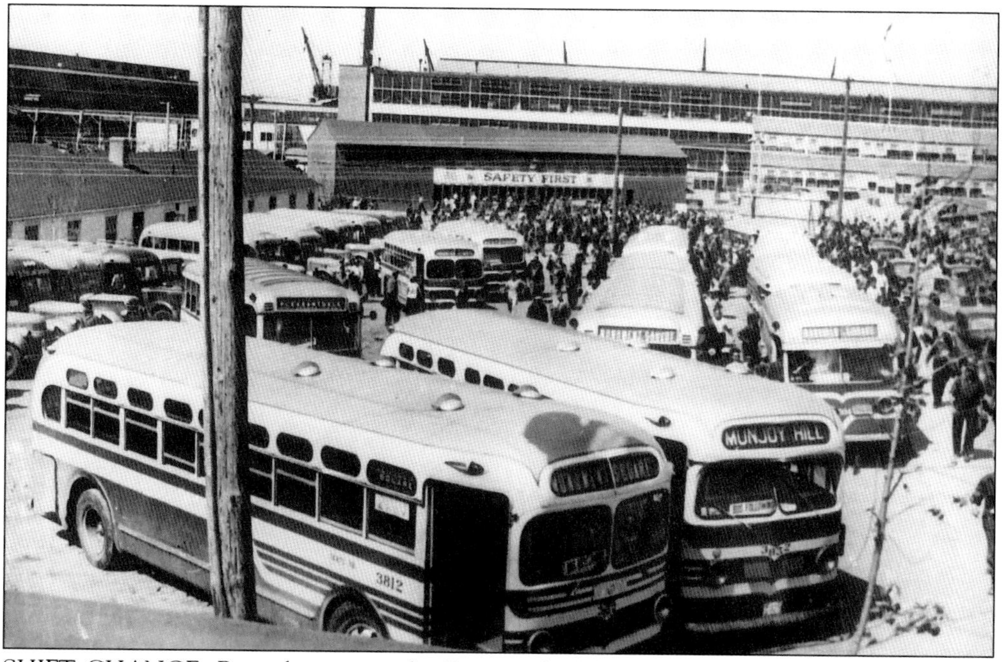

SHIFT CHANGE. Buses line up at the East Yard of the South Portland Shipyard to carry workers to and from their jobs, *c.* 1944. (George Thompson)

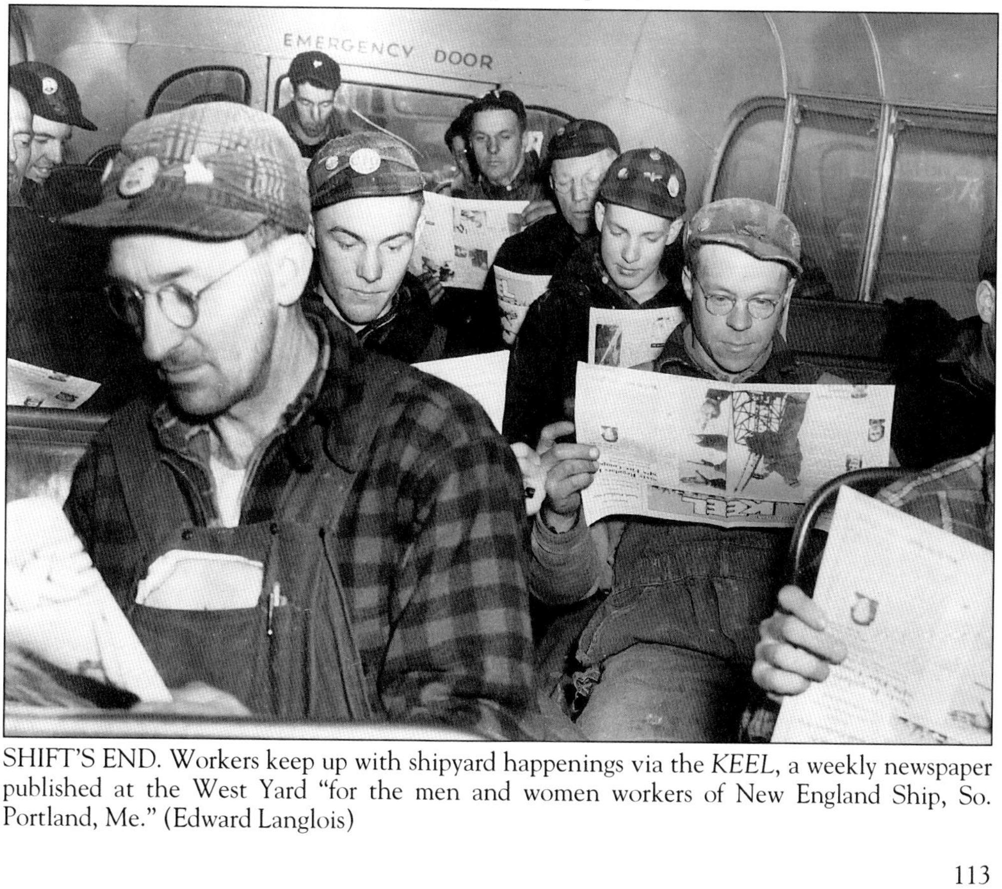

SHIFT'S END. Workers keep up with shipyard happenings via the *KEEL*, a weekly newspaper published at the West Yard "for the men and women workers of New England Ship, So. Portland, Me." (Edward Langlois)

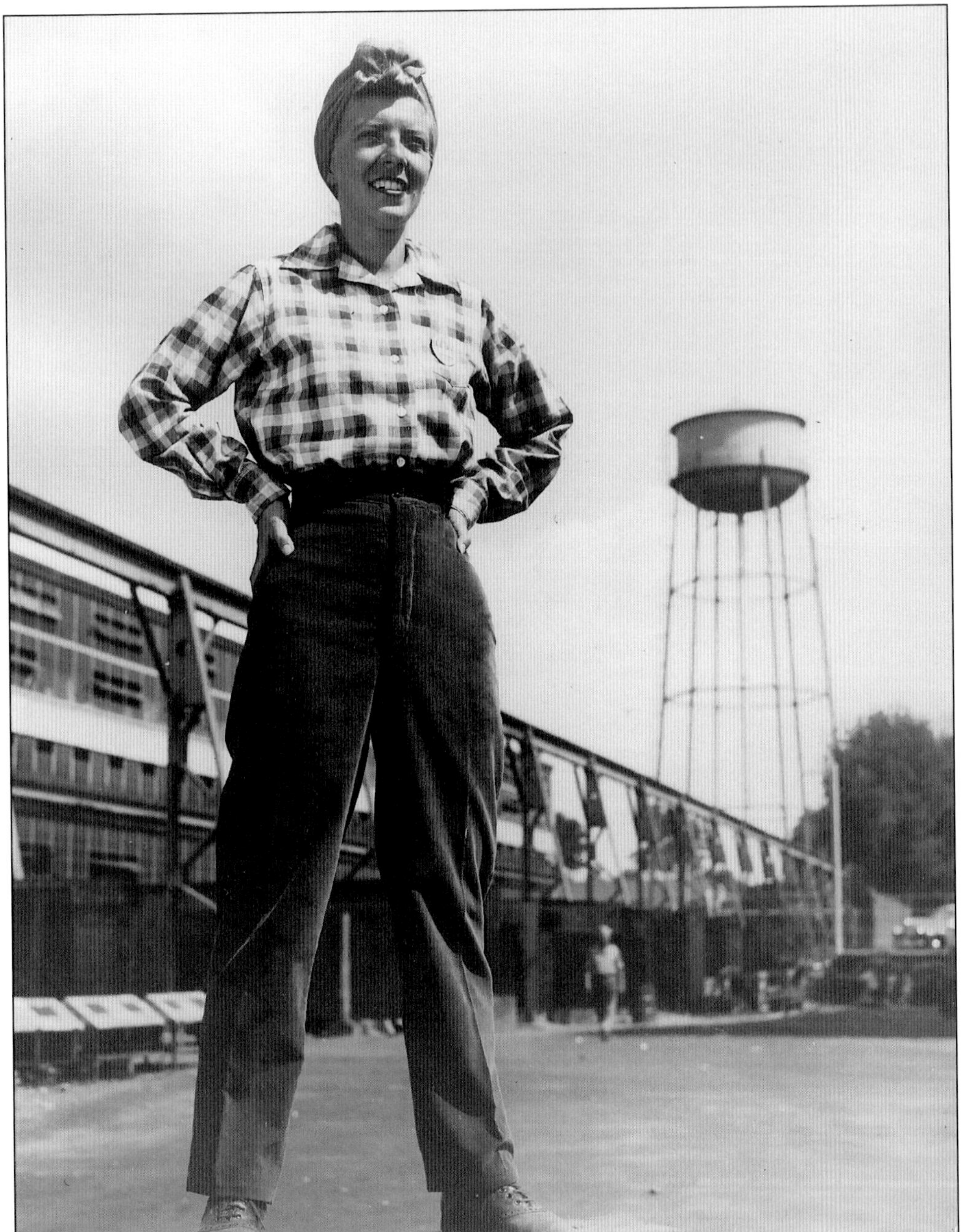

A "WENDY." Virginia Piston O'Toole of South Portland typifies the women who worked at the shipyards throughout America. The first non-clerical woman was hired in South Portland in 1942. Those assigned to the welding shop were known nationwide as "Wendy the Welder," a counterpart to "Rosie the Riviter." For most, it was their first taste of "men's work for men's wages," though they were handed pink slips when the men returned. (Edward Langlois)

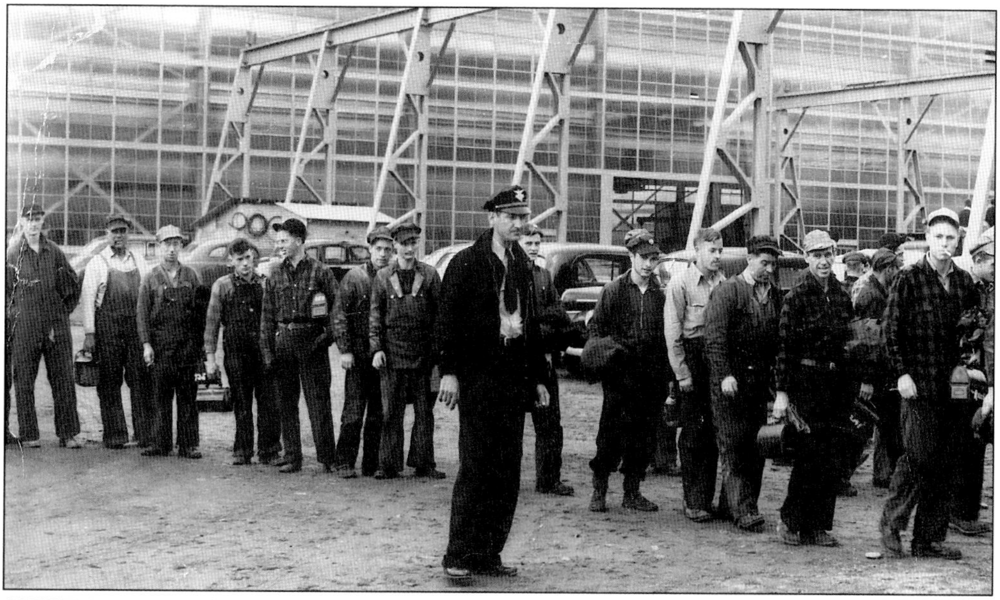

SHIFT START. Officer Fuller Hodgkins, chief of security at the shipyard, maintains order as workers line up for one of three scheduled shifts. Workers came from throughout Maine and, though most were inexperienced and received only about 30 hours training, production time for the Liberty Ships decreased from 279 days to 52 days within 2 years. (Edward Langlois)

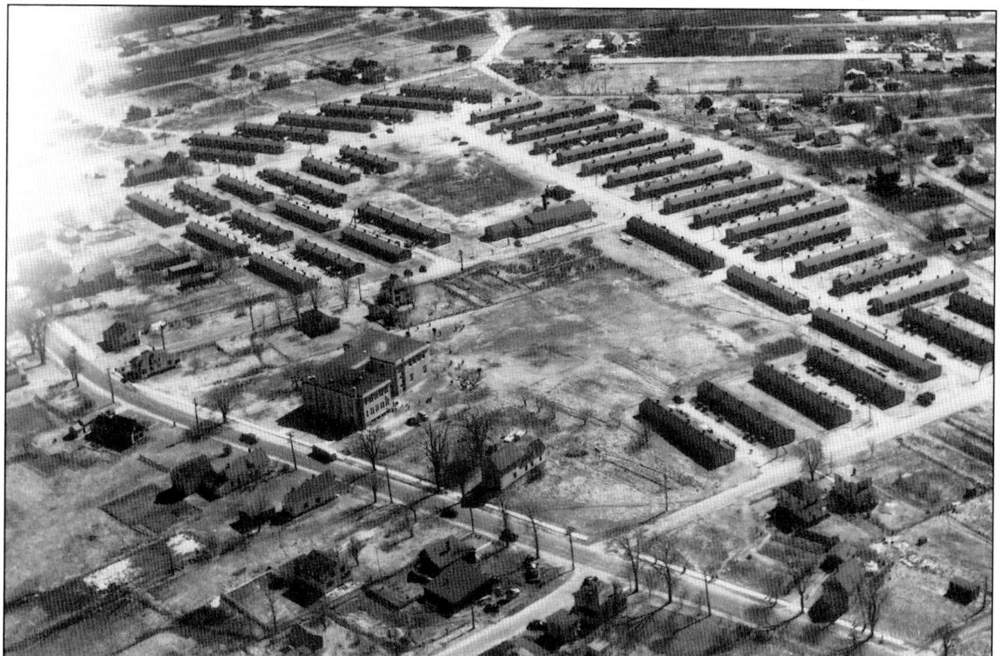

PEARY VILLAGE. Broadway crosses in front of the Lincoln School in South Portland, with the homes at Peary Village in the background. Peary Village was one of the area's temporary wartime housing units built in the early 1940s. The barrack-style units are gone and the site, currently home to the Veteran's of Foreign Wars Post 832, is known as Peary Terrace. (George Thompson)

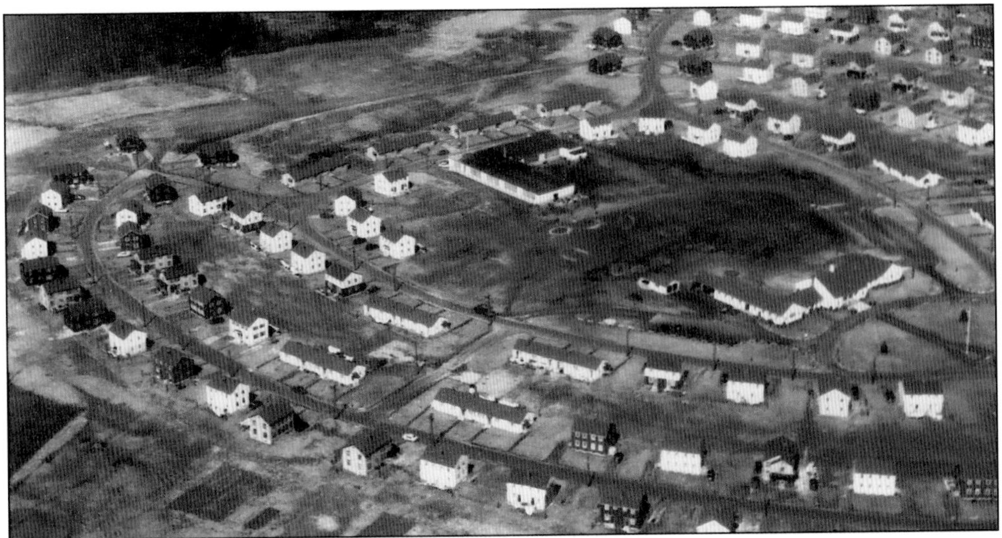

REDBANK. Redbank, a five-hundred-unit housing development, was built for defense workers in World War II, near what is now the Maine Mall area. Government-owned and operated, it provided a playground for children in the center area, a community building (at right), and its own school (at left). It has been privately owned since 1954 and renamed South Portland Gardens. (George Thompson)

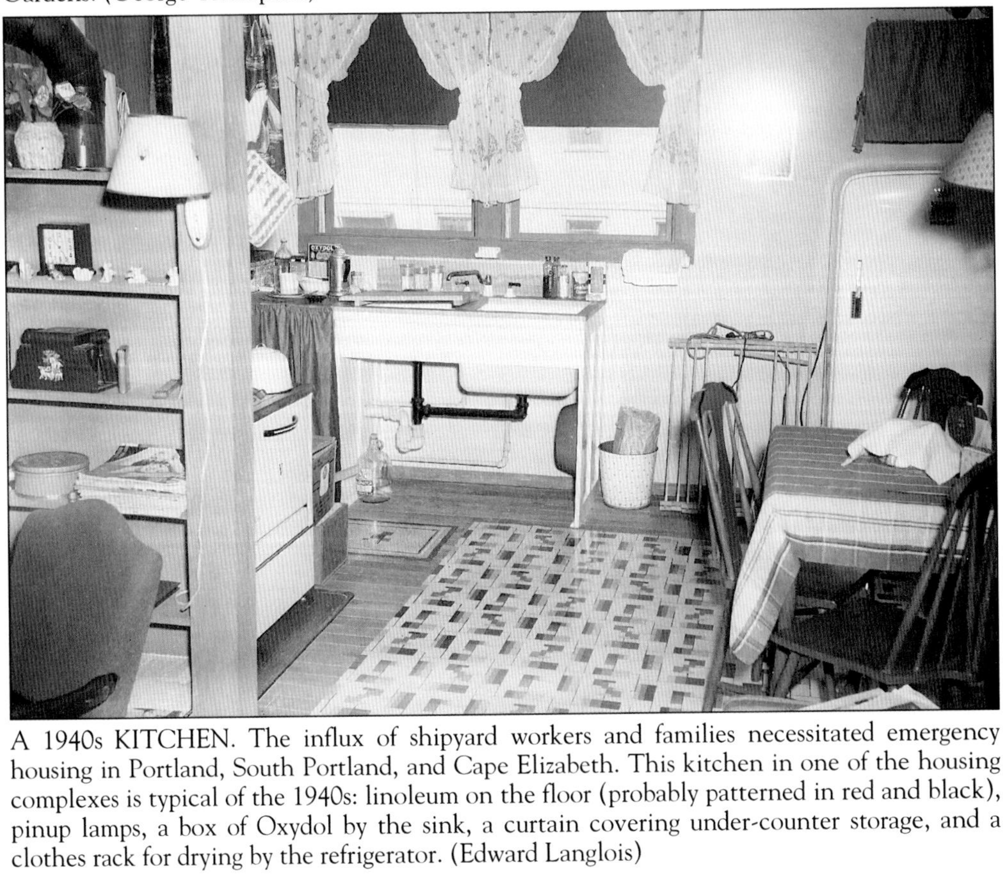

A 1940s KITCHEN. The influx of shipyard workers and families necessitated emergency housing in Portland, South Portland, and Cape Elizabeth. This kitchen in one of the housing complexes is typical of the 1940s: linoleum on the floor (probably patterned in red and black), pinup lamps, a box of Oxydol by the sink, a curtain covering under-counter storage, and a clothes rack for drying by the refrigerator. (Edward Langlois)

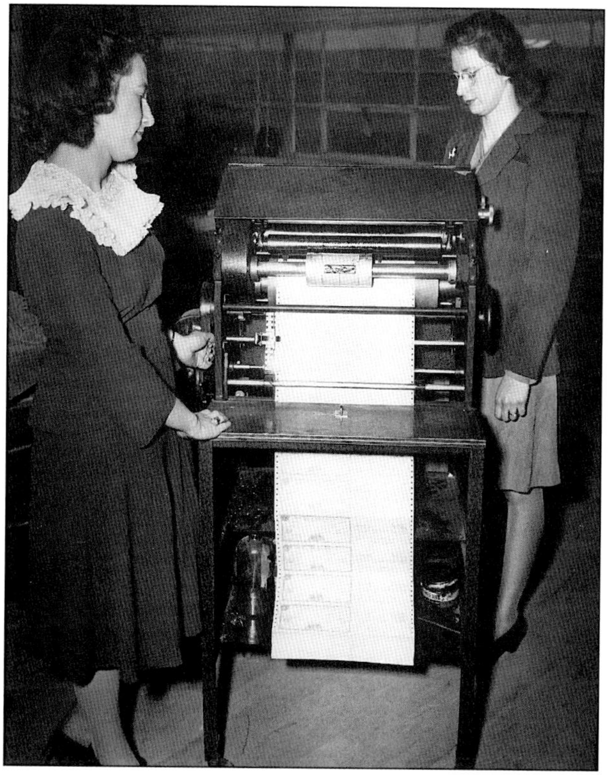

PAYCHECKS. A yearly payroll of $156 million in the mid-1940s contributed to a robust economy. Some shipyard workers saw paychecks rise from about $28 a week in 1941 to $98 weekly within two years. (Edward Langlois)

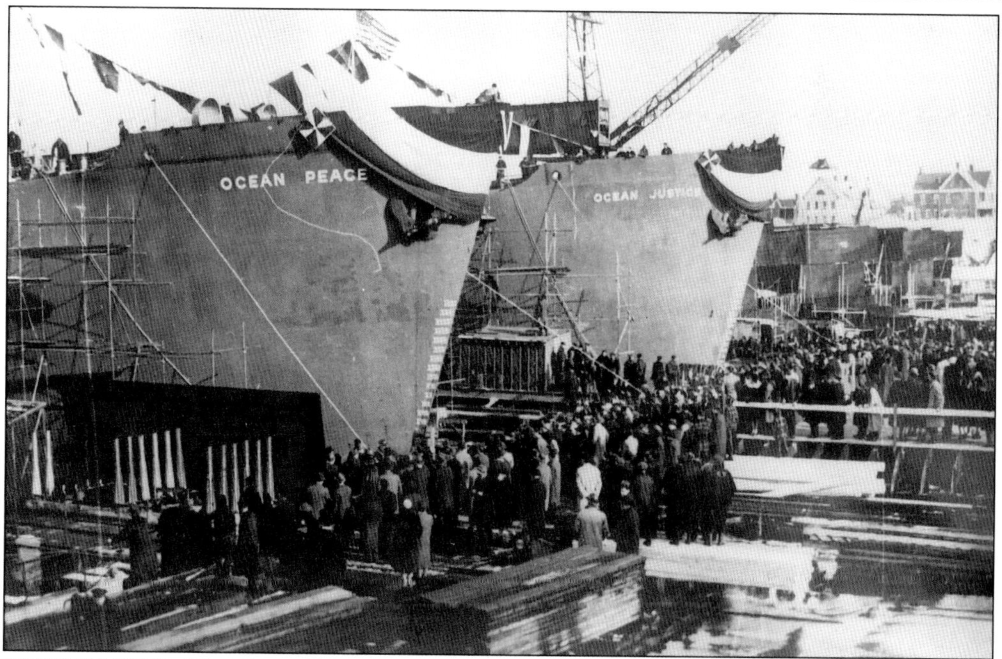

BRITISH SHIP. The *Ocean Peace* was one of the first thirty ships built for the British during the East Yard startup, *c.* 1942. U.S. ships were named after distinguished men until production outpaced distinction and ships began to be named after women, Amelia Earhart being the first. (George Thompson)

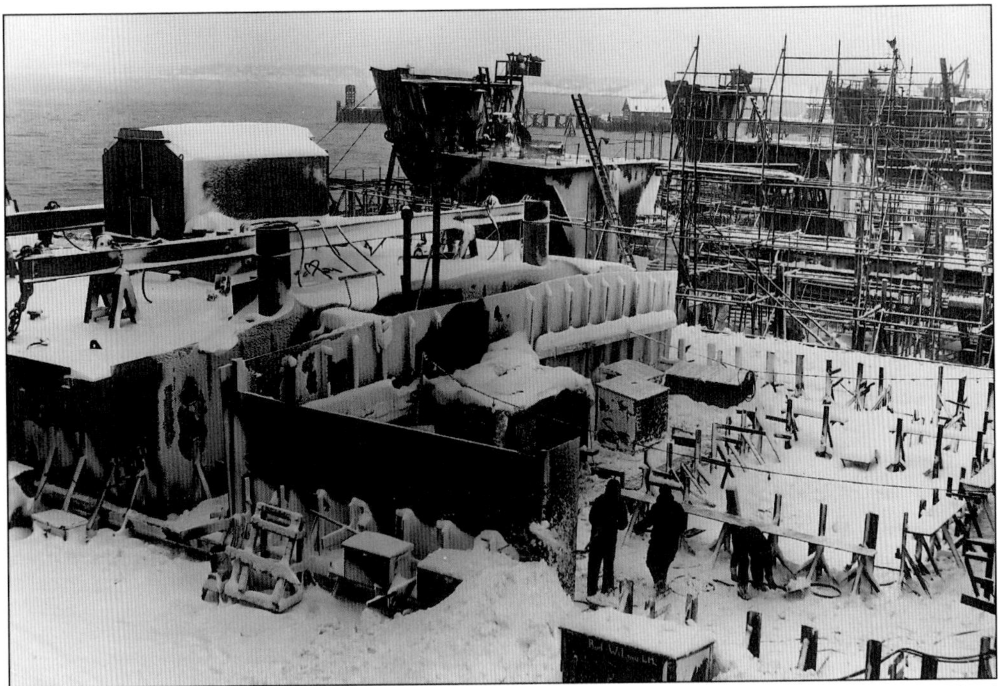

FRIGID. Leather or sheepskin-lined jackets helped protect workers at the East Yard from icy winter blasts that plummeted temperatures to as low as 45 degrees below zero. (Edward Langlois)

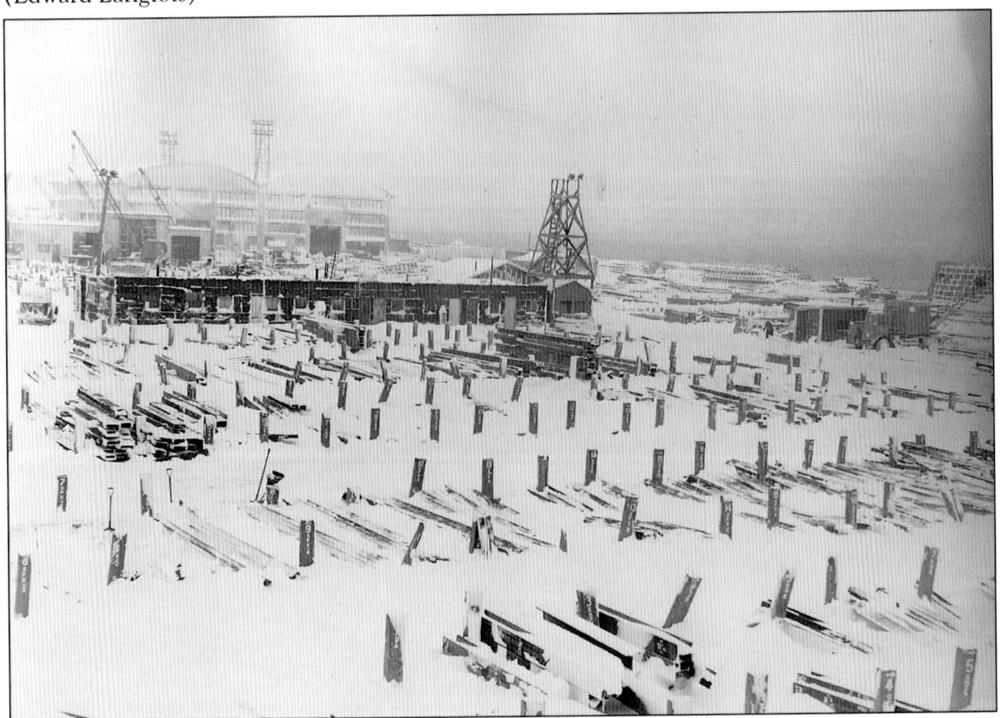

SURREAL. Brackets placed to support framework lend a tombstone effect to this winter shipyard scene. (Edward Langlois)

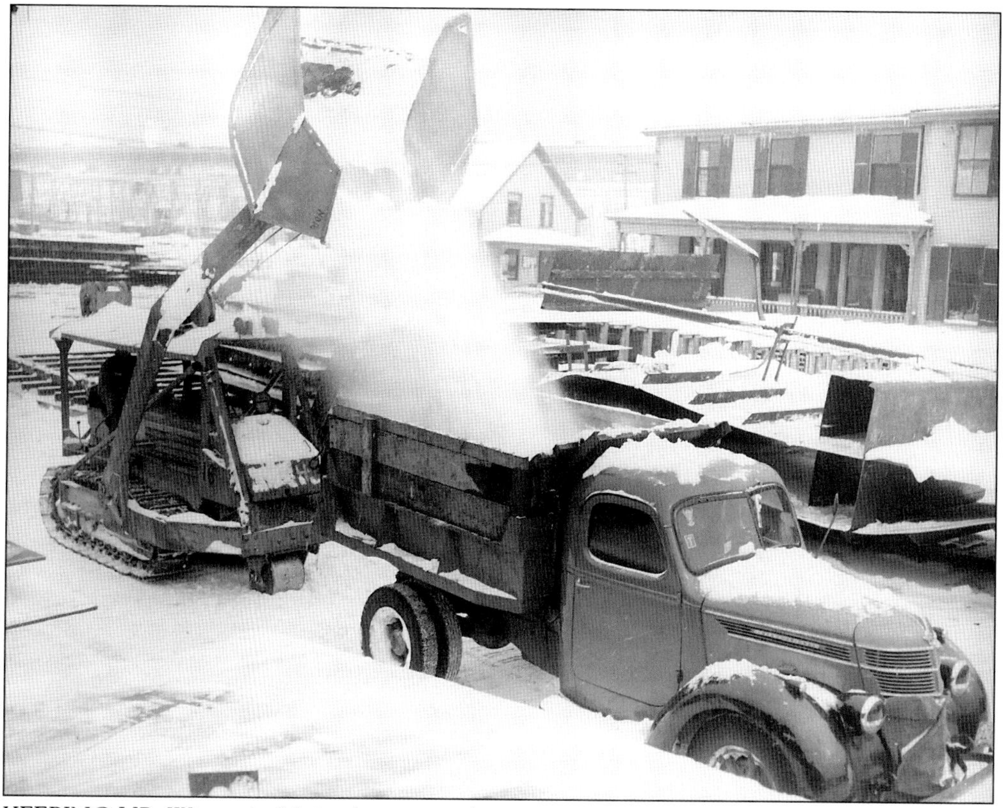

KEEPING UP. Winter in Maine kept crews busy removing snow from the bustling work areas. (Edward Langlois)

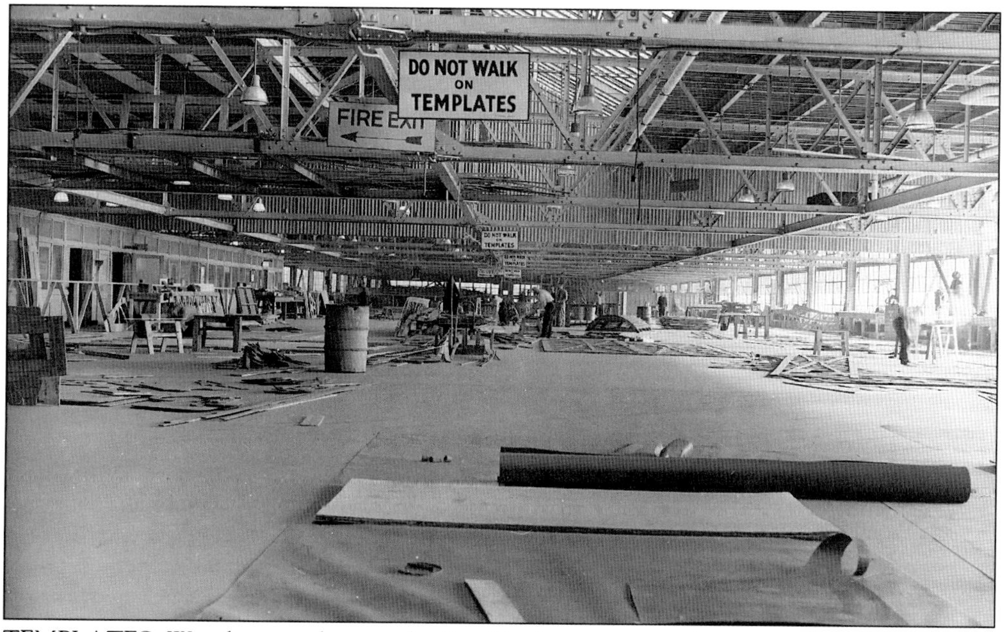

TEMPLATES. Wooden templates at the East Yard serve as a guide to stencil and hammer out steel parts for the Liberty Ships. (Edward Langlois)

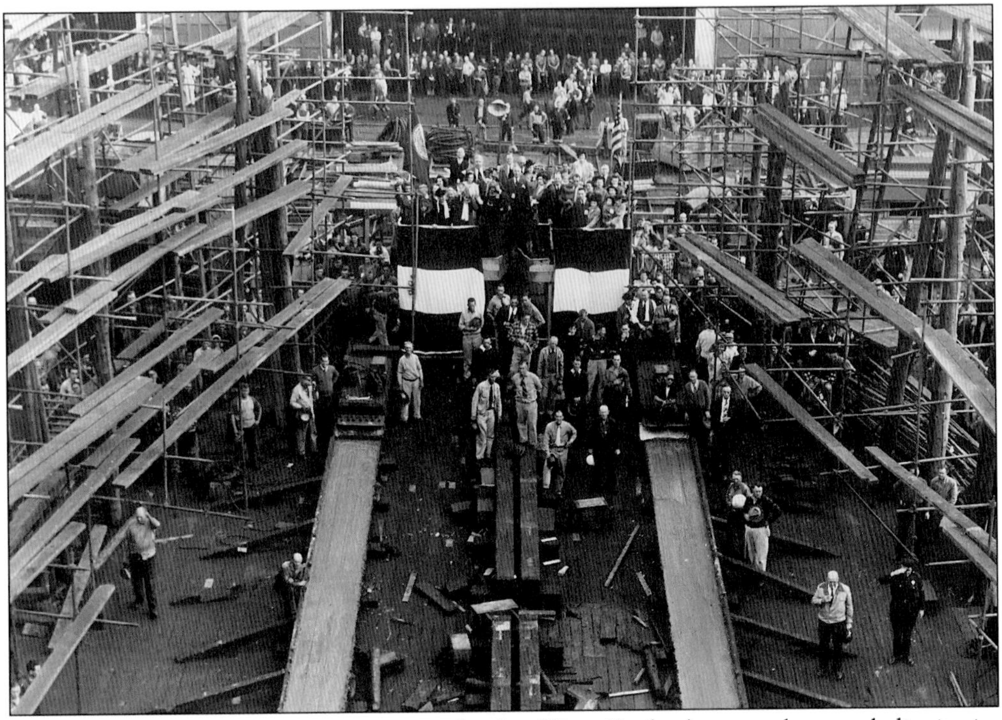

CEREMONY. A platform is set up inside the West Yard where workers and dignitaries turn out for a launching. The cost of building a Liberty Ship was approximately $1 million in South Portland, compared to up to $2 million in other shipyards throughout the country. (Edward Langlois)

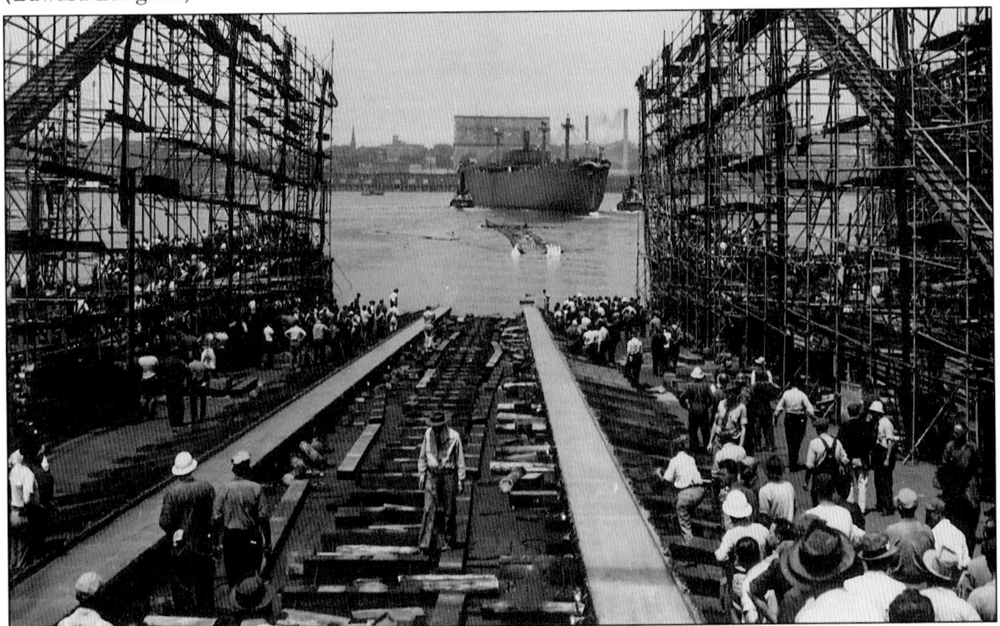

OFF TO WAR. On July 13, 1942, Hull 203 heads out to sea from the West Yard, with Portland's Grain Elevator in the background. That year, six Liberty Ships were launched at one time, a noteable feat. (Edward Langlois)

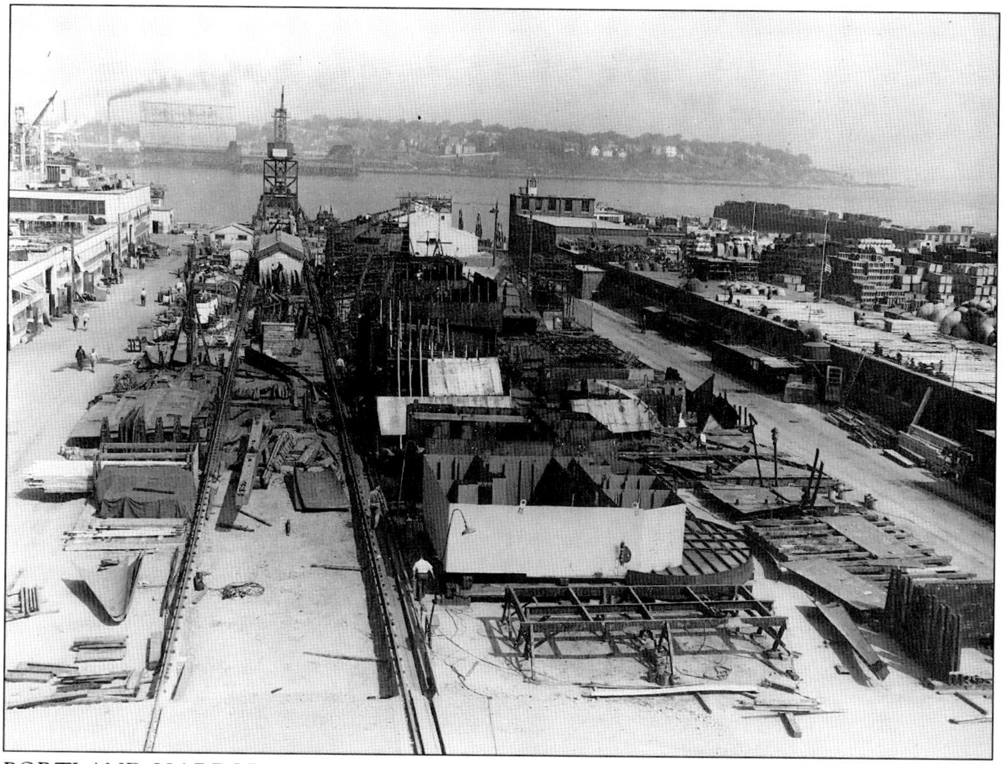

PORTLAND HARBOR. Crane tracks lead to Portland Harbor from the West Yard, where prefabricated parts were fitted to Liberty Ships prior to launching. (Edward Langlois)

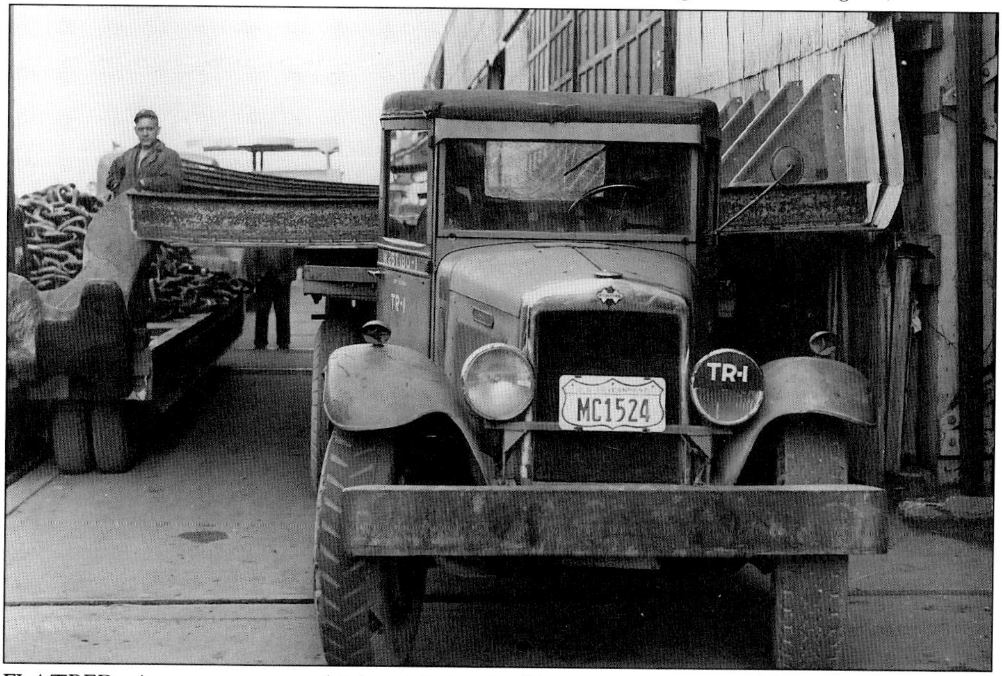

FLATBED. A government vehicle with hard rubber tires transports fabricated parts to the ships. (Edward Langlois)

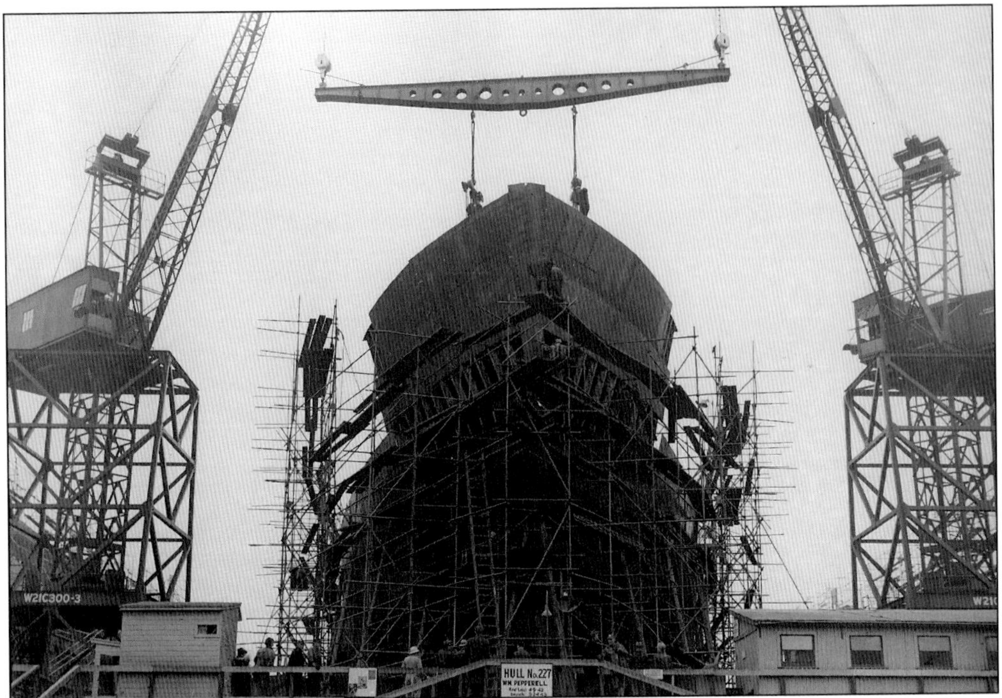

THE *WILLIAM PEPPERELL*. Two overhead cranes place a bow section onto Hull 227 at the East Yard. The launch date was May 24, 1943; the production time, forty-five days. This was the first time an assembled portion was built elsewhere and put into place at South Portland. (Edward Langlois)

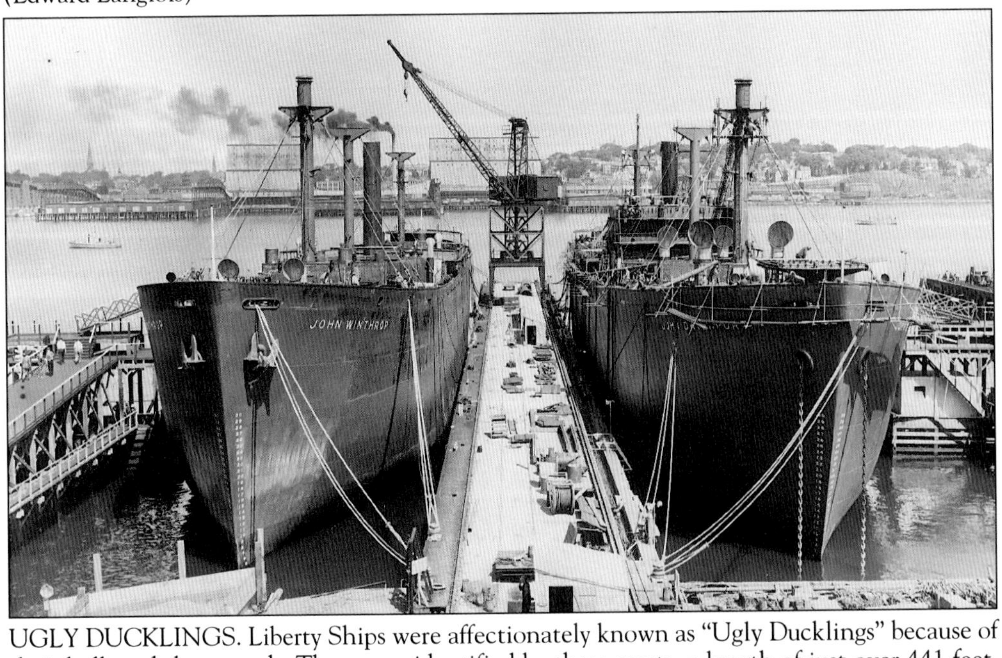

UGLY DUCKLINGS. Liberty Ships were affectionately known as "Ugly Ducklings" because of their bulk and slow speeds. They were identified by three masts, a length of just over 441 feet, and they weighed over 10,000 tons. Top speed under steam power was only 11 knots, with a capacity of 44 crewmen and a gun crew of 12. (Edward Langlois)

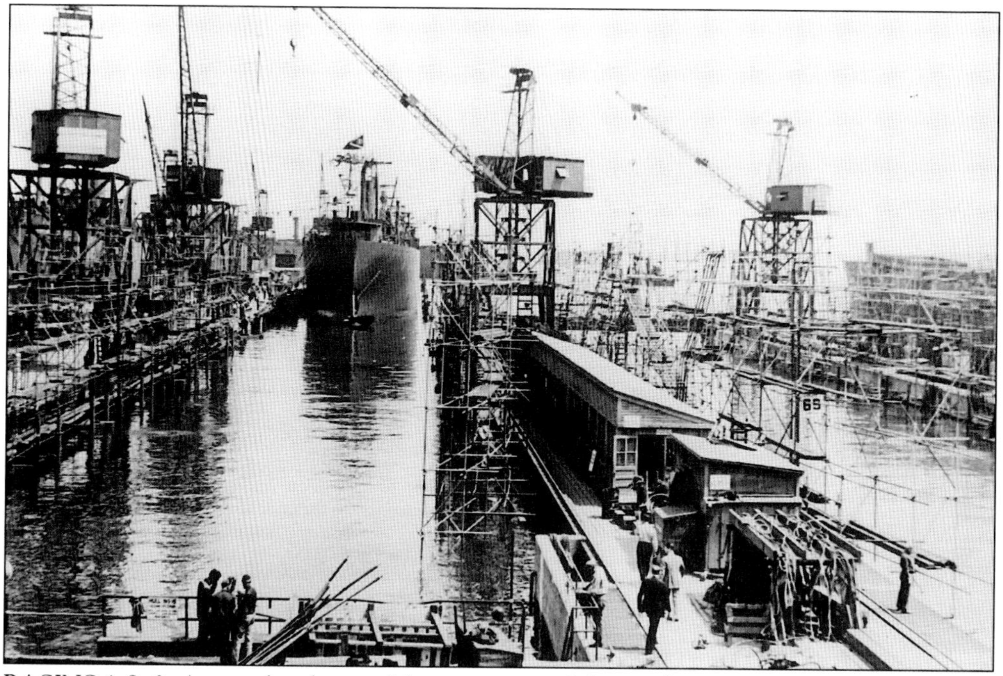

BASINS 1 & 2. An overhead crane lifts parts onto a Liberty Ship in Basin 1 at the East Yard. One of most dangerous missions during the war was the Murmansk Run to the Russian front. Nearly one hundred ships and countless men were lost. (Edward Langlois)

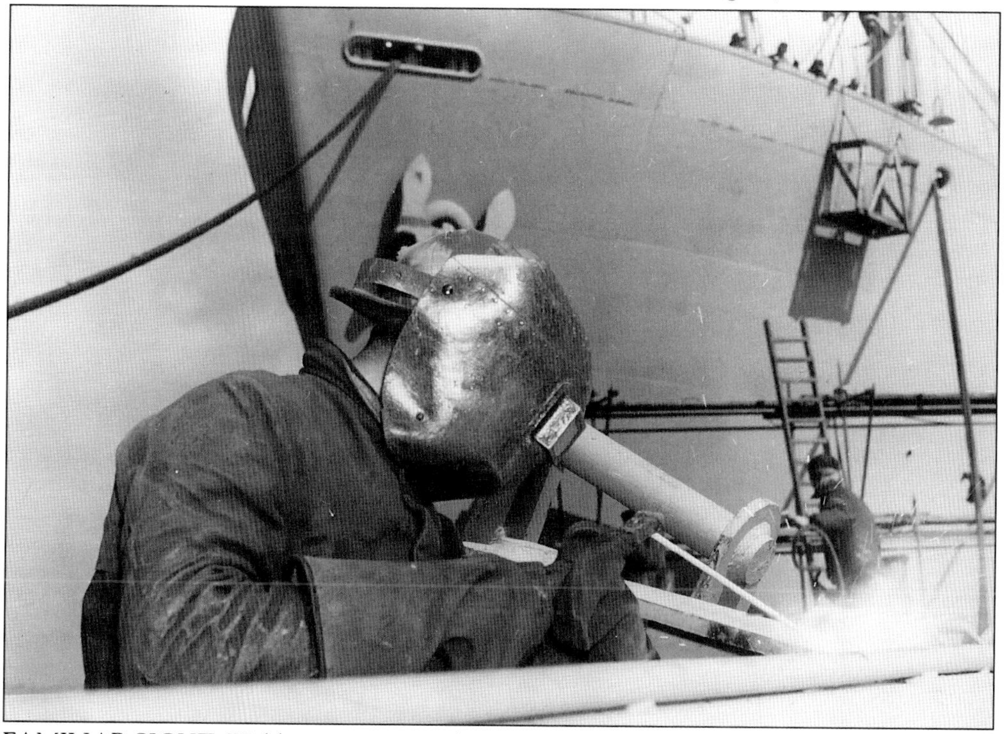

FAMILIAR SIGHT. Welders were required to meet stringent government standards in order to work on the Liberty Ships. (Edward Langlois)

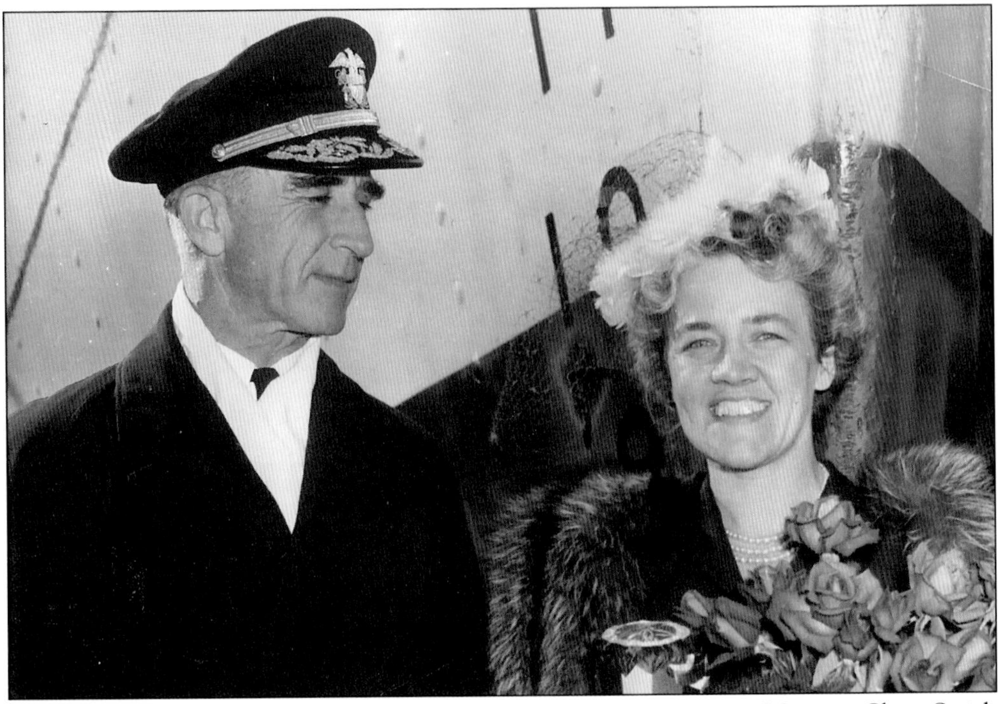

MARGARET CHASE SMITH. Admiral Land and U.S. Representative Margaret Chase Smith of Maine were on hand for Liberty Ship launchings in the early 1940s. Miss Smith was to be the first woman elected to both the U.S. House and Senate, serving thirty-two years. She died May 29, 1995, at her home in Skowhegan at the age of ninety-seven. (Edward Langlois)

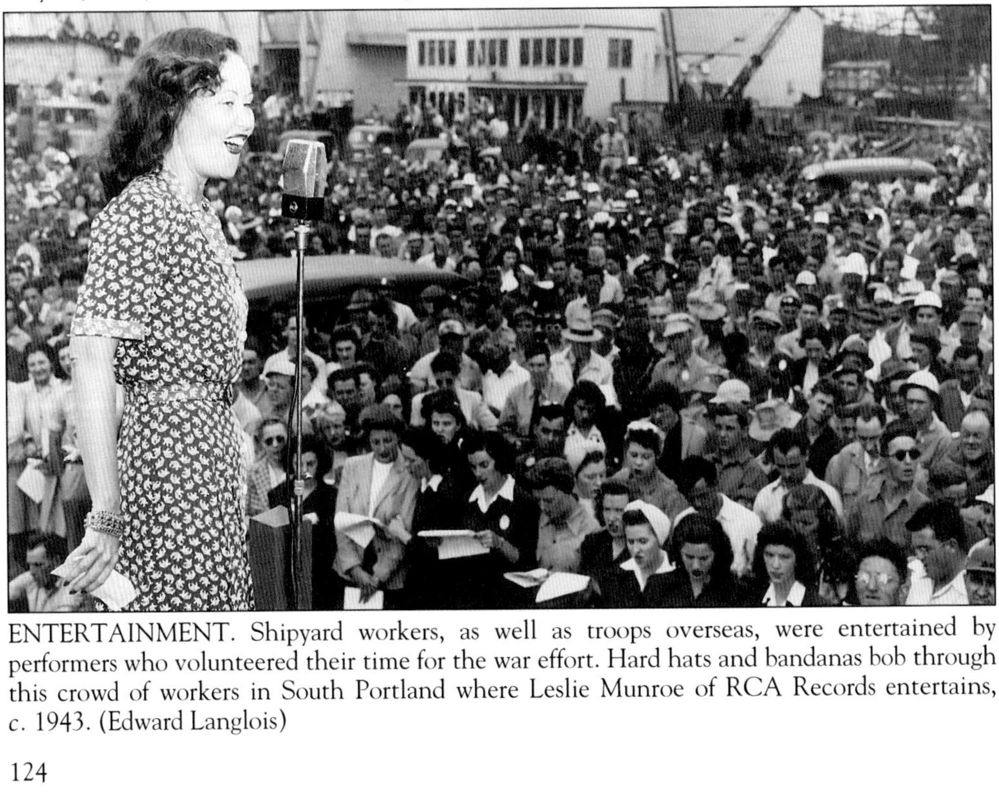

ENTERTAINMENT. Shipyard workers, as well as troops overseas, were entertained by performers who volunteered their time for the war effort. Hard hats and bandanas bob through this crowd of workers in South Portland where Leslie Munroe of RCA Records entertains, c. 1943. (Edward Langlois)

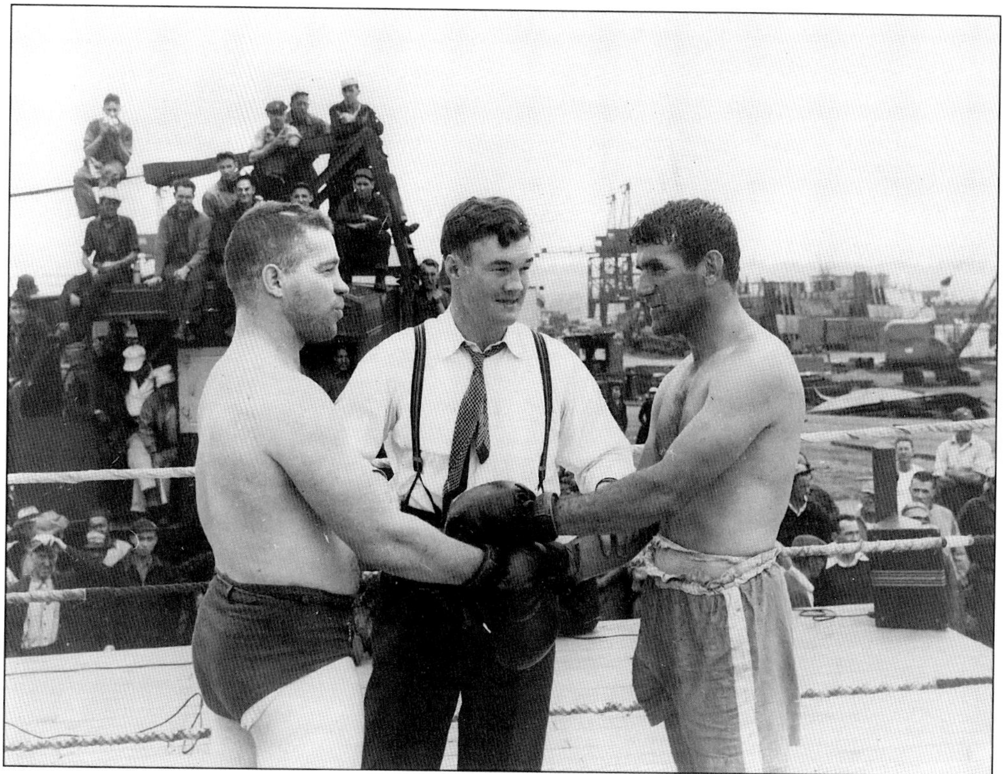

PUT 'EM UP. A *c.* 1941 photograph of Maine Welterweight boxing champion Coley Welch refereeing a fight between Paul Flaherty and John "Bull" Fisher. Jack Nichols, a world-class wrestler, was in charge of non-musical entertainment for the shipyard workers. (Edward Langlois)

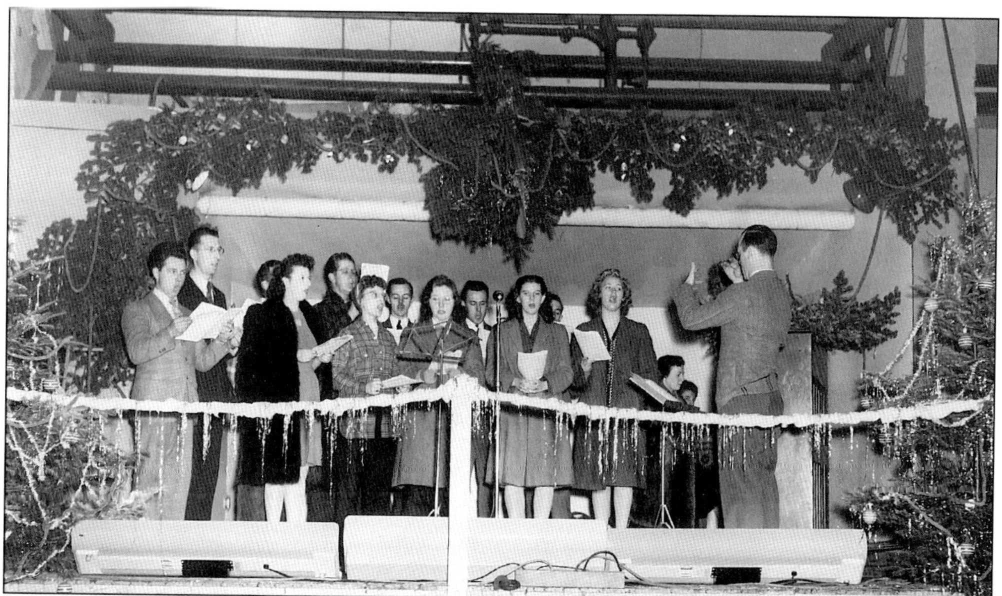

CAROLERS. Paul Guimont, director of musical entertainment at the shipyard, conducts a Christmas program staged for the workers, *c.* 1943. (Edward Langlois)

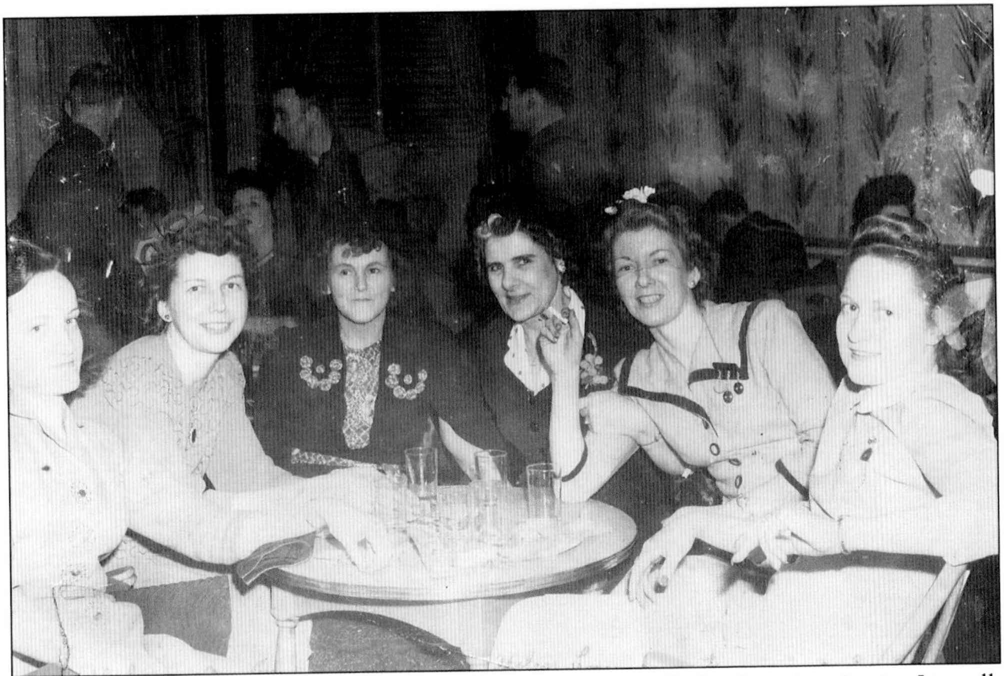

PAINT GANG. A c. 1943 photograph of Delores, Maxine, Helen Lovejoy, Louise Linnell, Francis, and Mary Young—the "paint department gang" at the shipyard—enjoying a Saturday night out at the Falmouth Hotel in Portland. Helen became a welder, but when the pink slips went out, she returned to "women's work" in the cafeteria of South Portland's junior and senior high schools. She worked there for twenty-eight years, retiring in 1970. She lives at Willard Beach and, at last count, had 142 grand and great-grandchildren. (Helen Goodine)

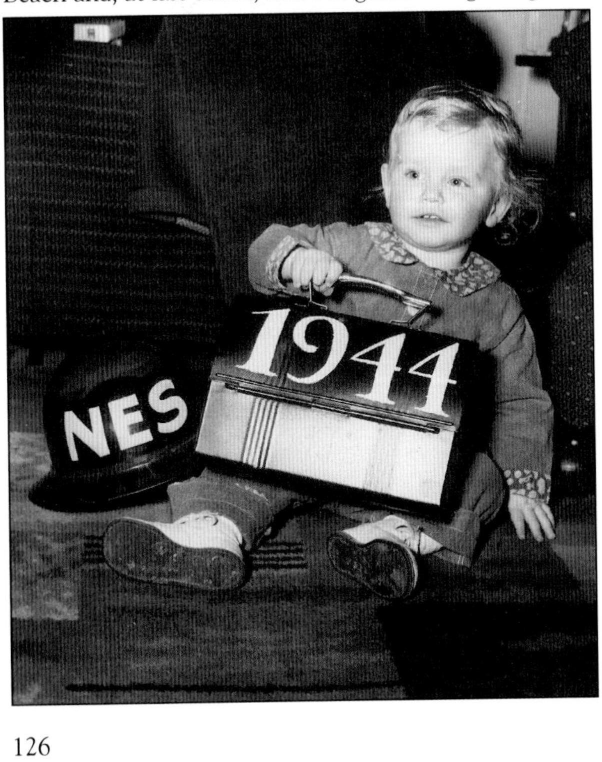

SIGN OF THE TIMES. This youngster, in hightop leather "walking" shoes, holds Dad's (or is it Mom's?) lunchbox, proclaiming the year 1944. (Edward Langlois)

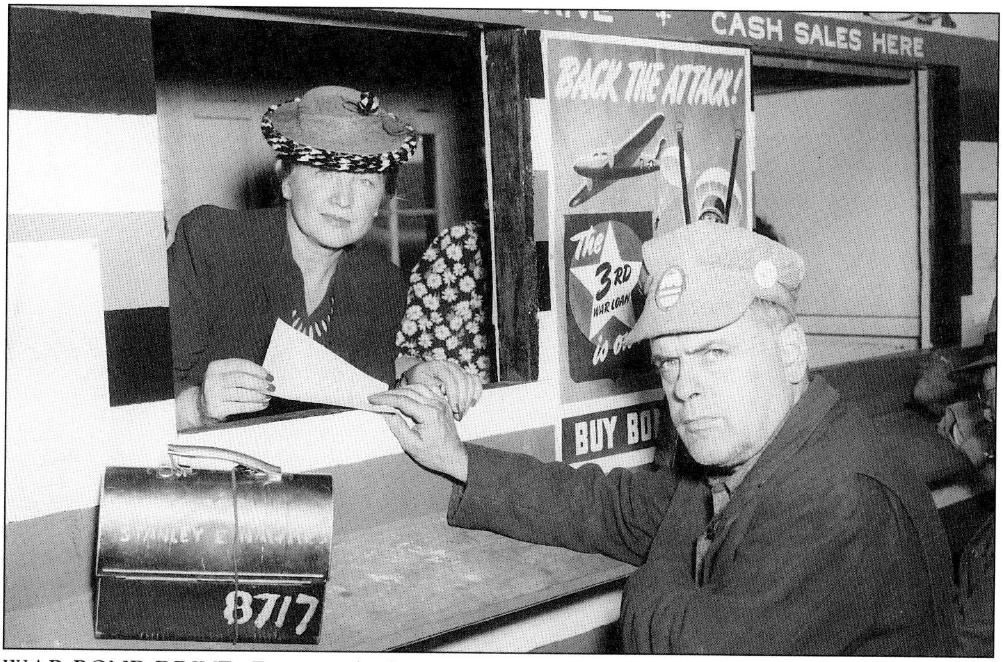

WAR BOND DRIVE . Everyone had a part to play during the war effort of the 1940s. Women volunteers sold war bonds to "back the attack" and shipyard worker Stanley E. Hawkes makes his contribution. (Edward Langlois)

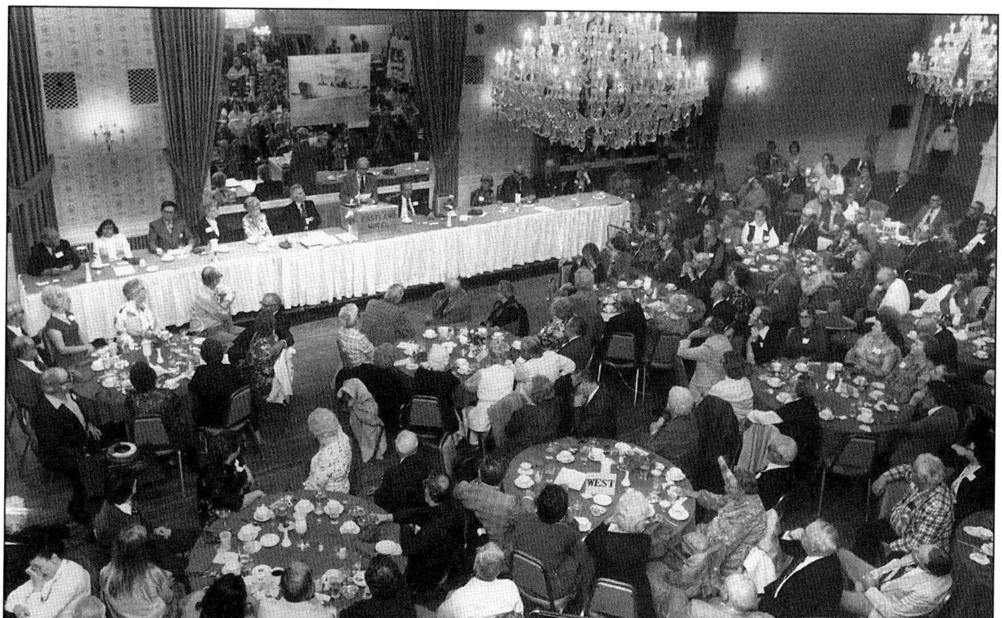

REUNION. The South Portland Shipyard Society holds its first reunion in October 1980 in the Eastland Hotel Ballroom, Portland. More than five hundred former shipyard employes attended. The Society publishes an annual newsletter and was formed "for the preservation of the historic World War II contribution of the workers of the Todd-Bath Iron and South Portland Shipbuilding corporations." Its mailing address is P.O. Box 161, Portland, ME 04112. (Edward Langlois)

Acknowledgments

To all of those who welcomed me into their homes, shared with me their memories, and allowed me to walk away with irreplaceable photographs and albums, my thanks. And a special thanks to those who went the extra step to locate photographs or do behind-the-scenes research without acknowledgment in the book:

The Robert Shuman family;
Rosella Loveitt, my American History teacher at South Portland High School where she taught for thirty-two years;
Ray Taylor and the gift of his book *Growing Up in Pleasantdale*;
Norm Sullivan of Sullivan Photo and Train, who has a vast collection of photographs of the Portland area available to the public;
Ed Langlois;
Ellen Knight;
Norm Jordan;
George Thompson;
Cynthia DeCapua;
The SPHS Class of 1955 Reunion Committee;
and two very special people:
Helen Goodine and Dot Wilkes.